Economic Development and Reform Deepening in China

T0298624

This book, together with *Macro-control and Economic Development in China* is a collection of papers written in recent years about maintaining economic growth, managing inflation, the relationship between growth and structural adjustment, control of price growth, maintaining stable economic development, and other relevant aspects of macro-control, economic development, and deepening reform. The Chinese Government adopted many of the recommendations put forward by the book.

Chen Jiagui (1944–2013) was Economist, Professor of the Academic Division of Economics of the Chinese Academy of Social Sciences, specializing in industrial economics and enterprise management.

China Perspectives Series

The *China Perspectives* series focuses on translating and publishing works by leading Chinese scholars, writing about both global topics and China-related themes. It covers Humanities and Social Sciences, Education, Media and Psychology, as well as many interdisciplinary themes.

This is the first time any of these books have been published in English for international readers. The series aims to put forward a Chinese perspective, give insights into cutting-edge academic thinking in China, and inspire researchers globally.

For more information, please visit https://www.routledge.com/series/CPH

Regulating China's Shadow Banks
Qingmin Yan, Jianhua Li

Macro-control and Economic Development in China
Jiagui Chen

Economic Development and Reform Deepening in China
Jiagui Chen

Forthcoming titles

Internationalization of the RMB: Establishment and Development of RMB Offshore Markets
International Monetary Institute, Renmin University of China

The Road Leading to the Market
Weiying Zhang

Research Frontiers on the International Marketing Strategies of Chinese Brands
Zuohao Hu, Xi Chen, Zhilin Yang

History of China's Foreign Trade, 2e
Yuqin Sun

Economic Development and Reform Deepening in China

Jiagui Chen

LONDON AND NEW YORK

CHINA SOCIAL SCIENCES PRESS

This book is published with financial support from Innovation Project of CASS

Translated by Yang Limeng and Wu Yisheng

First published 2017 by Routledge

2 Park Square, Milton Park, Abingdon, Oxfordshire OX14 4RN

52 Vanderbilt Avenue, New York, NY 10017

Routledge is an imprint of the Taylor & Francis Group, an informa business

First issued in paperback 2020

British Library Cataloguing in Publication Data
A catalogue record for this book is available from the British Library

Library of Congress Cataloging-in-Publication Data
Names: Chen, Jiagui, author.
Title: Economic development and reform deepening in China / Jiagui Chen.
Description: London; New York : Routledge, 2016. | Series: China perspectives series
Identifiers: LCCN 2016001149| ISBN 9781138898707 (hbk) |
    ISBN 9781315708416 (ebk)
Subjects: LCSH: Economic development—China. | China—Economic policy—2000- | China—Economic conditions—2000-
Classification: LCC HC427.95. C433335 2016 | DDC 338.951—dc23
LC record available at http://lccn.loc.gov/2016001149

ISBN: 978-1-138-89870-7 (hbk)
ISBN: 978-0-367-51664-2 (pbk)

Typeset in Bembo
by Apex CoVantage, LLC

Contents

Illustrations

Preface

My research life can roughly be divided into two stages: the research on micro-economic and macro-economic issues respectively. When I was an undergraduate, my major was national economic planning which should fall into the scope of macro-economy, but I was mainly engaged in business management after I graduated. Later, I studied business management for a master's and doctor's degree. Afterwards, I began work in the Institute of Industrial Economics of CASS and was mainly involved in the study of business management and industrial economy. I finally transferred my research interest to macro-economy to meet my job needs. In 1998, I was appointed Vice President of the Chinese Academy of Social Sciences. In 2003, I was elected a member of the NPC Standing Committee and the Financial & Economic Committee. In 2006 when CASS set up different departments, I was appointed Dean of the Department of Economics and Chief Editor of the *Blue Book of Economy*. Due to these job opportunities, in recent years, the issues I touched upon and discussed are basically about macro-economy. And the topics I researched and the academic activities I participated in are mainly on macro-economy as well. Therefore, the research findings I published are mostly about macro-economy.

This Collection (consisting of this volume and the companion volume *Macro-control and Economic Development in China*) mainly includes my published articles on macro-economy, and it includes issues such as macro-control, economic development, and reform deepening.

Between the two volumes there are 18 articles included on macro control. A majority of them were originally published in the Theory Section of *People's Daily* after the year 2008. These articles are concerned with the current economic situation and macro-control policy, call attention to some problems, and put forward policy suggestions. They specifically make an in-depth analysis on how to balance economic growth, restructuring, and price control. After a systemic reading, the readers would be able to grasp the evolution of China's economic situation and macro-control policies in recent years. In this sense, this is also an important reason why this Collection is published.

Regarding Economic Development, this Collection includes 19 articles on crucial issues that China faces during its economic development, namely, the international economic environment, energy and resources, the development of the manufacturing industry, industrial modernization, regional development, sustainable development, industrial structure, and the coordination of rural and urban development. As to development, my concern has always been on China's industrialization. We have made a detailed analysis of the industrialization process from 1995 to 2010, and come to a decision on which stage China's industrialization is in. The research finding has produced a tremendous influence and most issues I touch upon are on the major background of industrialization. In the meantime, as I frequently made field surveys to local cities, I also put forward suggestions on local economic development. This Collection contains my proposals on how to develop the Round Beibu Gulf Economic Zone, the Yangtze River Midstream Economic Zone, and the Economic Zone on the West Side of the Straits. The opinions I proposed about Round Beibu Gulf Economic Zone were ahead of the times and were adopted and put into effect.

This Collection contains 14 articles about Reform Deepening. I have long been concerned with the reform of state-owned enterprises, and published many articles about reform results. But the 14 articles are concerned with the reform of the macro-economic structure. It is worth mentioning that in 2008 at the 30th anniversary of the reform and opening-up, I summed up the characteristics of China's reform and opening-up, and analyzed its nature, direction, target model, methods, driving force, deployment, and measures; moreover, I am one of the earliest scholars that advocated a socialist market economy in China. This Collection specifically selects two of my articles about socialist market economy published in 1993. So far, the viewpoints of the two articles still serve as a guideline for China to build a mature socialist market economy.

The research has no ending. There are many problems need to be researched. With limited time put into unlimited research, mistakes and errors are unavoidable. Please don't hesitate to give your critical and constructive comments!

Chen Jiagui
December 1, 2012

Acknowledgements

We sincerely appreciate the input and support of China Social Sciences Press's President Zhao Jianying for this project and Xia Xia, Yang Yang, and Zhou Guanghuan in the department of international Cooperation & Publishing at CSSP served as the editors and proofreaders. They have done a lot of work in arranging the preparation of the English version.

We also sincerely appreciate the hard work of the translators, Mr. Yang Limeng and Wu Yisheng. Without their diligent work, this English version would not exist.

Finally we especially appreciate the financial support in the publication of this book from CASS Innovation Translation Fund.

December 3, 2015

Part I

On economic development

1 Advance the progress in the urban and rural integration steadily

1. China's economic society has entered a new stage of economic development, in which agricultural development is promoted by industry, and rural development is fueled by urban expansion; at the 4th plenary session of the 16th CPC central committee, secretary-general Hu Jintao put forward an important argument of "two tendencies", stressing that China has generally entered the stage of economic development in which industry nurtures agriculture and cities support countryside

Our studies have indicated that the new stage began with the 10th Five-Year Plan, the bases for which are as follows:

(1) The pace of industrialization and urbanization in China quickened significantly since the beginning of the 21st century

It is estimated that China's industrialization entered the second half of the middle period by 2005, with the synthetic index of industrialization level up to 50. Seven provinces and municipalities have already realized industrialization or entered the late stage of industrialization, including Shanghai, Beijing, Tianjin, Jiangsu, Zhejiang, Guangdong, and Shandong; 10 provinces, municipalities, and autonomous regions are at the late stage of industrialization, including Liaoning, Fujian, Shanxi, Jilin, Inner Mongolia, Hubei, Hebei, Heilongjiang, Ningxia, and Chongqing; and 13 provinces and autonomous regions remain at the initial stage of industrialization, including Shaanxi, Qinghai, Hunan, Henan, Xinjiang, Anhui, Jiangxi, Sichuan, Gansu, Yunnan, Guangxi, Hainan, and Guizhou. In the meantime, the pace of urbanization in China has also quickened significantly. By 2005, the urbanization rate in China has reached 42.99%, even up to 50% in nine provinces and municipalities such as Beijing, Tianjin, Liaoning, Jilin, Heilongjiang, Shanghai, Jiangsu, Zhejiang, and Guangdong.

(2) Financial scale expanding rapidly with increasing financial revenue

The average annual growth rate of China's financial revenue was 16.49% during the 9th Five-Year Plan (1996–2000), 20.43% during the 10th Five-Year Plan

(2001–2005), and 21.81% in the first three years (2006–2008) of the 11th Five-Year Plan. In this period, China's financial revenue was much higher than the average annual growth rate of 14.2% from 1979 to 2008. What's more, the scale of China's financial revenue expanded rapidly with accelerated pace of industrialization; the financial revenue exceeded RMB1 trillion in 50 years (1.1444 trillion in 1999), further increased to RMB2 trillion in four years, to RMB 3 trillion in two years, to RMB5 trillion in two years only, to RMB 6 trillion in one year, and is expected to draw near or exceed RMB10 trillion this year.

(3) Rapidly increasing financial funds for agriculture and expanding financial scale

The Central Government has begun to make large-scale investment and all-round compensation for "three rural issues" (concerning agriculture, farmers, and rural areas), e.g. direct grain-growing subsidy, selective seed subsidy, agricultural implements purchase subsidy, and general subsidies for purchasing agricultural supplies for all farmers, as well as additional investment into the construction of rural infrastructure and social undertakings. According to data from the Ministry of Finance, the absolute amount of the financial fund for agriculture increased rapidly since the year of 2000, i.e. only RMB123.154 billion in 2000 and nearly doubled to RMB245.031 billion in 2005. During the 10th Five-Year Plan, the growth rate of funds for agriculture averaged out at 14.9%, 1.6 percentage points faster than the 9th Five-Year Plan. The financial funds for agriculture amounted to RMB351.7 billion in 2006, up to RMB431.8 billion and 595.55 billion respectively in 2007 and 2008, to RMB725.31 billion in 2009, and further up to RMB2104.36 billion in the first four years of the 11th Five-Year Plan, outnumbering the total sum of previous 50 years.

(4) Agricultural taxes abolished throughout the country

In the 21st century, as the pace of industrialization quickens, China is turning from an agricultural country into an industrial one and the financial revenue of the Central Government is now dependent largely on industry and modern services. Of three industries, agriculture makes up a decreasing proportion in financial revenue, and the proportion of agricultural taxes in total government revenue dropped from nearly 40% in 1950 to about 3% in 2000. This indicates that abolition of agricultural taxes throughout the country has little impact on financial revenue. On this ground, agricultural taxes, including a tax on agricultural specialty products except tobacco, were cancelled in 2006 to alleviate farmers' burden amounting to about RMB50 billion, from which more than 700 million farmers have benefited. This marks the end of the history when farmers were obliged to contribute grain to the imperial palace and pay mandatory taxes, which has lasted more than 2600 years.

(5) The proposal of "building a new socialist countryside" conception quickened the infrastructure construction and development of social and cultural

undertakings in rural areas. In October 2005, the CPC Central Committee presented the *Proposal* for the 11th Five-Year Plan, specifying the objectives and tasks of building a new socialist countryside. Afterwards, the Political Bureau of the Central Committee and the State Council conducted monographic studies on this subject. It was emphasized in a series of documents and policy measures issued by the Central Committee that we would by all means increase investment in "three rural issues", alleviate burden on farms, increase farmers' income, and build a new socialist countryside with "well-developed production, well-off life, civilized rural customs, clean and tidy villages, and democratic administration".

The aforesaid facts have proven that China's economic society has generally entered a new stage at which agriculture is nurtured by industry, and the countryside is supported by cities. In this case, the CPC Central Committee and the State Council proposed in time that the urban construction be integrated with rural construction and overall consideration be given to both urban and rural development. However, it is also clear that conditions for the construction of urban–rural integration vary from one region to another due to the disparate development of China's economic society. For regions that have entered the late period of industrialization or have realized industrialization and whose urbanization rate has measured up to 50%, the conditions therein have become mature for the construction of urban–rural integration, so they are required to focus on upgrading the industrial structure and the acceleration of such integration. For regions that remain in the initial or middle period of industrialization and whose urbanization rate remains below 40%, they are required to quicken the space of industrialization and urbanization and carry out a pilot project of urban–rural integration in selected cities where conditions permit, and promote overall urban–rural integration later on when conditions become mature.

2. Several key issues that must be addressed during the construction of urban–rural integration

In the last two years, some authority ratified some regions to carry out pilot projects with regard to the construction of urban–rural integration; all provinces, municipalities, and autonomous regions made efforts in this regard; many experts and scholars conducted in-depth discussions on this issue. Practice and theoretical research have already proven that breakthroughs must be made in the following key issues, apart from a rather advanced level of industrialization and urbanization, in order to achieve fruitful results of urban–rural integration activities:

(1)   Equalization of public finance

It is affirmative that the State has increased investment in the "three rural issues (rural economy, rural development, rural demography)" in recent years, but the investment is insufficient as compared with investment in urban development. Besides, the growth rate of investment in rural areas remains lower than the growth rate of public finance, despite an increasing absolute amount of investment into "three rural issues". In addition, the national investment put in agricultural infrastructure is inadequate to ensure good maintenance of many water conservancy facilities in bad repair and smooth progression of rural social undertakings, especially the rural social security, thus leading to a big difference in urban–rural income gap and living environment.

(2) Reform of household registry system

This is a big trouble that has the hindered construction of urban–rural integration for a long period. More than 100 million rural migrant workers are perplexed by the problem of citizen identity when they are working in cities; rural college graduates, whether employed or unemployed in cities, do not feel at home when their household registers are sent back to their hometown in rural areas because they fail to find an employer who can help them settle in. The rural household registry, rigidly separated from urban household registry, has discriminated against rural residents in terms of education, employment, and wages/benefits. The Central Government has put forth some requirements stressing the reform of the household registry, but it is not easy to push forward the reform only through efforts of several sectors and local authorities; rather, a comprehensive supplementary reform must be implemented under unified deployment.

(3) Reform of land system

While rural land is owned by the collective as prescribed by law and is contracted to farmers for long-standing cultivation and management, it is difficult to implement the ownership and management rights of rural land in practice. Quite a few local governments infringed upon farmers' interests by the low-cost requisition of rural land and reselling to land developers, thus earning a large amount of land fund, much of which was spent on the construction of large- and medium-sized cities. In the past, local governments implemented urban construction with money accumulated by price scissors, but nowadays they achieve this purpose by the requisition of rural land. During land transfer, many problems have occurred, such as poor scale benefits and low labor productivity. According to data from the National Bureau of Statistics, the labor force population employed in rural areas accounted for above 38% of total employment in 2009, but the primary industry made up only 10.3% of the GDP.

(4) Complete coverage of urban and rural social security

Since the reform and opening up, the new rural social security system has not been established after the disintegration of the old system in China. In recent years, the Central Government has placed great emphasis on the construction of a new rural social security by trial implementation of "new rural endowment insurance system" in some regions; nevertheless, the system has a relatively narrow coverage and low security level, and the investment made in the rural security system by the Central Government remains at a low rate. A huge number of rural workers are employed in cities, but few of them are insured; for those insured, their endowment insurance relations cannot be transferred or renewed.

(5) Formation of a uniform market for urban and rural labor force

Due to restrictions on household registry, the labor market in China is in fact split into an urban labor market and a rural labor market, resulting in an unreasonable employment structure. In 2008, China's three industries presented a production value structure of 11.3:48.6:40.1, while the employment structure was 40.0:26.8:32.4. In developed countries, however, the production value structure and employment structure changed synchronously and coordinated generally with each other. As a result of the household registry barrier and split labor market, rural workers make up an overwhelming majority of blue-collar staff in many industries, a unique case around the globe; what's more, they are not treated in the same way as urban workers.

(6) Quickening construction of medium- and small-sized towns

As the pace of industrialization and urbanization quickens in China, there will be a great amount of the rural population migrating into cities.

Due to limited bearing capacity in large- and medium-sized cities and small towns, a majority of rural migrant workers have aggregated in medium- and small-sized cities and small towns that attract insufficient investment from the Central Government and receive the poor effect of industrial agglomeration. Therefore, it will be less likely to help rural migrant workers settle in large- and medium-sized cities and small towns unless the industrial development and living environment are improved.

(Published in *Chinese Academy of Social Sciences Brief Report for Leaders' Reference*, Oct 25, 2010)

2 The process of industrialization and the change of the financial revenue and expenditure structure

The process of industrialization has changed the situation where state revenue relied largely on agriculture and traditionally commercial circulation industries in the early period after liberation in 1949. In the 9th Five-Year Plan (1996–2000), the transition from an agricultural country into an industrial country quickened in China, and the state revenue was derived mainly from industry and modern services industry; as a result, the improved state revenue began to reduce farmers' burden substantially. Ever since the abolition of agricultural taxes throughout the country in 2006, farmers are no longer obliged to pay taxes for growing crops; instead, they can also obtain direct subsidy for growing crops, subsidy for growing superior crop varieties, subsidy for the purchase of fertilizer and farm implements as well as other subsidies from the Central Government, which has intended to increase investment in rural infrastructures, including water conservancy facilities and roads, and other social and cultural establishments. This marks China's access into the new stage in which agriculture is nurtured by industry and countryside is supported by the cities.

1. Process of industrialization and growth of financial revenue

Our studies show that the process of China's industrialization began to accelerate after the year of 1992. The composite index of China's industrialization level reached 18 in 1995, indicating China's entry into the second half of the initial period of industrialization. At the end of 2000, the composite index reached 26 with an average annual growth rate of 1.6, indicating that China entered an acceleration period of the industrialization process during the 9th Five-Year Plan (1995–2000), but remains in the second half of initial period of industrialization. At the end of 2005, the composite index reached 50, marking the advent of the middle and late periods of industrialization; in other words, China's industrialization process quickened at a high speed in the 10th Five-Year Plan, during which the composite index of industrialization level grew nearly five levels per year on average.

As the process of industrialization quickens, the secondary industry, especially the manufacturing industry, plays more important roles in the national economy and accelerates and makes increasing contribution to the growth of financial revenue (see Table 1.2.1).

It is shown in Table 1.2.1 and Fig. 1.2.1 that there are two periods for China's financial revenue in 28 years from 1981 to 2008:

Period I (1981–1992): unstable growth of financial revenue. The growth rate was 22.0% in 1985, the highest growth rate, and 20.2% in 1984, the second highest rate, but dropped to 1.4% in 1981, 3.1% in 1982, 5.8% in 1986, 3.6% in 1987, 7.2% in 1988, and only around 10% in other years, e.g. 11.6% per year

Table 1.2.1 China's Financial Revenue and Growth Rate during 1981 and 2008

Year	Financial revenue (RMB100 million Yuan)	Growth rate of financial revenue (%)	Year	Financial revenue (RMB100 million Yuan)	Growth rate of financial revenue (%)
1981	1,175.79	1.4	1995	6,242.20	19.6
1982	1,212.33	3.1	1996	7,407.99	18.7
1983	1,366.95	12.8	1997	8,651.14	16.8
1984	1,642.86	20.2	1998	9,875.95	14.2
1985	2,004.82	22.0	1999	11,444.08	15.9
1986	2,122.01	5.8	2000	13,395.23	17.0
1987	2,199.35	3.6	2001	16,386.04	22.3
1988	2,357.24	7.2	2002	18,903.64	15.4
1989	2,664.90	13.1	2003	21,715.25	14.9
1990	2,937.10	10.2	2004	26,396.47	21.6
1991	3,149.48	7.2	2005	31,649.29	19.9
1992	3,483.37	10.6	2006	38,760.00	22.5
1993	4,348.95	24.8	2007	51,322.00	32.4
1994	5,218.10	20.0	2008	61,330.00	19.5

Source: Based on data from *China Statistical Yearbook*.

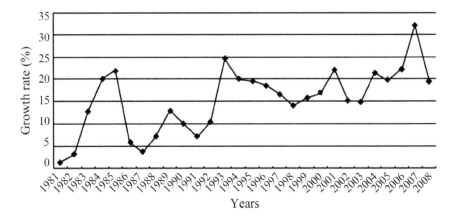

Fig. 1.2.1 Growth Rate of Financial Revenue from 1981 through 2008

on average during the 6th Five-Year Plan (1981–1985) and 7.9% per year on average during the 7th Five-Year Plan (1986–1990). In these 12 years, the rate remained below 10% for six years.

Period II (after 1993): stable and rapid growth of financial revenue. In these 16 years, the growth rate was below 15% for two years, e.g. 14.2% in 1998 and 14.9% in 2003; it was around 20% for nine years, e.g. the highest at 32.4% in 2007, 16.3% per year on average during the 8th Five-Year Plan (1991–1995), 16.49% per year on average during the 9th Five-Year Plan (1996–2000), 20.43% per year average during the 10th Five-Year Plan (2001–2005), and 21.81% in the first three years of the 11th Five-Year Plan (2006–2008). The process of industrialization in China went through a period of acceleration and rapid progress during the 8th Five-Year Plan when the financial revenue was much higher than the annual growth rate 14.2% from 1979 to 2008, 11.6% during the 6th Five-Year Plan and 7.9% during the 7th Five-Year Plan (see Fig. 1.2.2).

What's more, as industrialization is accelerating and progressing rapidly in China, the financial revenue is increasing rapidly, up to RMB1 trillion Yuan in 50 years (1.1444 trillion in 1999), from 1 to 2 trillion in four years, from 2 to 3 trillion in two years, from 3 to 5 trillion in two years, and from 5 to 6 trillion in one year (see Fig. 1.2.3).

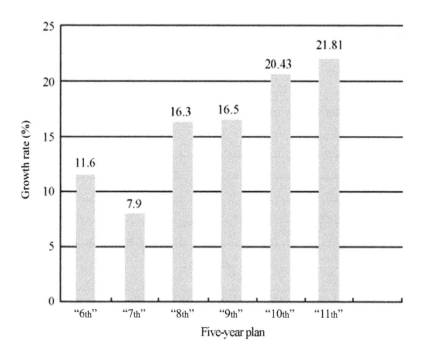

Fig. 1.2.2 China's Financial Revenue Growth Rates from the 6th Five-Year Plan to the First Three Years of the 11th Five-Year Plan

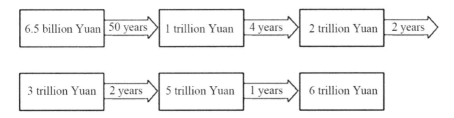

Fig. 1.2.3 Expansion of China's Financial Revenue from 1950 to 2008

If price factors are excluded, China's financial revenue in 1993 is RMB434.895 billion Yuan, 10% higher than the 391.97 billion during the 4th Five-Year Plan; 521.810 billion in 1994, exceeding 508.961 billion in the 5th Five-Year Plan; 740.799 billion in 1996, roughly equal to 740.275 billion in 6th Five-Year Plan; 1,339.523 billion in 2000, 1.09 times 1,228.06 billion in the 7th Five-Year Plan; 2,639.647 billion in 2004, 1.18 times 22,442.10 billion in the 8th Five-Year Plan; and 6,133 billion in 2008, 1.21 times 5,077.439 billion in the 9th Five-Year Plan.

2. Process of industrialization and the change of financial revenue and expenditure structure

The change of financial revenue structure reflects the change of the industrialization process and economic situation in China. The financial revenue structure can be investigated from several perspectives. This paper addresses how financial revenue structure is influenced by the industrialization process, so the financial revenue structure will be investigated from the perspective of sector structure and industrial structure.

(1) Sector structure change of financial revenue

Sector structure of financial revenue means income structure that forms financial revenue provided by sectors such of industry, agriculture, commerce, transportation industry, and building industry. Prior to 1996, complete statistical data were made available by National Bureau of Statistics (see Table 1.2.2 and Table 1.2.3).

By data in Table 1.2.2 and Table 1.2.3, we have reached the following conclusions:

(i)   In the early period after liberation in 1949, China's financial revenue relied largely on agriculture. In 1950, agriculture made up 39.17% of state revenue; industry, 30.22%; and commerce, 16.43%. In 1952, industry took the first place, followed by commerce and agriculture, and the sequence continued till the end of the 8th Five-Year Plan.

Table 1.2.2 Financial Revenues Provided by All Sectors (RMB100 million Yuan)

Period	Total financial revenue	Agriculture	Industry	Building industry	Commercial industry	Transportation	Others
1950	65.20	25.54	19.70	0.36	10.71	1.00	7.88
1951	133.10	33.70	41.69	0.79	27.98	5.17	23.81
1952	183.70	37.06	62.24	0.85	41.73	9.54	32.30
1950–1952	382.00	96.30	123.63	2.00	80.42	15.71	63.99
1st Five-Year Plan (1953–1957)	1,354.90	201.88	602.58	6.5	305.31	102.33	136.32
2nd Five-Year Plan (1958–1962)	2,116.70	176.92	1,244.62	4.03	375.62	230.50	84.93
3rd Five-Year Plan (1966–1970)	2,529.10	176.83	1,813.52	−2.90	292.54	188.61	60.50
4th Five-Year Plan (1971–1975)	3,919.70	151.63	2,907.95	−2.53	463.13	297.45	102.08
5th Five-Year Plan (1976–1980)	5,089.61	154.23	3,885.52	0.90	364.68	363.69	320.59
6th Five-Year Plan (1981–1985)	7,402.75	304.10	5,274.87	25.76	−6.78	441.28	1,363.52
7th Five-Year Plan (1986–1990)	12,280.60	559.75	6,474.90	176.10	2,476.00	748.08	1,845.77
8th Five-Year Plan (1991–1995)	22,442.10	1,183.91	10,364.63	403.75	6,837.65	940.14	2,712.02

Source: Based on data from *China Statistical Yearbook*.

(ii) From the 3rd Five-Year Plan to the 6th Five-Year Plan, agriculture contributed more than 70% to state revenue, e.g. 71.71% during the 3rd Five-Year Plan, 74.19% during the 4th Five-Year Plan, 76.35% during the 5th Five-Year Plan, and 71.26% during the 6th Five-Year Plan.

(iii) From the 3rd Five-Year Plan to the 6th Five-Year Plan, commerce's contribution to state revenue fell 10–20 percentage points as compared with that in a normal period, e.g. 11.57% during the 3rd Five-Year Plan, 11.82% during the 4th Five-Year Plan, 7.12% during the 5th Five-Year Plan, and down to -0.09% during the 6th Five-Year Plan. This is 10–20 percentage points lower than the 21.05% during 1950–1952, the 22.54% during the 1st Five-Year Plan, the 20.16% during the 7th Five-Year Plan, and the 30.47% during the 8th Five-Year Plan. In other words, the increasing proportion of the secondary industry in this period is due to the backward development of commerce rather than acceleration of the industrialization

Table 1.2.3 Financial Revenue Proportions Provided by All Sectors (%)

Period	Total financial revenue	Agriculture	Industry	Building industry	Commercial industry	Transportation	Others
1950	100	39.17	30.22	0.55	16.43	1.53	12.10
1951	100	25.32	31.32	0.59	21.02	3.88	17.89
1952	100	20.17	33.88	0.46	22.72	5.19	17.58
1950–1952	100	25.21	32.36	0.53	21.05	4.10	16.75
1st Five-Year Plan (1953–1957)	100	14.90	44.47	0.46	22.54	7.57	10.07
2nd Five-Year Plan (1958–1962)	100	8.36	58.81	0.19	17.75	10.89	4.00
3rd Five-Year Plan (1966–1970)	100	6.99	71.71	−0.11	11.57	7.46	2.39
4th Five-Year Plan (1971–1975)	100	3.87	74.19	−0.06	11.82	7.58	2.60
5th Five-Year Plan (1976–1980)	100	3.04	76.35	0.03	7.12	7.15	6.31
6th Five-Year Plan (1981–1985)	100	4.11	71.26	0.35	−0.09	5.96	18.41
7th Five-Year Plan (1986–1990)	100	4.56	52.72	1.43	20.16	6.09	15.04
8th Five-Year Plan (1991–1995)	100	5.28	46.18	1.8	30.47	4.19	12.08

process. There are two reasons for the backward development of commerce: many commercial enterprises were eliminated during the 3rd Five-Year Plan and the 4th Five-Year Plan as remnants of capitalism under the influence of the "extreme-leftists" policy; the original commercial circulation system and channels were altered due to some deviation in the guiding ideology of the reform; the new system and channels were not yet opened during the 5th Five-Year Plan and the 6th Five-Year Plan. Should a normal development trend be maintained in commerce, the proportion made by industry in state revenue would have dropped 10–20 percentage points to a normal level of 45–50%.

(2)　Change of industrial structure for financial revenue

The financial revenue structure consists mainly of industrial sectors in line with three industrial structures: the primary industry (agriculture), the secondary industry (manufacturing and building), and the tertiary industry (services and circulation sector). Analyzing sector structure of financial revenue allows us to foster revenue sources, adjust structure, improve effects, and achieve increasing production and income.

According to Table 1.2.2 and Table 1.2.3, due to the slow development of building trade in the secondary industry and transportation service in the

Table 1.2.4 Three Industries' Contribution to Financial Revenue (RMB100 million Yuan)

Period	Total financial revenue	Primary industry	Secondary industry	Tertiary industry
1950	65.2	25.54	20.06	19.60
1951	123.1	37.70	42.69	42.71
1952	183.7	37.06	63.09	83.55
1950–1952	382.05	96.30	123.99	161.76
1st Five-Year Plan (1953–1957)	1,354.9	201.88	609.08	543.96
2nd Five-Year Plan (1958–1962)	2,116.7	176.92	1,248.65	691.05
3rd Five-Year Plan (1966–1970)	2,529.1	176.83	1,810.62	541.65
4th Five-Year Plan (1971–1975)	3,919.7	151.63	2,905.42	8,62.66
5th Five-Year Plan (1976–1980)	5,089.6	154.23	3,886.51	1,048.96
6th Five-Year Plan (1981–1985)	7,402.75	304.10	5,300.63	1,798.02
7th Five-Year Plan (1986–1990)	12,280.6	559.75	6,651.00	5,069.85
8th Five-Year Plan (1991–1995)	22,442.1	1,183.91	10,768.38	10,489.81

Source: Based on data from *China Statistical Yearbook*.

Table 1.2.5 Three Industries' Proportion in Financial Revenue (%)

Period	Total financial revenue	Primary industry	Secondary industry	Tertiary industry
1950	100	38.96	30.77	30.27
1951	100	30.63	34.68	34.69
1952	100	20.17	34.34	45.49
1950–1952	100	25.21	32.89	41.90
1st Five-Year Plan (1953–1957)	100	14.90	44.93	40.17
2nd Five-Year Plan (1958–1962)	100	8.36	59.00	32.64
3rd Five-Year Plan (1966–1970)	100	6.99	71.60	21.41
4th Five-Year Plan (1971–1975)	100	3.87	74.13	22.00
5th Five-Year Plan (1976–1980)	100	3.04	76.38	20.58
6th Five-Year Plan (1981–1985)	100	4.11	71.61	24.28
7th Five-Year Plan (1986–1990)	100	4.56	54.15	41.29
8th Five-Year Plan (1991–1995)	100	5.28	47.98	46.74

tertiary industry, their proportions in financial revenue were too low to alter the aforesaid conclusions.

In the early period after New China was founded, China's financial revenue was derived mainly from the primary industry, i.e. agriculture. In 1950, agriculture made up nearly 40% of state revenue; later on, the secondary industry increased its proportion and gradually became the largest contributor, followed by the tertiary industry.

3. Impact of "price scissors" on the financial revenue structure

Direct reference to figures in *China Statistical Yearbook* that describe the contributions of each sector and industry to financial revenue is usually questioned by many specialists and scholars, especially those who are specialized in studies of agricultural economy. They argue that agricultural contribution has been less reckoned due to "price scissors". There is some truth in this argument. To solve this problem, factors of "price scissors" must be considered.

The definition of "price scissors" may vary from one specialist or scholar to another. As our studies are designed to define contributions of agriculture and industry to financial revenue, the concept "price scissors" mentioned herein means agriculture's contribution to financial revenue that is less reckoned due to the government intentionally bringing down the prices of agricultural products by means of mandatory price and other administrative means. The "price scissors" prevailed during 1953 and 1983, the period that started at the beginning of state monopoly for purchase and marketing and continued to the initial stage of the reform and opening up.

Specialists and scholars have conducted a number of studies on this problem and produced various calculating methods, but results vary.

This paper adopts the calculating method of Wu Li (2001) to adjust the amount and proportion contributed by agriculture to state revenue (see Table 1.2.6) because:

(1) this scientific method is acceptable to the majority of people due to use of difference between planned price and market price for calculation; (2) the calculated result is roughly equal to research result, i.e. RMB14.74 billion Yuan per year on average; and (3) balance over years listed links up with our studies. See Table 1.2.7 and Table 1.2.8 for adjusted contribution and proportion of three industries to financial revenue.

The price difference computed by Wu Li has included 25–30% spreads resold to farmers, which is deducted in the right column. While providing data listed in the table, he made an analysis that the following five points need to be clarified when treating with aforesaid data based on experience and historical materials: (1) suppose the market price is consistent with state purchase price in 1952 when the state monopoly for purchase and marketing policy was implemented. In fact, the market price at that time was fluctuating within a narrow range around the state-fixed price; (2) the state purchase price was higher

Table 1.2.6 Changes of Price and Quantity of Agricultural and Sideline Products during 1952 and 1983

Years	Market trade price index (100 in 1952)	Combined index of state purchase price of agricultural and sideline products (100 in 1952)	Purchase volume of agricultural and sideline products from rural areas (RMB 100 million Yuan)	Index difference between market price and state purchase price	Difference between two prices of agricultural and sideline products from rural areas (RMB 100 million Yuan)	Actual difference after deduction of return selling to farmers (RMB 100 million Yuan)
1953	103.9	109.0	155.7	−5.1	−7.9	−7.90
1954	106.3	112.4	179.2	−6.1	−10.9	−10.90
1955	106.1	111.1	180.9	−5.0	−9.0	−9.00
1956	105.9	114.5	180.6	−8.6	−15.5	−15.50
1957	108.9	120.2	208.1	−11.3	−23.5	−23.50
1958	117.5	122.9	222.2	−5.4	−11.9	−11.90
1959	119.0	125.1	265.2	−6.1	−16.2	−16.20
1960	136.6	129.4	208.0	7.2	14.9	9.83
1961	491.8	165.6	196.0	326.2	639.4	422.0
1962	319.6	164.6	203.0	155.0	314.7	207.70
1963	241.2	159.9	232.0	81.3	186.9	123.50
1964	167.8	155.8	263.0	12.0	31.6	20.86
1965	173.2	154.5	299.3	18.7	55.9	36.89
1966	175.3	161.0	336.9	14.3	48.2	31.81
1967	178.2	160.8	335.4	17.4	58.4	38.54
1968	178.2	160.5	328.9	17.7	58.2	38.41
1969	178.1	160.3	314.7	17.8	56.0	36.96
1970	178.1	160.4	337.7	17.7	59.8	39.47
1971	193.8	163.1	358.0	30.7	109.9	72.53
1972	209.6	165.4	364.3	44.2	161.0	106.26
1973	220.7	166.8	421.3	53.9	227.1	149.89
1974	224.8	168.2	430.9	56.6	243.8	160.91
1975	233.8	171.6	457.3	62.2	284.4	187.70
1976	243.1	172.5	448.8	70.6	316.9	209.15
1977	237.2	172.0	478.0	65.2	311.7	205.72
1978	221.6	178.8	530.1	42.8	226.9	149.75
1979	211.6	218.3	677.6	−6.7	−45.4	−45.40
1980	215.8	233.9	797.7	−18.1	−144.4	−144.40
1981	228.3	247.7	908.0	−19.4	−176.2	−176.20
1982	235.8	253.1	1,031.0	−17.3	−178.4	−178.40
1983	245.7	264.2	1,206.0	−18.5	−223.1	−223.10

Source: *China's Trade Price Statistics (1952–1983)*, China Statistical Publishing House, 1984.

Note: The last line is added by the author.

than market price before 1960; during 1953 and 1957, there were two considerations: (i) reduce farmers' resentment against monopolized purchase and marketing and cooperatives to achieve socialist transformation successfully and (ii) learn a lesson from former Soviet Union to minimize "price scissors" between agricultural products and industrial products; but during 1958 and

Table 1.2.7 Contributions of Three Industries to Financial Revenue after Adjustment (RMB100 million Yuan)

Period	Total financial revenue	Primary industry	Secondary industry	Tertiary industry
1950	65.2	25.54	20.06	19.6
1951	123.1	37.70	42.69	42.71
1952	183.7	37.06	63.09	83.55
1950–1952	382.05	96.30	123.99	161.76
1st Five-Year Plan (1953–1957)	1,288.10	135.08	609.08	543.96
2nd Five-Year Plan (1958–1962)	2,728.13	788.35	1,248.65	691.05
3rd Five-Year Plan (1966–1970)	2,717.30	362.02	1,810.62	541.65
4th Five-Year Plan (1971–1975)	4,596.89	828.92	2,905.42	862.66
5th Five-Year Plan (1976–1980)	5,464.52	529.05	3,886.51	1,048.96
6th Five-Year Plan (1981–1985)	7,098.65	−273.00	5,300.63	1,798.02
7th Five-Year Plan (1986–1990)	12,280.60	559.75	6,651.00	5,069.85
8th Five-Year Plan (1991–1995)	22,442.10	1,183.91	10,768.39	10,489.81

Note: Financial revenue, with "price scissors" factors considered, is greater than actual financial revenue.

Table 1.2.8 Proportions of Three Industries in Financial Revenue after Adjustment (%)

Period	Total financial revenue	Primary industry	Secondary industry	Tertiary industry
1950	100	38.96	30.77	30.27
1951	100	30.63	34.68	34.69
1952	100	20.17	34.34	45.49
1950–1952	100	25.21	32.89	41.90
1st Five-Year Plan (1953–1957)	100	10.49	47.29	40.17
2nd Five-Year Plan (1958–1962)	100	28.30	45.77	32.64
3rd Five-Year Plan (1966–1970)	100	13.32	66.63	21.41
4th Five-Year Plan (1971–1975)	100	18.03	63.20	22.00
5th Five-Year Plan (1976–1980)	100	8.31	71.11	20.58
6th Five-Year Plan (1981–1985)	100	—	74.67	25.33
7th Five-Year Plan (1986–1990)	100	4.56	54.16	41.28
8th Five-Year Plan (1991–1995)	100	5.28	47.98	46.74

1959, the reason might be stagnant market trade as a result of the people's commune system "large in size and collective in nature"; (3) during the Great Chinese Famine (1961–1963), the market price of agricultural products deviated greatly from the state purchase price due to the great famine, which cannot be viewed as a normal trend; (4) with regard to market the trade price index mentioned herein, the price should be higher than the market price under open conditions as there were few agricultural products available for trading; and (5) after 1979, with the rise in purchase price and an increasing supply of agricultural products, the ratio between market price and purchase price returned to the situation before 1957, so it is hard to argue that the state benefits from "price scissors" by arbitrary pricing.

Three conclusions can be reached from Table 1.2.8 and Figs. 1.2.4 and 1.2.5:

(1)   The structure of revenues provided by three industries has changed, with the greatest change in the primary industry. During the 2nd Five-Year Plan, the primary industry made up 28.3% of state revenue, 19.94 percentage points higher than it did before adjustment; during the 3rd Five-Year Plan, it made up 13.32%, 6.33 percentage points higher; during the 4th Five-Year Plan, it made up 18.03%, 14.16 percentage points higher; and during the 5th Five-Year Plan, it made up 9.68%, 6.64 percentage points higher. In the meantime, the proportions of the secondary and tertiary industries dropped at varying degree, with a greater drop rate in the secondary industry. After adjustment, the proportion of the secondary industry dropped

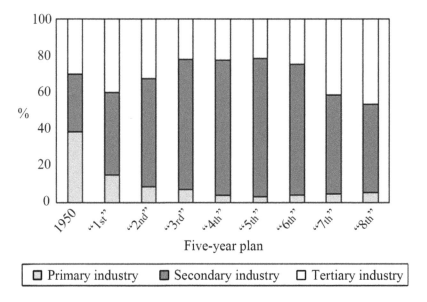

Fig. 1.2.4 Proportions of Three Industries in Financial Revenue before Adjustment

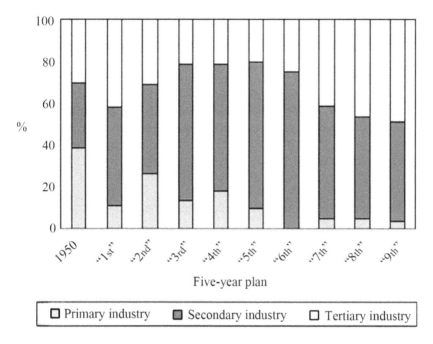

Fig. 1.2.5 Proportions of Three Industries in Financial Revenue after Adjustment

from 59% to 45.77% during the 2nd Five-Year Plan, down 13.23 percentage points; from 71.6% to 66.63% during the 3rd Five-Year Plan, down 4.97 percentage points; from 74.13% to 63.20% during the 4th Five-Year Plan, down 10.93 percentage points; and from 76.38% to 71.11% during the 5th Five-Year Plan, down 5.27 percentage points.

(2) This adjustment has not changed the step-down trend of agriculture's contribution to state revenue or the uptrend of the secondary industry's contribution (based on manufacturing) to state revenue.

(3) From the 3rd Five-Year Plan to the 6th Five-Year Plan, as we analyzed in previous paragraph, the proportion of the secondary industry in state revenue was on the high side, up to 70%, because the commerce of the tertiary industry dropped about 20% as against normal period; with this factor deducted, the secondary industry should have made up around 45% of state revenue. From the 7th Five-Year Plan to the 8th Five-Year Plan, the proportion of the three industries in state revenue seemed realistic when the "price scissors" factor became less influential and commerce recovered to a normal growth rate.

In the 9th, 10th, and 11th Five-Year Plan periods, China's industrialization paced up and financial revenue grew at a high rate. It is certain that the financial revenue structure has changed a lot in this period, but we regret not conducting studies on it in this article. Unfortunately, the *China Statistical Yearbook* has no longer provided concrete figures of financial revenue contributed by each sector and industry since 1996; but fortunately, the *China Taxation Yearbook* began to publish concrete figures of taxes paid by each industry from the 10th Five-Year Plan. Tax revenue has made up more than 90% of state revenue. For instance, during the 10th Five-Year Plan, China's total tax revenue was RMB10.703308 trillion Yuan, accounting for 93% of state revenue (RMB11.5050 trillion); in the first three years of the 11th Five-Year Plan, the total tax revenue was RMB14.338627 trillion, accounting for 94.7% of state revenue (RMB15.1412 trillion). Therefore, the proportion of taxes paid by each industry can basically reflect its contribution to financial revenue (see Table 1.2.9 and Table 1.2.10).

These figures have indicated the following:

(1) As the industrialization increased during the 10th Five-Year Plan and the 11th Five-Year Plan, the primary industry contributed less and less to financial tax revenue; especially after the exemption of agricultural taxes, its contribution would be negative should public subsidies for agriculture be included.

(2) During the 10th Five-Year Plan and the 11th Five-Year Plan, the secondary industry, the manufacturing industry in particular, contributed the most to China's state revenue, stabilizing at above 50% and up to 59.01% during the 10th Five-Year Plan. This shows that, with the accelerating pace of industrialization that stimulated the rapid growth of financial and tax revenue, the secondary industry made up an increasing proportion of financial and tax revenue during the 10th Five-Year Plan and the 11th Five-Year Plan, more than 10 percentage points higher than it did before this period.

Table 1.2.9 Tax Revenues Paid by Three Industries during the 10th Five-Year Plan and in the First Three Years of the 11th Five-Year Plan (100 million Yuan)

Year	Total financial revenue	Primary industry	Secondary industry	Tertiary industry
10th Five-Year Plan	107,033.08	23.64	63,160.42	43,836.31
2001	14,910.68	1.46	8,489.32	6,407.20
2002	16,633.03	6.29	9,858.54	6,768.20
2003	19,991.80	4.81	11,844.18	8,142.81
2004	25,188.80	4.72	15,002.52	10,181.55
2005	30,308.78	6.37	17,965.86	12,336.54
11th Five-Year Plan (2006–2008)	143,386.27	40.41	77,978.58	65,253.48
2006	36,949.59	14.22	21,293.15	15,642.22
2007	48,574.92	13.54	26,041.68	22,519.70
2008	57,861.76	12.64	30,643.76	27,091.56

Source: Based on data from *China Taxation Yearbook*.

Table 1.2.10 Proportions of Taxes Paid by Three Industries during the 10th Five-Year Plan and in the First Three Years of the 11th Five-Year Plan (%)

Year	Total financial revenue	Primary industry	Secondary industry	Tertiary industry
10th Five-Year Plan	100	0.03	59.01	40.96
2001	100	0.09	56.94	42.97
2002	100	0.04	59.27	40.96
2003	100	0.02	59.25	40.73
2004	100	0.02	59.56	40.42
2005	100	0.02	59.28	40.70
11th Five-Year Plan (2006–2008)	100	0.03	54.38	45.51
2006	100	0.04	57.63	42.33
2007	100	0.03	53.61	42.33
2008	100	0.02	52.96	46.82

(3) Since 2006, the secondary industry maintained an up to 50% contribution rate to financial and tax revenue, but the proportion seemed to decline, with an average decline of 1.38, 5.4, and 6.05 percentage points during 2006 and 2008 as against the 10th Five-Year Plan period; by contrast, the tertiary industry showed an uptrend in its contribution to state revenue. Is it a behavior that emerges in the middle and late period of industrialization process? This needs further investigation.

4. Process of industrialization and change of financial expenditure structure

Now let's look at the relationship between the industrialization process and the financial expenditure structure, focusing on the change of financial funds for agriculture.

According to Fig. 1.2.6 and Table 1.2.11, the absolute amount of financial funds for agriculture increased rapidly after the year of 2000; it was only RMB123.154 billion in 2000 but nearly doubled to RMB245.031 billion in 2005. During the 10th Five-Year Plan, despite drastic fluctuations, financial funds for agriculture grew at an average rate of 14.9%, 1.6 percentage points higher than the 9th Five-Year Plan. The expenditure for supporting agriculture in 2006 alone amounted to 1.4 times expenditure during the 8th Five-Year Plan and 64% of expenditure during the 9th Five-Year Plan.

Proportions of financial funds for agriculture are given in Table 1.2.12 and Fig. 1.2.7. The financial expenditure on agriculture was only 7.5% during the 10th Five-Year Plan. Ever since the exemption of agriculture taxes in 2004, the amount of agricultural taxes reduced by RMB13.551 billion, and the tax on agricultural specialty products reduced by RMB4.631 billion, totaling RMB18.182 billion in 2004 as compared with tax revenue in 2003;

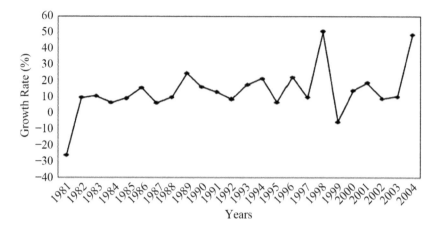

Fig. 1.2.6 Growth Rates of Financial Funds for Agriculture

Table 1.2.11 Amount Growth Rate of Financial Funds for Agriculture since 1981

Year	Financial expenditure on agriculture (RMB100 million)	Expenditure growth rate (%)	Year	Financial expenditure on agriculture (RMB100 million)	Expenditure growth rate (%)
1981	110.21	−26.3	1994	532.98	21.0
1982	120.49	9.3	1995	574.93	6.4
1983	132.87	10.3	1996	700.43	21.8
1984	141.29	6.3	1997	766.39	9.4
1985	153.62	8.7	1998	1,154.76	50.7
1986	184.20	15.2	1999	1,085.76	−6.0
1987	195.72	6.1	2000	1,231.54	13.4
1988	214.07	9.4	2001	1,456.73	18.3
1989	265.94	24.2	2002	1,580.76	8.5
1990	307.84	15.8	2003	1,574.45	9.7
1991	347.57	12.9	2004	2,337.63	48.5
1992	376.02	8.2	2005	2,450.31	8.7
1993	440.45	17.1	2006	3172.97	29.5

Source: Based on data from *China Statistical Yearbook*.

the former reduced by RMB32.142 billion and the latter 4.3 billion, totaling RMB36.442 billion in 2005 as against in 2003. Should all these revenues be included, the proportion of financial funds for agriculture would come near to 8% during the 10th Five-Year Plan.

A clear relationship between the industrialization process and agriculture is revealed by the comparison between financial revenue provided by the primary industry and financial funds for agriculture (see Table 1.2.13).

Table 1.2.12 Proportion of Financial Funds for Agriculture

Period	Total financial expenditure (RMB100 million)	Expenditure on agriculture (RMB100 million)	Proportion in total expenditure (%)
1950	68.1	2.74	4.0
1951	122.1	4.19	3.4
1952	176.1	9.04	5.1
1950–1952	366.6	15.97	4.4
1st Five-Year Plan	1,345.6	99.58	7.4
2nd Five-Year Plan	2,288.7	283.65	12.4
3rd Five-Year Plan	2,518.6	230.45	9.1
4th Five-Year Plan	3,917.94	401.22	10.2
5th Five-Year Plan	5,282.44	693.55	13.1
6th Five-Year Plan	7,483.18	658.48	8.8
7th Five-Year Plan	12,865.67	1,167.77	9.1
8th Five-Year Plan	24,387.46	2,271.95	9.3
9th Five-Year Plan	57,043.46	4,938.88	8.7
10th Five-Year Plan	128,022.85	9,579.88	7.5

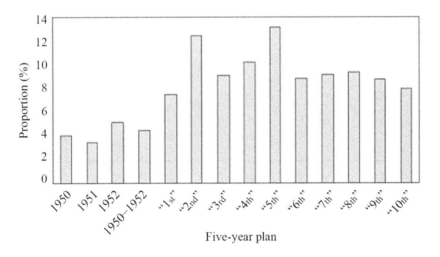

Fig. 1.2.7 Proportion of Financial Funds for Agriculture

According to Table 1.2.13 and Fig. 1.2.8, China's national policy for agriculture was implemented in three stages:

Stage 1: From the founding of the People's Republic of China in 1949 to implementation of the reform and opening up policy, and the national policy then was "agriculture supports industry and countryside supports cities". In this period, the state government collected a lot of money from the countryside for industrial and urban construction. Before the 5th Five-Year Plan, the money

Table 1.2.13 Comparison between Financial Revenue Provided by Primary Industry and Financial Expenditure on Agriculture

Period	Financial revenue provided by the primary industry (RMB100 million)	Expenditure on agriculture (RMB100 million)	Net expenditure (RMB100 million)
1950	25.54	2.74	−22.80
1951	37.70	4.19	−33.51
1952	37.06	9.04	−28.02
1950–1952	96.30	15.97	−80.33
1st Five-Year Plan (1953–1957)	135.08	99.58	−35.50
2nd Five-Year Plan (1958–1962)	788.35	283.65	−504.70
3rd Five-Year Plan (1966–1970)	362.02	230.45	−131.57
4th Five-Year Plan (1971–1975)	828.92	401.22	−427.0
5th Five-Year Plan (1976–1980)	529.05	693.55	164.50
6th Five-Year Plan (1981–1985)	−273.00	658.48	931.48
7th Five-Year Plan (1986–1990)	559.75	1,167.77	608.02
8th Five-Year Plan (1991–1995)	1,183.91	2,271.95	1,080.04
9th Five-Year Plan (1996–2000)	2,054.55	4,938.88	2,884.33
10th Five-Year Plan (2001–2005)	23.64	9,579.88	9,556.24
11th Five-Year Plan (2006–2008)	40.40	13,790.50	13,750.10

Notes

(1) The financial revenue listed in the table and provided by the primary industry means revenue with "price scissors" factors deducted, which is higher than actual financial revenue;

(2) The financial revenue provided by agriculture and listed in the table after the 9th Five-Year Plan was replaced with the revenue of agricultural taxes because data on financial revenues provided by the three industries were no longer published by National Bureau of Statistics after the 9th Five-Year Plan.

withdraw from the countryside was much more than the money put into agriculture by the state during the 1st Five-Year Plan and the 4th Five-Year Plan. In the two decades, the net amount of money withdrawn from the countryside by the state was roughly RMB110 billion, about 5.5 billion per year on average; the biggest amount of 93.24 billion occurred during the 2nd Five-Year Plan and the 4th Five-Year Plan, with about 84.8% of total money withdrawn.

Stage 2: From the implementation of the reform and opening up policy to the year 2000, and the national policy for agriculture then was reducing tax burden and increasing investment, i.e. a flexible policy of "giving more to,

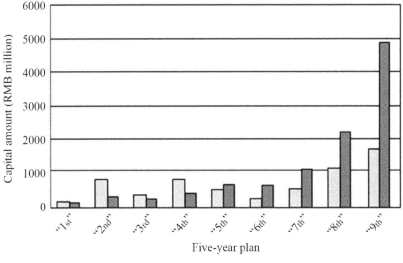

☐ Comparison between Financial Revenue Provided by the Primary Industry
▨ Financial Funds for Agriculture

Fig. 1.2.8 Comparison between Financial Revenue Provided by the Primary Industry and Financial Funds for Agriculture

withdrawing less from and loosening control of rural economy". As a result, the money put into "three rural issues" (countryside, agriculture, and farmers) was more than money withdrawn; in the 25 years, by rough calculation, the net investment by the state into the countryside amounted up to RMB539.566 billion, 21.583 billion per year on average.

Stage 3: Starting from the 10th Five-Year Plan, the fundamental policy of the state then was "giving full support to address three rural issues without taking any money away from countryside". In addition to an exemption of agricultural taxes, the state launched large-scale investment into agriculture and the countryside to make full compensation for the three rural issues. According to data from the Ministry of Agriculture, the financial funds for agriculture amounted to RMB351.7 billion in 2006, 431.8 billion in 2007, 595.55 billion in 2008, 725.31 billion in 2009, and up to 2,104.36 billion in the first four years of the 11th Five-Year Plan, exceeding the sum in the past 50 years.

5. New stage of industrialization and economic development

At the 4th Plenary Session of the 16th CPC Central Committee, Secretary General Hu Jintao proposed an important argument of "two tendencies", stressing that China has generally entered the stage of economic development in which industry nurtures agriculture and cities support the countryside. Our studies have proved that the new stage started from late period of the 9th Five-Year Plan on five bases as follows: (1) the accelerating pace of industrialization since the beginning of the 21st century; (2) the rapid growth of financial revenue and increase of finance size; (3) the rapid growth of financial funds for agriculture; (4) the accelerating rural infrastructure construction and socio-cultural undertaking development after the new concept of building a new socialist countryside was created; and (5) the abolition of agricultural taxes.

The following analysis will focus on the last two points, for we have addressed the first three points in previous paragraphs.

(1) Put forward the idea of building a new socialist countryside and accelerate rural infrastructure construction and socio-cultural construction

There was a cognitive process from the Central Government to local governments when the idea of building a new socialist countryside was created. For quite some time, most people advocated the transfer of rural surplus labor into small towns or medium- and small-sized cities; as a result, great emphasis was placed onto accelerating the construction of small towns rather than on rural construction. This might be a good choice to reduce the rural surplus labor; however, no matter how many rural people migrate into small towns or medium- and small-sized cities, it is inevitable that there will be hundreds of millions of people engaged in agricultural or sideline production in the countryside. A continuous and important problem facing China is how to promote rural construction, agricultural development, and improve farmers' living level. For this reason, the Central Government set out to increase support of the "three rural issues" from the late period of the 9th Five-Year Plan in order to alleviate the burden on farmers, promote rural economic development, and increase farmers' income. The fund for rural capital construction amounted to RMB46.07 billion in 1998, roughly equal to 47.2 billion of investment during the 8th Five-Year Plan. In the last three years of the 9th Five-Year Plan, the state investment into rural capital construction amounted to RMB123.216 billion, much higher than the sum of investment in the two decades during the 5th, 6th, 7th, and 8th Five-Year Plans. The investment into rural capital construction during the 10th Five-Year Plan amounted to RMB248.696 billion, 1.6 times that during the 9th Five-Year Plan and 3.25 times that during the 8th Five-Year Plan.

In 2000, close attention was paid to farmers' income at the 5th Plenary Session of the CPC Central Committee of the CPC. These words "make every endeavor to increase farmers' income" were included into documents of the Central Committee. Thereafter, the 1st Meeting of the 16th National Congress of the CPC proposed harmonizing economic and social development in urban and rural areas. In 2003, the Central Rural Work Conference was required to implement the policy of "giving more to, withdrawing less from and loosening control of rural economy" for agriculture.

At the beginning of 2005, the CPC Central Committee released the No. 1 Document – *Several Opinions of the Central Committee of the Communist Party* of China and the State Council on Further Strengthening Rural Work and Improving Overall Agricultural Production Capacity – to deploy work on the "three rural issues". In October, objectives and tasks of building a new socialist countryside were put forward in the *Proposal for the 11th Five-Year Plan* made by the CPC Central Committee. Later on, the Political Bureau of the Central Committee and the State Council conducted subject researches on building a new socialist countryside. It was stressed in a series of documents and policy measures issued by the Central Committee that we should expand investment into "three rural issues", try to alleviate burden on farmers, make every endeavor to increase farmers' income, and gradually build the countryside into a new socialist countryside with "developed production, well-off living, rural civilization, clean and tidy villages and democratic management".

Since then, building a new socialist countryside has been put in full swing: (i) carry out rural tax reform and abolish agricultural taxes to alleviate burden on farmers; (ii) push forward comprehensive pilot reforms in rural areas and increase transfer payment from the exchequer; (iii) improve direct subsidies for farmers by increasing subsidy items from three to four items (i.e. direct grain subsidy, general subsidy for agricultural supplies, subsidy for superior crop varieties, and subsidy for agricultural implements purchase). Direct grain subsidy and general subsidy for agricultural supplies have benefited 728 million farmers; direct grain subsidy has reached up to 50% of the total grain risk fund nationwide; subsidy for improved varieties of paddy rice has covered all rice-growing areas and the area receiving subsidy for growing wheat and maize has escalated; the subsidy for agricultural implements purchase has extended to all agricultural/animal husbandry counties/ranches throughout the country; agricultural implements entitled to the subsidy have increased to 50 kinds of 18 subclasses under nine categories, such as power machinery, tillage machines, sowing and planting machines, and harvesting machines, covering all necessary machines for agricultural production; (iv) actively support construction of overall agricultural production capacity, focusing on "six categories of small projects in rural areas"; (v) set up and improve new social security system in countryside, and expand new rural cooperative medical pilot reform to the whole country. By 2009, the number of farmers participating in new rural cooperative medical system has reached up to 833 million, with a participation rate of 94%. From 2009, 320 counties have been selected as pilot sites of the new rural endowment insurance system, and the number of pilot counties will be increased to cover the whole country in 5–10 years. The minimal living security system and the rural "five guarantees" system (i.e. providing free services of clothing, housing, medical care, and burial for rural residents without labor capability or living security) will be improved gradually; and (vi) continue to increase support for public health, compulsory education, technological development, environmental protection, and cultural construction in rural areas. In 2004, the state set about promoting experiments on free compulsory education in part of central and western regions, exempted all tuition fees, textbook fees and other fees charged for students with economic difficulty, and granted living allowances for resident students. In 2006, the state decided to exempt all tuition fees and textbook fees for rural students at the stage of compulsory education in western regions, and in 2007 the exemption extended into the central and eastern regions.

(2) Reform of abolishing agricultural taxes

Before the founding of the PRC, China had been a largely agricultural country where the important historical position of agricultural taxes was determined by the dominant position of agriculture. In the rather long historical course of the feudal and semi-feudal society, agricultural taxes had been the main source of government financial revenue; however, heavy taxation had been the most important reason for farmers to fight against oppression and exploitation and even launch uprisings. To alleviate this contradiction, the Rulers had carried out five significant reforms on the agricultural taxation system. The first reform: the feudal labor rent system of "Gong (i.e. in-kind rent, about one tenth of average yield in several years, imposed on tenants by the Ruler), Zhu (i.e. the Ruler allowed people to cultivate public land and then held all grain yield), and Qie (practice of both Gong and Zhu)", was modified to be the rent-in-kind system of "initial tax on land per *mu* (1*mu*=0.0667 hectare)" (i.e. tax levied per *mu* on both public and private land) during Xia, Shang, and Zhou dynasties (2070 B.C.–771 B.C.). The second reform: the proportional agricultural taxation system during Qin Dynasty and Han Dynasty (221 B.C.–220 A.D.) was changed to the quota taxation system in the period from Wei and Jin Dynasties (220–420 A.D.) to the early period of Tang Dynasty (618–907 A.D.), i.e. the taxation system paying commissions by land yield was changed to pay quota tax by land quantity. The third reform: the household-based "Zu Diao" taxation system ("Zu" refers to rent; "Diao" refers to other tributes such as silk, cotton, and linen) in Wei, Jin, Sui, and Tang dynasties (581–907 A.D.) was reformed to Two-Tax Law in the middle and late period of Tang Dynasty, by which corvée and miscellaneous tax were levied after being incorporated into land quantity per *mu*. The fourth reform: the Two-Tax Law in late Tang Dynasty was reformed to "One-Whip Law" (i.e. a uniform taxation system that combined taxes and corvée) in Ming Dynasty (1368–1644), symbolizing that the feudal taxation system, which unified head tax and produce tax and had been in effect for more than 2 thousand years in Chinese history, was transformed into a rent taxation system specific to the in-kind object of farmland, and ever since then, the corvée system has been totally abolished. What's more, it was stipulated in this reform that the tax on agricultural products would be collected per *mu* of land in silver currency, realizing the transition of agricultural tax from paid-in-kind tax system to paid-in-money tax system. The fifth reform: the "One-Whip Law" during the Ming Dynasty was reformed to the taxation system "Tan Ding Ru Mu" (integrating various poll taxes into feudal land tax) during the Qing Dynasty (1616–1912), which is the continuity of the "One-Whip Law" that further completed the incorporation of taxes and corvée and linked the tax burden to tax bearing capacity, and under which, the more land an able-bodied man rented, the more tax he would be levied.

In history, agricultural taxes were totally abolished six times in China. The longest abolition, which had lasted for 11 years, occurred in the period of Emperor Jing of the Han Dynasty; and aside from that, it had lasted only one or two years in all other dynasties. The most fundamental reason for the failure to eradicate agricultural taxes in feudal society is the economic conditions of a country. For an agricultural country where the state revenue is derived mainly from agriculture and traditional commerce, exempting agricultural taxes means cutting off the main source of state revenue; this is why the state government cannot ban agricultural taxes but reduce taxes. After the founding of New China, the Chinese Government had paid close attention to alleviating farmers' burdens, but achieved little effect due to the absence of necessary conditions. In 1990 when the 50th anniversary of the founding of New China was celebrated, the Central Government intended to cheer up farmers with the idea of a one-year exemption of agricultural taxes so that they could share the happiness of achievements of the reform and opening up policy, but did not mean to abolish agricultural taxes thoroughly. The idea was aborted for the fear that it would be more difficult to collect taxes at the expiration of the one-year exemption term; after all, the economic development remained at a low level and the national financial resources remained insufficient.

At the beginning of the 21st century, China realized the transformation from a major agricultural country into an industrial power as the pace of industrialization accelerated, and the state revenue was derived mainly from industry and the modern service industry that serves manufacturing. Among the three industries, the agriculture contributed less and less to state revenue, and the proportion of agricultural taxes in total state revenue dropped from nearly 40% in 1950 to around 3% in 2000. Since the nationwide abolition of agricultural taxes no longer exerted any significant impact on state revenue, pilot reforms on the rural taxation system were initiated in Anhui Province in 2000, including the cancellation of administrative service fees and governmental fund and finance raising, such as the social pooling fund and rural education funding specially imposed on farmers, the cancellation of the butchery tax, the cancellation of voluntary labor service as uniformly required, the adjustment of the policy on agricultural taxes and agricultural specialty products tax, and the modification of collection and use method of "village reserve" (i.e. the administrative fee and collective accumulated fund paid to the village collective economic organization by villagers or enterprises who have contracted the management of collective land or other production projects). Later, the pilot reforms extended to all regions in China in 2003.

In 2004, the Central Government decided to abolish taxes on animal husbandry and agricultural specialty products (except tobacco leaf), carry out a pilot reform of abolishing agricultural taxes and expand the scope of pilot reform, grant direct subsidies for grain-growing farmers and grant subsidies for farmers growing superior grain varieties and purchasing large agricultural implements in major grain producing areas, exempt in whole or in part the agricultural taxes in eight provinces including Jilin and Heilongjiang, reduce by 3 percentage points of the agricultural tax rate in 11 grain producing provinces or regions including Hebei, and reduce by 1 percentage point the agricultural tax rate in other provinces and regions.

In the first half of 2005, agricultural taxes were exempted in 22 provinces; at the end of 2005, these taxes were exempted in 28 provinces, regions, and municipalities as well as 210 counties (cities) in Hebei, Shandong, and Yunnan.

In February 2006 when there were mature conditions for the nationwide abolition of agricultural taxes, the 9th Plenary Session of the 10th NPC Standing Committee made a resolution that the *Regulations for the Agricultural Taxes of the People's Republic of China* was officially abolished as of January 1, 2006. Abolition of agricultural taxes and tax on agricultural specialty products (except tobacco leaf) can reduce about RMB50 billions of burden on farmers and benefit more than 700 million farmers. It marks the end of the history when farmers were obliged to contribute grain to the imperial palace and pay mandatory taxes, which lasted more than 2,600 years in China, and it also marks the consolidation of China's historical role as an industrial power and the beginning of a new stage in which "industry nurtures agriculture and cities support the countryside".

6. Brief summary

With accelerating process of industrialization, China has entered the middle and late period of industrialization and has changed from an agricultural power into an industrial power; what's more, great changes have taken place in fundamental economic realities and in the financial revenue and expenditure structure. Before the implementation of the reform and opening-up policy, the construction fund was mainly accumulated from agriculture by means of "price scissors" to support national industrial construction. After the reform and opening up, especially in the 21st century, with the accelerating process of industrialization, China's financial revenue was derived mainly from the secondary industry, especially the manufacturing industry, and grew at a rapid and stable rate. Being financially strong, the Central Government decided to abolish agricultural taxes and increase investment into the "three rural issues". Therefore, China has comprehensively entered a new stage in which industry nurtures agriculture and cities support the countryside.

(Published in *China Industrial Economics*, 3rd issue 2010)

3 Alleviate the contradiction between the supply and demand of energy; ensure our energy security

1. Increasingly prominent contradiction between the supply and demand of energy

In China, industry makes up 70% of energy consumption in China. According to our prediction, China now lies in the middle period of industrialization and is faced with regional development imbalance. By 2005, only two cities of 31 provinces, municipalities, and autonomous regions evolved into the late period of industrialization; 10 provinces remained in the middle period of industrialization; 13 provinces and municipalities stayed in the initial period of industrialization; and several regions lingered in the pre-industrialization period. In other words, there are still 24 provinces, municipalities, and autonomous regions in the middle, initial, and pre-industrialization periods. We have predicted that China will basically realize industrialization and urbanization around the year of 2018. Only then will the energy consumption demand likely decline. Before this deadline, there will be a long way to go for China to utilize energy-saving technologies due to the rapid development of heavy industry, a huge number of high-energy-consuming enterprises, the unreasonable business organization structure, and a difficulty in reducing the number of high-energy-consuming medium- and small-sized enterprises. For this reason, the demand for energy will be increased by industrial development; along with urban development and growth in the living standard, the demand for energy will grow rapidly in next two decades in China. According to prediction, if the average of the energy consumption elasticity coefficient is not lower than 0.7 during 2007 and 2010 or 0.5 during 2010 and 2020, the total consumption of primary energy will reach 2.9 billion tons of standard coal in 2010 and will hit 3.8 billion tons of standard and quasi-standard coal in 2020. At present, however, the energy consumption index remains as high as around 1.0. If we follow the old pattern of economic and social development in the advanced countries and make no effort to quicken the transformation of China's economic development pattern and let this trend evolve at will, it is unlikely to meet the demand for primary energy that will have exceeded 5 billion tons of standard coal by 2020.

With regard to the supply of energy resources, we are faced with insurmountable hardship in terms of energy and environment. It is estimated that, with the current proved reserves of resources and the existing capability of resource exploitation and utilization, the average exploitable life of resources in the world may be about 230 years for coal, about 45 years for petroleum, and about 61 years for natural gas; but China's per capita possession of resources is much lower than the world's average, with the exploitable life of above resources exploitation being only 80 years, 15 years, and 30 years respectively. In reality, this is an optimistic estimate; with regard to proven reserves, for instance, the residual exploitable reserve of coal is currently 114.5 billion tons, less than 20 years of supply though calculated by exploiting 2 billion tons per year at a recovery rate of 30%. We will soon be confronted with a critical shortage of energy resources if we do not accelerate resources survey or improve recovery rate and utilization rate of resources.

In addition, environmental pollution and water pollution will become intolerable due to the unreasonable exploitation and utilization of coal and expansion of high energy-consuming enterprises (direct combustion of most coal without washing). In 2006, China's GDP made up only 5.5% of the world's GDP and energy consumption exceeded 10% of the world's total consumption, but China's emission of carbon dioxide was the highest in the world, beyond the bearing capacity of China's environment. According to some experts' estimation, 2.5 tons of underground water will be contaminated per ton of coal exploited; this is a serious situation for a country like China, which is facing a critical shortage of water resources.

2. Strengthen exploitation and development of China's energy resources and assure domestic energy supply

At present, coal makes up the largest proportion in China's energy structure. According to incomplete statistical caliber, so far in 2004, coal made up 75.6% and 67.7% respectively in production and consumption structure of primary energy; petroleum, 13.5% and 22.7%; natural gas, 3.0% and 2.6%; and hydropower, 7.9% and 7.0%. However, new energy and renewable energy sources, such as nuclear energy, solar energy, wind energy, and biomass energy, made up a very tiny proportion in the energy structure.

Henceforth, China's energy policy will still be based on coal. Coal resources need to be developed and utilized in a high-yield and clean manner so as to develop large-scale thermal power stations, optimize the thermal power production structure, promote coal liquefaction and gasification, and encourage gas extraction and utilization. Both the central and local initiatives should be brought into play to quicken hydropower construction. In addition, the production and consumption structure of energy resources should be adjusted to promote the development of new energy and renewable energy sources, such as nuclear energy, solar energy, wind energy, and biomass energy.

Nuclear energy is a clean, controllable modern energy and also an economically reasonable alternative energy in recent years; thanks to technical progress, safety can be assured in the use of nuclear energy. Internationally, some advanced countries including France have done quite well in the development and utilization of nuclear energy. We should learn from them. Like China, France is also short of traditional energy resources; by developing nuclear energy from a strategic height, France has increased its self-sufficiency rate of energy supply from 27% to 50%, and thus effectively reduced dependence on imported petroleum. In France, at present, nuclear energy has made up 75% of the installed power-generating capacity and 85% of total electric energy production. The use of nuclear energy in China has begun earlier, but it develops slowly due to hysteretic technical route policy and restrictive investment system; the currently installed capacity of nuclear power in commercial operation is only 5–6 million kW, accounting for only 1–2% of the energy supply, about 20 years behind advanced countries. There is huge potentiality in this respect.

The emerging, new-type renewable energy resources, such as solar energy, wind energy, and biomass energy, are developing rapidly in the world. The prospect is beyond measure, though emerging energy sources have not yet been put into wide and large-scale commercial applications due to such constraining factors as technology and cost. According to the prediction by an authoritative international energy organization, the traditional fossil energy available worldwide will reach the peak of production during 2020 and 2040 due to limited reserve, and will possibly be used up during 2040 and 2050; for this reason, fossil energy will make up less and less in the energy structure. In contrast, the renewable energy resources, typically the solar energy, wind and biomass energy, will increase their share in the energy structure, up to 50% by 2050 and 85% by 2100. This is why advanced countries have deemed the development and utilization of renewable energy resources as strategic commanding height for the future acquisition of energy resources in order to take the initiative in the competition for clean, renewable, and distributed energy. For instance, in the merely four years from 1999 to 2003, the solar photovoltaic power-generating market grew tenfold and the cost dropped by 20% in Germany. The photovoltaic power generation has spread rapidly around the world, with an average annual growth rate of 33% in the last decade, 43% in the last five years, and 61.2% in 2004, over 50% of which was grid-connected to march into the mainstream market. According to a prediction by the European Photovoltaic Industry Association, photovoltaic power generation will make up 1% of the world's electric energy production in 2020 and will grow to 21% in 2040 when photovoltaic energy becomes the main source of energy in the world. The world's wind energy grew 30% per year on average during 1996 and 2004, with a total installed capacity up to 47.60 million kW (additional 8.30 million kW in 2004). Wind energy has made up 0.5% of the world's electric energy production, and will exceed 12% in 2020.

China has exploited and utilized the renewable energy resources to some extent. It is estimated that there is a reserve of about 300 million tons of standard coal (including energy resources used by rural households, not included in statistics). In comparison with advanced countries, however, China holds a low strategic position and provides insufficient policy support for the development of renewable energy at its primary stage featuring spontaneous, disperse, and small-scale exploitation and utilization rather than large-scale commercial application.

3. Improve energy use efficiency and save energy

As compared with developed countries, China still has huge potential in saving energy. With regard to energy exploitation, the flourishing small coal mines that adopt destructive mining methods with a low recovery rate (no more than 10–15%) have caused a destructive effect on large mines. A few profit-driven countries even make the distinction between rich and poor large mines. The comprehensive recovery rate of coal in China now averages out at around 30%, much lower than the international advanced level of 60–80%.

With regard to unit energy consumption per output value, the energy consumed for the GDP per million US dollars calculated by the exchange rate in 2000 was 1,274 tons of standard coal in China, 2.4 times the world's average, 2.5, 4.9, 8.7, and 0.43 times that in the United States, EU, Japan, and India respectively.

With regard to energy consumed per unit product, the average unit energy consumption of main products manufactured by electrical power, steel and iron, non-ferrous industry, petrochemical industry, building materials, chemical industry, light industry, and textile industry in China was 39% higher than the international advanced level in 2005; for instance, the comprehensive energy consumption of the copper smelting industry was 65% higher than the international advanced level; large-sized synthesis ammonia plant, 30%; and paper and board, 115%.

According to an international comparison of the energy efficiency of major energy-consuming equipment, the average operating efficiency of industrial coal-fired boiler in China was around 60% in 2005, 15–20 percentage points lower than the international advanced level; the average efficiency of medium- and small-sized electric motors was 87% and the average design efficiency of fan and water pump was 75%, both 5 percentage points lower than the internationally advanced level, with the system operating efficiency being nearly 15–20 percentage points lower than the international advanced level; the fuel economy of motor vehicles was 25% lower than Europe, 20% lower than Japan, and 10% lower than the United States; the fuel consumption of trucks per hundred ton kilometer was 7.6L, doubling the international advanced level; and the fuel consumption of inland transport ships was 10–20% higher than the international advanced level.

According to an international comparison of energy consumed per unit building area, the energy consumed for heating per building area in China has doubled or tripled that in developed countries with similar climatic conditions. According to experts' actual calculation of thermal loss in high-rise apartments in Beijing, Harbin, and Toronto, the thermal loss on the outer wall of buildings in Beijing is 4.4 times; on windows, 2.2 times; and on roofs, 4.2 times that in Canada. Whereas in Harbin, the thermal loss on outer wall of buildings was 3.6 times; on windows, 1.1 times; and on roofs, 2.6 times that in Canada respectively. By experts' analysis, it is practical and workable that saving 50% energy is required for all public and residential buildings in China; as compared with developed countries, there will be huge potential for saving energy even when the goal of 50% has been reached.

According to an international comparison of the overall energy efficiency, China's energy efficiency is 10 percentage points lower than the international advanced level. For instance, the average efficiency of a thermal power generating unit is 33.8%, 6–7 percentage points lower than the international advanced level. With enormous loss and severe waste of energy at intermediate links (e.g. processing, transition, and storage), the overall production efficiency and economic efficiency of China are 12–15 percentage points lower than the international advanced level in the case of the same quantity of materials consumed.

By theoretical analysis and estimation and by comparing energy consumption per unit product and energy consumption per end-user equipment with the international advanced level, we have discovered that China now has the energy-saving potential of about 600 million tons of standard coal per year. Fully exploiting this potential, however, will be not as easy as expected, for it requires a strong energy-saving awareness among all the people, an investment of a huge amount of money, advanced energy-saving technologies, advanced and reasonable technical criteria for energy consumption, the rationalization of prices of energy and resource products, an economic policy for saving energy, and a complete system of laws and regulations. We still have much to do in this respect.

In brief, only by increasing supply and reducing consumption can we alleviate the contradiction between the supply and demand of energy resources so as to ensure energy security in China.

4. Enhance international energy cooperation

The proper use of overseas energy resources through international trade and upstream exploration and development can make a necessary supplement for domestic energy supply. With the rapid process of modernization, China's dependence on external energy supply will intensify constantly; thus, enhancing international energy cooperation is deemed as one of the important approaches to China's energy shortage. We did a lot in this respect. In recent years, China has carried out bilateral or multilateral dialogues with some countries on the energy issue; Chinese petroleum enterprises have entered into agreements on the development of petroleum and natural gas with enterprises in some other countries. China will continue to take an active part in the bilateral and multilateral international energy cooperation, strengthen dialogue and cooperation with international organizations and transnational corporations, and make joint efforts to safeguard the stability of the international energy market.

In addition, China will speed up the establishment of a national petroleum reserve system to prevent petroleum supply risk. China has now embarked on building crude oil reserve bases in Zhoushan, Ningbo, Qingdao, and Dalian, setting up management organizations and preparing related laws and regulations in order to increase the petroleum reserve capacity in a short term.

(Published in *China Economic & Trade*, No. 27, 2008)

4 Provide intellectual support for economic development and environmental protection

At the current stage, China's economic development is confronted with some constraints from resources and environment, including: (1) insufficient energy resources; (2) environmental pollution; (3) ecological degradation; and (4) climate change. These problems are produced by a series of characteristic national conditions:

First, low per capita possession of resources due to a large population. The total amount of resources, however large, will become small if divided per capita by a large population. For quite some time, China has been boasting of its vast territory and abundant resources; but, more than half of the territory consists of plateau, desert, and gobi, low in productivity or unable to be cultivated, while only 30% of the land is endowed with a favorable ecological environment and abundant resources and is considered livable.

Second, prominent contradiction between economic growth and environmental protection due to an accelerating process of industrialization and urbanization. China's economic development now has entered a crucial period of modernization; industries are led by heavy chemical industry that consumes a considerable quantity of natural resources; and urbanization now lies in the medium term of fast advancement. Tens of millions of people flocking into cities every year have increased demands for housing, transportation, electricity and infrastructure, jobs, schooling opportunities, and social security, and have also stimulated the development of heavy chemical industries such as metallurgy, chemical industry, building materials, and power and energy resources. Due to the enormous consumption of natural resources and the severe pollution of environment, these industries will give rise to some problems, such as a shortage of resources and environmental disruption, which have adverse impact on sustainable development.

Third, limited economic strengths of state finance and inadequate investment into environmental protection. At present, China's investment into environmental protection infrastructure accounts for around 1% of the GDP. Due to the low utilization rate of funds for environmental protection, some environmental protection equipment has a low rate of operation and a low comprehensive utilization rate of wastes.

Fourth, extensive pattern of economic development and inadequate capability of technological innovation. As a result, the extensive economic development patterns that have existed for many years remain unchanged; the energy consumed per unit of production remains high in heavy chemical industries such as metallurgy, chemical industry, building materials, electricity, and energy resources. This shows, on the one hand, that there is a huge energy-saving potential in these major energy-consuming sectors, and that, on the other, these sectors lag in energy-saving technology and have poor capability of independent innovation.

Finally, people's awareness of environmental protection needs to be strengthened; the system and mechanism of environmental protection need to be transformed without delay. There is a phenomenon that has remained unchanged for years: local governments have sought after short-term economic benefits but lost sight of long-term sustainable development. Despite people's strong desire for blue sky and green mountains and rivers, they are tolerant towards economic behaviors that have ruined environment.

As required by the 17th CPC National Congress, the concept of ecological civilization must be established to "create the industrial structure, growth pattern and consumption pattern that save resources and protect environment". For this purpose, the following research activities must be carried out:

First, fundamental research is needed on the relationship between economic development and resource environment and on basic laws concerning economic development and environmental protection, with priorities given to achieving a number of high-quality research findings in industrial ecology, resource economics, and environmental economics.

Second, research is needed on a system and mechanism conducive to the conservation of resources and energy sources, protection of the ecological environment, and the realization of sustainable development in order to provide theoretical support for improving the legislation on resource environment and creating a responsibility and accountability system.

Third, comprehensive interdisciplinary research is needed to strengthen cooperation between social scientists, naturists, and engineering scientists, as the project of economic development and environmental protection is a complex systematic one such that it requires close cooperation among multi-disciplinary researchers.

Finally, research is needed on issues such as economic development and environmental protection from a global perspective through international exchange and cooperation. The issue of resources and environment has become a concern throughout the world. We need to expand academic exchanges with external experts via dialogue and try to reach a consensus regarding win-win strategies.

(Published in *Guangming Daily*, May 14, 2008)

5 Improve the quality and level of the manufacturing international operation

1. Achievements made in China's manufacturing international operation

As the economic globalization evolves and the economic reform and opening up policy deepens, China has become one of the major nations in foreign trade. In 1980, the total import-export volume was only RMB57 billion and the dependence on foreign trade was 12.6%. In 2004, however, the total volume jumped to RMB955.51 billion, ranking the third in the world and preceded only by the United States and Germany; the dependence on foreign trade was about 69.8%. In 2006, the total volume of imports and exports rocketed to US$1.7604 trillion, cementing China's position as one of the major nations in foreign trade. In 2008, the total volume was expected to exceed US$2 trillion, and China would hopefully surpass Germany and become the second largest nation in foreign trade. With the expanding scale of foreign trade, immense changes have taken place in the structure of foreign trade and considerable progress has been achieved in manufacturing internationalization.

(1) Export commodities

First, the finished products have occupied a large portion in export commodities. In 1980, the export amount of primary products of export commodities accounted for 50.3% of the total amount of export commodities, and the manufactured goods accounted for 49.7%. After the year 2000, the proportion of manufactured goods went up to 90%, while that of the primary products went below 10%. In 2006, the former went up to 94.5%, while the latter went below 6%.

Second, the proportion of mechanical and electrical products in manufactured goods has been on the rise: 34.5% in 1995, up to 47.1% in 2000, and further up to 56.7% in 2006.

Third, the proportion of hi-tech and new products in manufactured goods keeps rising constantly: only 6.0% in 1995, up to 22.2% in 2002, and further up to nearly 30% in 2006.

Finally, the international competitiveness of products is enhanced gradually. Since 1994, the trade competitive index of China's manufactured goods has been positive, i.e. 0.08, 0.06, 0.16, 0.16, 0.11, 0.11, 0.10, 0.09, and 0.09 respectively from 1995 to 2003; whereas, that of the primary products has been negative since 2005.

The share of China's manufactured goods on the international market keeps rising: 8.3% in 2004, surpassing Japan in worldwide ranking, and next only to the EU and the US and making China the third largest economy of manufactured goods in the world, which is 81% of the US and 104% of Japan. In 2003 and 2004, China's market share grew at the rates of 36% and 37% respectively.

(2) Foreign direct investment (FDI)

Foreign direct investment is a win–win strategy, which not only can create jobs to promote economic development in the host country but also can diversify the country of origin to reduce trade friction. Since 2002, China's foreign investment has entered a rapid development period as the Government constantly perfected the promotion and service system for foreign direct investment, accelerated the process of FDI facilitation, and encouraged and supported enterprises with comparative advantages under different ownerships to "go outside".

At the end of 2006, there were over 30,000 enterprises engaged in transnational investment and management in more than 160 countries. Chinese enterprises involved in foreign investment are transforming from simply building stations or "windows" to such internationally popular transnational investment patterns as establishing factories, merger and acquisition, equity replacement, overseas listing, and setting up strategic cooperation alliance. At the end of 2006, the stock of China's FDI amounted to US$75 billion, 3.3 times that by the end of 2002, with a net increase of US$52 billion. From 2002 to 2006, the FDI flow was US$2,700 million, US$2,900 million, US$5,500 million, US$12.3 billion, and US$17.6 billion respectively. The FDI flow in 2006 was 6.5 times that in 2002.

(3) Introduction of foreign capital

A large quantity of appropriate technology introduced through the utilization of foreign direct investment has facilitated the optimization and upgrading of the industrial structure. From 2003 to 2006, a total amount of US$29.3 billion of foreign direct investment was put into manufacturing communication equipment, computers, and other electronic devices, including US$8,200 million in 2006, increasing 5.9% over the previous year. At present, factories are being built in China by major IT manufacturers around the globe; some of them have even moved their R&D center into China; as a result, China's electronic and communication equipment manufacturing has technologically improved, and products in these industries have become more competitive in the international market.

2. Several issues concerning improving manufacturing international operation

(1) Establish standards and fight for international discourse power

There are enterprise standards, industrial standards, local standards, and national standards in China. In order to launch products in overseas markets, China must upgrade its standard system and observe the international standards and advanced overseas standards, including those established by the International Standardization Organization (ISO), the International Electrotechnical Commission (IEC), the International Telecommunication Union (ITU), and those formulated by other international organizations but confirmed and published by ISO. As an important technic-economic policy of China, the adoption of international standards serves as an essential measure for enterprises to promote technical progress, improve the quality of products, open wider to the outside world, become compatible with internationally accepted practices, and facilitate the development of a socialist market economy. China has achieved certain progress in this regard. By the end of 2001, 8,621 out of 19,744 national standards have adopted international standards or advanced overseas standards, with the adoption rate up to 43.7%; 6,300 out of 16,745 existing standards released by ISO and IEC have been transformed into national standards of China, with the transformation rate up to 38%. There is obviously a gap between China's standardization level and the international level. In addition, with the economic globalization and technical progress in China, no longer shall we be passively accommodated to foreign standards; instead, we should fight for the discourse power and initiative to create international standards.

(2) Focus on independent innovation and core technology development

Since the economic reform and opening up to the outside world, a large number of Chinese enterprises have made success in independent innovation. Some of them have occupied the international market by industrializing their original innovations, and some others have achieved this purpose by creating proprietary brands through introduction, assimilation, and re-innovation. In general, however, the capability of Chinese enterprises for independent innovation remains not as strong as expected due to a lack of core technology competence as a result of low input of R&D expenditures and an imperfect organizational mechanism of innovation. According to data provided by the National Bureau of Statistics, the R&D fund of large- and medium-sized industrial enterprises only accounted for 2.6% of industrial value added in 2005, about one third of that in the developed countries, e.g. 8.3% in the United States (2000), 7.4% in Germany (2000), and 8.6% in Japan (1998). Only 23.7% of the large- and medium-sized enterprises in China have established a scientific research institution, and only 38.7% have ever carried out scientific and technology activities. According to data published by the State Intellectual Property Office, of all domestic enterprises so far, only 3‰ have proprietary intellectual property rights; only 1.1% are granted patents, including 0.17% with patents for invention; half of 130,000 invention patents in 2006 were granted to transnational corporations abroad. At the international level, Chinese enterprises are falling behind the developed countries in technical innovation input and output. For this reason, two important and urgent tasks in making China an innovation-orientated nation is enhancing the independent innovation capability of enterprises and establishing their dominant position in technical innovation.

Although China is a major manufacturer of household appliances, the patented technology of many products is in the possession of foreign corporations. For instance, more than 60 million DVDs are produced per year in China, with 80% of them exported; however, China owns only 20 of over 200 patented technologies related to this line of products; for each piece of these products exported, 3–5 US dollars are paid to a foreign corporation as patent royalty. Similar problems are more or less found in export products such as color TVs, refrigerators, and washing machines.

In recent years, the Chinese Government has deemed independent innovation as a national strategy and planned, by 2020, to increase the percentage of R&D input in the GDP from the current 1.35% to 2.5%, increase the contribution rate of scientific and technological progress to the GDP from the current 39% to 60%, and increase the number of cited Chinese patents and papers from the current 20th to fifth place in the world.

(3) Expand production of high-quality and high-value-added products

Obviously, Chinese products are faced with severe challenges though they are somewhat competitive.

i   The competitive force of Chinese products is also based on low prices and high environmental costs. First, the price of energy resources is low. In China, the tax rate of petroleum, natural gas, and coal is only 1%; iron and monohydrallite, 2%; terrestrial heat, 3%; and gold ore, 4%; but in foreign countries, the compensation standard of petroleum, natural gas, and mineral resources is usually 10–16%. At the end of 2005, when the crude oil price on the international market reached US$420 per ton, Russia took more than $180, about 42% of the oil price; the United States took $134, about 32% of the oil price; but China only took $4, less than 1% of the oil price. This unpaid use of resources has encouraged the over-development of high energy consumption and high pollution enterprises, intensified the malformation of the industrial structure, and led to the waste of energy resources. According to research, the energy consumption per $1 million GDP calculated at the prevailing rate in China is 1,274 ton standard coal, 2.4 times higher than the world average level, and 2.5, 4.9, 8.7, and 0.43 times higher than the US, EU, Japan, and India respectively. Second, the wage of laborers is low. The current labor cost of China is only equivalent to about 3% of developed countries. In the 10 years from 1996 to 2005, the total wage of workers in China grew 9.15% per year on average, less than one-third of the 28.62% growth rate of corporate profit in the same period; in addition, the wage of migrant workers grew much slowly. Finally, the externalization of internal costs is based on the sacrifice of the environment. According to monitoring results of the State Environment Protection Administration of China, 27% of 411 surface water monitoring sections of seven river systems in China were classified as Class V (seriously polluted water). About one in two urban districts witnessed seriously polluted groundwater; in some areas, either rivers dried up or the water was polluted.

ii   China's export products are mainly produced by foreign-funded enterprises, of which processing trade occupies a heavy proportion. In 2006, the processing trade products of the mechanical industry in China contributed to more than 50% of the total amount of export products, with 84.4% produced by foreign-funded enterprises.

iii Low additional value of products and shortage of products with high additional value. China's export products are mainly labor-intensive products while hi-tech products occupy a small proportion of exports.

iv   Shortage of products with world-renowned brand. After over 20 years' effort, some brands with international influence have emerged in China, such as Haier, Lenovo, and Chang Hong, and some traditionally famous brands are going global. In general, however, the development of self-owned brands at the present stage is out of proportion to China's position in the world economy and trade; most enterprises adopt a development mode based on low-price competition and low-cost scale expansion, and thus they make less profit from product brand. The Made-in-China toys account for 70% of total production in the world; footwear, 50%; color TVs, 45%; air conditioners, 30%; textile and garment trade, 24%; and the production of nearly 200 product varieties takes the first place in the world; nevertheless, China has very few brands with international competitiveness. At present, less than 20% of import and export enterprises in China own proprietary trademarks; less than 10% of export enterprises have proprietary intellectual property rights; as a result, the development of self-owned brands is lagging behind. It is estimated that the value created by brands in the United States accounts for 60% of the GDP, but it is less than 20% in China.

(4) Lay stress on human capital and enhance workers' qualities

Human capital plays an important role in improving enterprise benefits and competitiveness. Schurz once calculated the development of the American economy: the material resources increased 4.5 times in the 70 years from 1890 to 1959; investment made in laborers' education and training increased 8.5 times; the former resulted in a 3.5 times rise in profits and the latter resulted in a 17.5 times rise in profit. According to Japanese research data, the number of additional technical innovators rises by 6% per grade of worker's education level raised, a proposal for technical innovation can reduce cost by 5%, a proposal made by a specially trained technician can reduce cost by 10–15%, the creation and promotion of advanced management technology by a well-educated/trained manager can reduce cost by at least 30%, and engineering technicians who have received re-education of technology can raise their work efficiency by 40–70%. In China, experts from Jilin Academy of Social Sciences also conducted surveys on the relationship between workers' quality and economic benefits. According to a survey in Changchun First Automobile Factory (FAW), the production efficiency of workers with a junior middle school diploma is 26% higher than those with primary school diploma, and the production efficiency of workers with a high education diploma is 20–30% higher than those only with junior middle school diploma. A survey on bench workers who have completed their apprenticeship in three years at the machine shop of Changchun Passenger Bus Factory shows that the workers with a higher degree of education can achieve the same efficiency rate in a shorter time than can those with a lower degree. It is revealed in both theory and practice that human capital is a key factor helping in improving workers' accomplishment and qualities, and that the formation of human capital is based on enterprise re-investment in addition to regular diploma education.

In brief, China must create a huge number of high-quality talents and senior skilled workers in order to become a great power of manufacturing industry and enhance its overall competitiveness in the world. The State Government needs to put more funds into vocational and technical education; the education authority needs to turn the focus on college/university education to technical training schools; and the enterprises and the whole community need to strengthen workers' on-the-job training, constantly update their knowledge, and improve their capabilities. These joint efforts will pave the way for China's manufacturing enterprises to compete in the international arena.

(Published in *Economic Management Journal*, Issue 5, 2008)

6 Expansion from quantity to quality

A critical period of industrial development in China

Over decades of construction, especially since the economic reform and opening up to the outside world, China's industry has been expanding from quantity to quality. This is a critical period of industrial development in China. When this period began remains unknown. Some argue that it began from the middle 1980s due to the considerable production capacity of machinery and textile industries. Some suggest that it began from the early 1990s due to the significant symbol of industrial structure adjustment from 1991 to 1992. Some others hold the view that it began when the idea of "two fundamental changes" was put forward. Whatever the exact time, the advent of this critical period is already an unquestionable fact.

China now has a considerable overall size of industry, which marks the end of expansion in quantity.

(1) Many industrial sectors have grown out of nothing and become stronger and stronger. Now an industrial system has formed, covering a full range of energy, machinery, auto manufacture, mining, metallurgy, electronics, chemical industry, petrochemical industry, aerospace, shipbuilding, construction and building materials, pharmaceutical, textile and garment, household appliance, and food and beverages.

(2) Regardless of considerable industrial production capacity, low capacity utilization rate encountered by a majority of industrial sectors has given rise to an immense waste of idle equipment. At the end of 1995, for example, the correspondences between production capacity and utilization rate went as follows: for 169 million tons of steel materials, the utilization rate was 56.2%; for 3.28 million automobiles, the rate was 44.3%; for 14.89 million motorcycles, the rate was only 55.4%; for 21.83 million washing machines, the rate was 43.4%; for 18.21 million refrigerators, the rate was 50.4%; for 2.03 million air conditioners, the rate was 33.5%; and for 41.90 million cotton spinning ingots, the rate was 77.0%. According to an investigation and analysis of the production capacity of 80 major industrial products by a relevant authority, the utilization rate of 28 products falls below 60%, making up 35%.

(3) The production of major industrial products such as crude steel, raw coal, cement, cotton cloth, and televisions has ranked first in the world while

that of electric energy production, fertilizer, and chemical fiber has risen to the second place.

(4) In China, the oversupply of most industrial products has decreased sales-output ratio but increased inventory of many enterprises. Statistical data have indicated excessive inventory in textile industry, light industry, household appliances, packaging industry, steel industry, and automobile manufacture. At the end of 1996, for example, excessive inventories include 10 million wrist watches, 20 million bicycles, and 110,000 automobiles as well as household appliances and garments.

However, the industrial quality needs to be improved:

(1) Unreasonable industrial structure. Basic industries such as energy and raw materials remain weak; traditional industries make up a large proportion and hi-tech industries remain under development; and the processing industry suffers from overcapacity and remains at a low level. There is also low-level redundant development.

(2) An incomplete variety of products with poor quality, a shortage of products with high technical content and famous brands being widely accepted by consumers, a less competitive presence in the global market. For example, a survey on backbone enterprises of machinery industry shows that there are only 17.5% of them whose leading products have reached up to the level of the 1990s, 52.0% of them whose leading products have reached up to the level of the 1980s, and 30.0% of them whose leading products have reached up to the level of the 1960s or 1970s. In 1996, China's steel production ranked first in the world, up to 101.10 million tons, but the quality remained low, only about 10% up to the international standard; the variety was not complete, so more than 40% of quality steel products demanded in the domestic market were depending on imports, including hot rolled steel coil, cold rolled sheet, tinplate strip, and galvanized sheet. There are only 1,800 varieties of products in large petrochemical enterprises, while there are thousands of types of petrochemical products in industrially developed countries. The difference ratio of synthetic fiber in China is only 10%; in contrast, the ratio is up to 30–40% in foreign countries. In China, products with high technical content take a small proportion and their output value only makes up about 3% of the gross national product; in contrast to developed countries, the proportion is usually above 10%.

(3) Unreasonable industrial organization structure. The industrial concentration ratio remains low; in some industries that require higher economic scale, the enterprises have a small and disperse scale; most enterprises fail to realize a reasonable economic scale, so the scale economic effect seems quite poor. In the automobile industry, for example, there are 112 assembly plants that produced 1.49 million cars in 1996, only 12,000 cars per plant on average; the economic scale of cars seems better, but lags far behind that of foreign countries. In addition, there is an irrational division of labor

and collaboration among enterprises and regions, leading to the fact that enterprises tend to be large or small but all inclusive, that sectors are segmented, with each creating a system of its own, and that the problem of structural assimilation worsens between regions. According to an analysis of statistical data in 1995, products including yarn, plastics, fertilizer, iron and steel, and tobacco are produced in 29 provinces, cities, and districts; chemical fiber is produced in 28 provinces, cities, and districts; TV sets are produced in 27 provinces, cities, and districts; automobiles are produced in 26 provinces, cities, and districts; bicycles and washing machines are produced in 23 provinces, cities, and districts; and refrigerators are produced in 19 provinces, cities, and districts. In addition, these popular products are also produced in newly-built factories in some regions. According to an estimate by the State Development Planning Commission, the similarity coefficient of the industrial structure is 93.5% in the central region and eastern region while it is 97.9% in the western region and central region.

(4) Low quality of enterprises. First, equipment level is low. According to typical investigation, 20% of state-owned enterprises have equipment levels pertaining to 1960s or 1970s, 20–25% have equipment that is outmoded but serviceable, and 55–60% whose equipment should have been obsolete. Second, qualities of enterprise leaders and employees need to be enhanced. Some leaders have such low qualities that they are dedicated to or responsible for nothing; they run their businesses with out-of-date professional and managerial knowledge, act with no democracy but autocracy, get involved in entirely unprincipled disputes over trifles, and always pass the buck. In 1994, when an examination was conducted for 158 enterprise leaders on business management in a province, 58% of examinees had no idea about VAT (value added tax). The money-driven ideology has grown among employees due to their incorrect understanding of a market-oriented economy; consequently, employees were not responsible for a lack of work ethics, dedication, and entrepreneur spirit. Many an enterprise needs to build an employee force that is both ideologically and technically competent. Finally, management quality of enterprises is low. The managerial level in China has worsened in recent years. A survey shows that 45% of enterprises have witnessed a decline in fundamental management level, 37% do the same in professional management, and 53% in site management.

(5) Low economic benefit of industry caused by emphasis on expansion in quantity that hinders improvement of overall qualities of industry in China. In 1996, the profit-tax rate of capital and production value of all industrial enterprises or state-owned industrial enterprises dropped 1–2 percentage points as compared with the early 1990s. The percentage and amount of losses was rising year by year; in 1996, the percentage of industrial enterprises at the township level or above was up to 23.00% under independent accounting, 5.27 percentage points higher than 1991 and 1.7 percentage points higher than 1995. The amount of losses made up 24.8% of total realized profit, 6.2 percentage points higher than 1995. The economic benefit

of state-owned enterprises was much less desirable. In 1996, the percentage of losses of state-owned enterprises came close to 40%, including about 20% of long-run losses and 20% of losses incurred in recent years. According to the information above, China's industrial economy has indeed come into a transition from expansion in quantity to quality. In this period, some new features will emerge in the economic development of China; some of them have appeared preliminarily and some others are about to appear.

First, the shortage of commodities has come to an end, and the buyer's market that features oversupply has taken shape. A positive result of expansion in quantity is that people's basic needs are satisfied. Shortage of commodities has passed, followed by people's need for improvement of life quality, which raises a higher requirement for the supply of commodities. Therefore, enterprises must rely on product quality, variety, service, and credit for consumers' recognition with the advent of the age that "User is God".

Second, the economic growth rate has slowed down. At this stage, the rate of industrial development in China may fluctuate, but the general trend shows a slowdown in growth rate. According to statistical data, the average annual growth rate of China's gross industrial output value was about 19% in the 17 years from 1978 to 1996, including a two-digit growth rate in 12 years and a rate greater than 20% in six years. Such a high growth rate is a miracle in the history of world economic development. It can be foreseen that a higher growth rate will be maintained for China's industrial economy and national economy in a rather long period. For example, a research group from Chinese Academy of Social Sciences predicted that the growth rate of China's industry was expected to be 12.5% during the "9th Five-Year Plan" and expected to be 9–10% in the first 10 years of the 21st century, both much lower than the actual growth rate since the economic reform and opening up to the outside world.

Third, the environment for enterprise survival and development is getting tougher. In terms of the external situation, the competition among enterprises will intensify due to a sufficient supply of commodities, the gradual formation of a buyer's market, the powerful role of market mechanism, and the increasing degree of China's economic internationalization. This competition comes not only from domestic enterprises but also from large transnational corporations around the globe. In terms of the internal situation, enterprises are encountered with a severe test about how to reinforce management and reduce costs in response to the rising prices of raw materials, the raise of employees' salaries, and the rocketing cost of products.

Fourth, corporate mergers and acquisitions will spring up and the industrial organization structure will be improved. Fierce competition will inevitably lead to an amalgamation and a merger of enterprises. In the future three to five years, there will be an upsurge of such mergers, when production factors centralize into dominant enterprises; as a result, there will be higher concentration ratio and more large enterprises and business groups.

Fifth, the rapid development of hi-tech and new industries will become new sources of economic growth. Since the 1980s, the light textile industry, especially the household appliance industry, has played a special role in the rapid development of the Chinese economy. In the late 1990s, the speed of the development of these industries reduced significantly due to market saturation. Henceforth, the development of industries other than cars and building materials will promote China's economic development; in addition, industries such as electronics and communication will also see a broad prospect for development. They will become new sources of economic growth, provided that they can manage to do so through fierce competition.

Finally, China's foreign trade is getting more difficult and will grow at a slower rate. With the increasing cost of labor and competition from the third world countries, China will lose the upper hand in exporting primary products and labor-intensive products. Consequently, exports will become more difficult; the growth rate of exports will slow down; upgrading and updating of export products will be unavoidable; and options for importing products will also become wider.

Considering the current situation and above foreseen characteristics of China's industrial development, one of the key problems concerning economic development is to change the growth pattern and improve the overall qualities of industry. This is an urgent and arduous task for us. It will be a complex and systematic project to improve the overall qualities of industry, for it involves all aspects of industry and requires us to make long and unremitting efforts in undertakings, for example, as those listed below:

First, improving the overall qualities of industry should be focused on the realization of "two fundamental changes", i.e. economic system changes from traditional planned economy system to a socialist market economic system; economic growth pattern changes from an extensive to an intensive pattern. As the key to promoting the sustainable, rapid, and healthy development of the national economy, these two changes also are the key to improving the overall qualities of industry. For this reason, in order to improve the overall qualities of industry, we must deepen the reform of the industrial economic system, especially the reform of state-owned enterprises, accelerate the pace of demutualization, and set up a modern corporate system adequate to the social market economy. We must do this so as to create an ideal system environment for improving the overall qualities of industry, to give full play to the fundamental roles of market mechanism in resources allocation, to promote the adjustment of the industrial structure, and to improve industrial efficiency. In order to change the pattern of economic growth, we must change the extensive growth patterns including the one-sided expansion in quantity instead of quality, the one-sided pursuit of high growth rate instead of economic performance, the one-sided pursuit of increasing the number of new enterprises instead of technical transformation, and the one-sided pursuit of denotative expanded reproduction instead of connotative expanded reproduction so that the industrial development moves under intensive management.

Second, improving the overall qualities of industry should be focused on structural optimization. For this purpose, we must abide by the national industrial policy and take advantage of market mechanisms to strengthen the development of basic industries including energy and raw materials, and give adequate support to pillar industries such as machinery, electronics, petrochemical, automobile, and building materials. We must strive to develop hi-tech industries and upgrade traditional industries. We must make adjustments of the product structure and give priority to undersupplied products and marketable products as needed on the market. We must try to launch a series of highly correlated products with high technical content, large market capacity, good export prospect, and high added value, especially the brand-name products, new products, and new variety; curtail the production of oversupplied products and reduce stock of unsalable products. We must eliminate outmoded products of inferior quality, high price, and high consumption of raw materials and energy. We must facilitate the merger and acquisition of enterprises to enlarge the scale and improve scale economic effects of enterprises. We must initiate a corporation system reform to promote the development of enterprises and the formation of trans-regional and cross-sector large enterprise groups or, if conditions permit, transnational corporations and groups. And we must strengthen the cooperation and coalition among enterprises so as to supplement each other's advantages.

Third, improving the overall qualities of industry should be focused on qualities of industrial enterprises. As the basic unit of the industrial economy, the qualities of industrial enterprises have a direct effect on the overall qualities of industry. For this reason, we must enhance the qualities of industrial enterprises; carry out a technical transformation of enterprises by means of new technology, new processes, and new machinery equipment to improve the quality of technical equipment; enhance the ideological, technical, and cultural qualities of enterprise leaders and employees by means of education and training; properly deal with the relationship between reform and management and get them closely combined; summarize and publicize advanced experiences of business management; learn and borrow advanced management methods and means from abroad; and strive to enhance the management quality and level of Chinese enterprises.

Finally, improving the overall qualities of industry should be aimed to improve economic effects. Economic effects can reveal the level of overall industrial qualities and act as an important standard to measure the results of improving the overall qualities of industry. For this reason, improving the overall qualities of industry should always center on improving economic effects, including the economic efficiency of enterprises and economic effects of the entire industry.

(Co-written by the author and research fellow Huang Qunhui; published in *Social Sciences in China*, Issue 3, 2003)

7 Problems of informationization in promoting industrial modernization

The 5th Plenary Session of the 15th CPC Central Committee pointed out that "realizing informationization is an arduous historic task in the process of modernization and promoting informationization of national economy and society is a strategic measure for modernization construction". The 16th CPC National Congress further defined the objectives for building a moderately prosperous society in all aspects and depicted the grand blueprint for the first 20 years of the 21st century. It was clearly pointed out in the report of the 16th CPC National Congress that "realization of informationization remains an arduous and historic task in the process of modernization" and that "informationization is an inevitable choice for accelerating realization of industrialization and modernization in China". Correct understanding of the relationship between informationization and industrial modernization will be of great importance to the economic construction and social development of China in the 21st century.

1. Relationship between informationization and industrialization

A. Discussion on the concept and connotation of informationization

In 1966, the concept of "informationization" was first created by Japanese scientists and economic research institutes to describe the evolution of human society while discussing the development of the information industry and information society. There is so far no consensus about the connotation of this concept. It is generally defined as: (1) an evolutionary process of social-economic formation after industrialization, typically as "a process of human evolution from a society where values are created from tangible material products to a society where values are created from intangible information", which is associated with concepts such as post-industrial society and information society; or (2) a revolutionary change of information acquisition and communication means caused by computer networking development, which is associated with concepts such as information super highway, network era and network economy; or (3) a process of utilizing and popularizing modern information technology, information products, information acquisition means and methods in social economy, which is characterized by the use of computer, the Internet, and mobile communication, and the revolutionary changes caused therein in people's production mode, working manner, and life style.

We accept the third definition, for it better reflects the reality. Despite some rationality in the first two definitions, they seem kind of one-sided. A deduction for the definition that informationization is deemed as an evolutionary process of production means and social-economic formation after industrialization is that informationization is either preceded by industrialization or attained directly without the need of industrialization. This conclusion is inadvisable because it is derived from developed countries' experiences and is not compliant with the reality and needs of China as well as the majority of developing countries; furthermore, it may be misleading to some extent. The viewpoint that associates informationization with descriptive economic phenomena such as an information super highway and new economy is apparently too parochial to interpret or instruct realistic practice.

Whatever understanding of the definition of informationization, the following consensus has been reached for China's informationization and its process through extensive discussion:

First, an evitable choice for developing countries to catch up with developed countries and realize great-leap-forward development is to seize the opportunity of the IT revolution for development and utilization of the most advanced productivity. In the wave of economic globalization and informationization, the developing countries are disadvantaged for competition. With the tendency of globalization, on the one hand, the world economic development reveals an evident imbalanced feature; on the other hand, as a booster for economic globalization, the wave of informationization is widening the digital gap between developed and developing countries. However, informationization in developed countries is also faced with the upgrading and updating of technology as modern IT is a high new technology and develops very rapidly. For this reason, developing countries are standing on the same starting line as developed countries for application of new technology, new equipment, and new methods. In the international competitive situation where opportunities and challenges exist side by side, only by sticking to reform and the opening up policy and by accelerating information construction can China not be dissociated from economic globalization and informationization. China's entry into WTO is the organizational guarantee for its economy to go global; but, a better and faster integration into the world economy is dependent on a number of conditions, an important one of which is the level of China's informationization. Today, widespread application of such technologies as the Internet, e-mail, e-commerce, e-bank, e-customs, e-taxation, and modern communication has enabled enterprises to rise above spatial and temporal differences, allowed a smooth flow of products, services, technology, and funds from one country to another, and facilitated cross-border organization of production. This is a new opportunity for developing countries to realize great-leap-forward development. The United Nations Industrial Development Organization (UNIDO) estimated that by the year of 2005, the proportion of developed countries' manufacturing in global manufacturing will drop from 86% in 1970 to 67.6%; by contrast, the proportion of developing countries will rise from 10.3% in 1970 to 30.6%. China must seize this opportunity to promote IT and its industry, accelerate the construction of informationization, and strive for a commanding height in the international arena so as to meet the opportunities and challenges brought about by economic globalization.

Second, accelerating construction of informationization is a systematic project that involves all aspects of national economy and the society. In 1996, the Leading Group for Information Technology Advancement under the State Council expressly defined "national informationization" as a "process of application of modern information technology into agriculture, industry, science and technology, national defense and social life, in-depth exploitation and widespread use of information resources, and rapid realization of the country's modernization under unified planning and arrangement by the State".

In addition to the unified planning and arrangement by the State, cultivation and improvement of six major elements (including information resources, national information network, information technology application, information technology and industry, informationization talents, and informationization policy, regulations, and standards) are needed to accelerate the construction of national information system. Cultivating and improving these elements will require great concern from people from all walks of life, as well as active involvement and joint effort from all sectors such as industry, agriculture, commerce and trade, finance, insurance, cultural education scientific research institution, national defense, press and publication, and health department.

Finally, China's informationization construction must be closely combined with national conditions and characteristics of economic development because its starting point differs from developed countries. In developed countries, informationization is based on industrialization. According to the acceleration theory of industrial investment expenditures, during a recession of traditional industries, capitals withdrawn from traditional industries can be put in part into the information industry via accumulative redistribution of national income to realize an indirect transfer of production elements.[1] Since China is now in the middle of industrialization and at the beginning of informationization, the foundation for development remains weak and there is quite a gap with developed countries; what's more, China is now faced with both industrialization and informationization. This means that China's industrialization will not follow the traditional path of developed countries, i.e. informationization preceded by industrialization. Instead, we should combine informationization with industrialization and industrial modernization; make full use of information technology means with multiplicative, highly permeable and driving functions; go directly into the difficult points currently facing China's industrialization and industrial modernization; focus on solutions to bottleneck problems, such as low technical level, low managerial efficiency, low cooperation level of socialized production, unreasonable industrial structure, low efficiency of market operations, and poor competitiveness of enterprises in the international market; and constantly improve the industrial technical level, expand the range of economic activities, reduce transaction cost, improve economic efficiency, and promote institutional innovation.

B. *Relationship between informationization and industrial modernization*

The industrial modernization is a dynamic process and informationization is a constantly developing process; the informationization under dynamic development is not only closely related to China's industrialization but also directly associated with the speed, process and level of development of China's industrial modernization. For this reason, it is not adequate to state that industrialization should be driven by informationization; instead, we must stress that China's industrial modernization should be promoted by informationization.

(1) The development level of information technology and information industry is an important symbol to measure the level of a country's industrial modernization. The process of industrial modernization is a process that witnesses an upgrade of the industrial technical level, the development of emerging industries, and the rising proportion of them in the economic structure. Frequent innovation and widespread applications of information technology as well as development and utilization of information resources have changed the economic growth pattern, accelerated the process of economic globalization and marketization, and incubated a large number of emerging industrial sectors. As the representative of emerging industries in today's world, the information industry has been on the rise for years and its proportion in the economic structure keeps rising in all countries. This is already a main symbol that the industrial structure is upgraded and gets into the advanced stage of industrialization.

Under the impetus of information technology revolution, all countries in the world have increased their inputs in research and study of information technology and in relevant basic researches. In the 1980s, as a fastest-growing forerunner in global economic development, information technology took an increasing proportion of more than 20% in the national economy of developing countries, and became an important, forerunning, and even leading industry to drive economic growth. Since the middle of 1990s, the actual contribution rate of information industry to GNP growth has exceeded 50% in developed countries, e.g. more than 75% in the United States. In 2000, the information industry has contributed more than 30% to the world economic growth.

In developed countries at higher level of industrial modernization, close attention is paid to the development of both the information technology and information industry that form an important part of national strategies. The United States is a representative that benefits a lot from the development of information technology and information industry. In financial budgets for the years of 1999 and 2000 alone, the US Government has increased its investment more than twice in R&D of information technology; the country's rapid economic growth for 10 consecutive years depends on the rapid development of information industry. This was pointed out in *Digital Economy in 2000* by the US Department of Commerce; the information technology and the Internet have become the impetus for the US economic development.

(2) Transformation of traditional industries by information technology is the key to promoting industrial modernization. The traditional industries remain the backbone industries for China's national economy in its current stage; but great changes have been taking place in traditional industry due to the popularization of information technology as well as the scientific knowledge and technical inventions accumulated in the 20th century. The information technology is creating a totally new industry through comprehensively transforming and upgrading the traditional industry and giving new contents to all industrial sectors.[2] We must seize this opportunity for widespread application of information technology to tackle various problems during industrial economic operation and recover traditional industries. This is the only way to enhance the international competitiveness of China's industry, and is also the key to promoting industrial modernization.

The history of the development of many industries has proved that transforming traditional industries by high and new technologies including information technology will bring about new vitality and competitiveness to traditional industries. The iron and steel industry was once called sunset industry. After the world's oil crisis in the 1970s, the iron and steel industry began widespread application of information technology. In this period, new technology and processes emerged one after another. The development of information technology created good conditions for improvement of the iron and steel industry. In developed countries, the iron and steel industry widely used computers in production and operation management, adopted a three-in-one new process of "steelmaking – external refining – continuous casting", employed new rolling technology that features control of plate-type precision as well as controlled rolling and cooling, promoted short flow process, and used an ultra-power electric furnace and thin slab casting and rolling. From then on, the iron and steel industry in developed countries was modernized and removed the bad reputation as a "sunset industry". The automobile industry was also a typical traditional industry, but it now becomes a backbone industry driving the world economic development ever since technologies including the semi-conductor, computer, and modern communication, along with many new materials and new processes, have been introduced into the production process and products of automobile industry.

According to practices in all countries, Japan replaced the United States in the leading competitive position in the world manufacturing industry from the 1970s to 1980s; in the 1990s, the widespread application of information technology in the American traditional industrial sectors enabled the US to maintain a more than 25% growth rate of its labor productivity and a more than two-thirds contribution rate of traditional industries to economic growth.[3] In the middle and late 1990s, the recessionary trend of the American traditional industries was totally reversed, and the American industries such as automobiles and computers regained international competitive advantages. In the same period, however, Japan held on to the traditional manufacturing industry but gave less concern to the development of the information industry and applications of information technology in traditional industries; as a result, it lost its competitive advantages in the manufacturing industry, thus resulting in a decline in international competitiveness and a 10-year-long economic downturn. The reversal of the competitive position in the manufacturing industry between Japan and the United States reveals the key roles of information technology in transforming traditional industries and in a country's industrial structure adjustment and international competitiveness.

(3) An efficient approach to promoting industrial modernization is developing and utilizing information resources. Materials, energy resources, and information are strategic resources for the development of modern society. As compared with other strategic resources, information resources exist in all activities of the national economy and in all walks of life. With economic development and social progress, information resources become increasingly important.

The development and utilization of information resources have provided new possibilities for industrial modernization and economic growth and made it possible for humans to break away from restrictions and constraints of material resources as much as possible. First, information is the only means of production that fails to observe the law of diminishing returns. In the information age, the value of any products can increase when intelligence and contents are added. Second, consumption of information resources is sustainable. New products filled with information resources will create many more market opportunities and sustainable consuming behaviors than original products. Finally, possession of information resources can realize control of the future economic activities. If economic fields are divided into the material energy conversion field and the information conversion field, then the impetus for future industrial modernization will be derived more from the development and utilization of information resources in the information field than from consumption of material resources in the material conversion field.

In the information age, an abundant reserve of information resources as well as the efficient development and utilization of information resources may serve as the foundation for alleviation and elimination of the imbalance of the economic structure and for long-term development and comprehensive utilization of other material resources to realize sustainable economic growth. If a country is short of information resources, or its information resources are in the possession of more than one sector, which are utilized on a simple, low-level, and dispersed basis so much so that they can hardly be subject to unified development, public sharing, and sustainable utilization, then informationization and industrial modernization in the country will be out of the question. For this reason, the implementation of the strategy by which industrialization is driven by informationization must be premised on extensive sharing, rapid circulation, and in-depth exploitation of information resources. An effective approach to industrial modernization is to make a practical strategy for information resources, vigorously develop and utilize information resources, reduce consumption of materials and energy per unit GNP, and balance and optimize the economic structure.

(4) Enterprise informationization is one of the important contents of industrial modernization. An enterprise is a microcell of the industrial society. Modernization of enterprise operation and management based on information technology application is an important part of industrial modernization. Enterprise informationization, which reflects "industrial modernization driven by informationization" at a microeconomic level, not only helps solve prominent problems in enterprise management and promotes the innovation of enterprise management and improvement of management level, but also is the main means to promote a wide application of information technology in all industries and accelerate the informationization process crucial to important areas of economic outlook; in addition, it is an important part of the industrial modernization in China.

The enterprise informationization level is high in developed industrialized countries. In these countries, information technology is largely used in the whole process of production and operation as well as in various external and internal economic activities so as to realize the management of modernization and enhance overall industrial competitiveness.

(i) During the research and development of new products, systems such as Computer Aided Design, Concurrent Engineering, Project Data Management, Simulation, and Virtual Prototyping are used for the management of the whole process of product R&D in order to shorten the R&D circle, improve the success rate, raise the functionality and reliability of new products, and minimize R&D cost.

(ii) During procurement and manufacture, the widespread application of information support systems such as Material Requirement Planning, Production Planning & Scheduling Systems, Computer Aided Process Planning, Computer Aided Manufacturing, and Computer Aided Quality Control can significantly reduce the inventory of raw materials, parts/components, and equipment as well as the number of WIP so that the procurement cost and business risks are minimized.

(iii) In making operation decisions, the widespread application of Management Information System, Decision Support System, Executive Information

System, and Office Automation System has ensured making scientific decisions and improved decision-making efficiency.

(iv) In marketing, the comprehensive application of information technology means and methods, such as Electronic Data Interchange, Customer Relationship Management, and Electronic Commerce, has provided prompt information support for the fastest response to customers' demands and the utmost development of potential customers, which plays a key role in stabilizing customers and expanding new markets.

(v) With the advancement of information technology and the need of enterprise management and development, the enterprise informationization tends to be integrated across enterprises when an increasing number of enterprises begin to use Computer Integrated Manufacturing System, Continues Acquisition and Life-cycle Support, and Commerce at Light Speed. The application of these comprehensive IT systems has given rise to a fundamental change in the process of production and operation, provided a powerful means for the innovation of enterprise management, and paved the way for the transformation of the enterprise organization structure from a pyramidal centralized organization pattern to a network-based decentralized pattern, thus improving the operation efficiency, flexibility, and competitiveness of the business organization.

2. Status quo of informationization and problems in the process of promoting industrial modernization in China

China's informationization began in 1984, when the State Council established the Task Force Team in Response to New Technology Revolution, which initiated widespread application of electronic computer technology and used it as an effective means to transform traditional industrial and commercial enterprises, accelerate the construction of four modernizations, and promote the development of national economy, and issued the "China's Electronic and Information Industries Development Strategy". After the preparatory phase of the national informationization project in the 1980s and the initial phase in 1993, China's information construction now has entered the implementation phase of the strategic guideline "using informationization to promote industrialization" in 2000.

Over the past two decades, tremendous achievements have been made in construction of informationization, including the perfection of the information infrastructure, the remarkable progress in key projects of informationization, the steady advancement of enterprise informationization, and the initiation of e-government affairs. As compared with developed countries, however, there are quite a few problems in the process of China's informationization due to a late start, a weak basis, and a short development time, which may be adverse to implementing the strategy of using informationization to promote industrial modernization in China.

A. Insufficient investment in informationization

An important reason for the low degree of informationization in China is insufficient investment in information infrastructure, information technology, and information products. The United States completed infrastructure construction of informationization in the 1990s, when the total investment in computer, software, and other products related to informationization exceeded US$200 billion. In 1996, for example, the United States made an investment in information technology and information industry 16 times the investment amount in other industrial equipment, accounting for 35.7% of total fixed assets of American enterprises and for 40% of the similar investment in the world.

In China, insufficient investment in the construction of informationization remains very common. According to a survey on 300 key enterprises from various countries by the Economic Center under the State Economic and Trade Commission, 70% of domestic enterprises hold the view of insufficient investment in enterprise informationization. By the end of 1998, the cumulative amount of investment made by 300 enterprises into information technology and equipment made up only 0.3% of their total assets; in China, the cumulative amount of investment made by Top 100 enterprises made up only 2.8% of their total assets. By contrast, the amount of investment in informationization made by enterprises in development countries including the United States and Japan reached up to 8–10% of their total assets. In addition, a research report from the International Data Center (IDC) indicates that 65% of Fortune 500 companies have made more investment in information technology than in production equipment. This shows a big difference in emphasis on information investment between China and multinational incorporations.

B. Low level of IT popularity and application

Only under a critical quality condition for popularity and application will information technology be able to promote economic growth in the true sense. Up to now, however, the popularity of information technology in social and economic activities remains on the low side, so there is still a long distance to the critical point at which informationization is used to promote industrial modernization in an all-round way. Whether the current situation with a low level of IT popularity and application can be changed thoroughly in the future will be contingent on three factors: (1) the prices of telecommunication infrastructure and IT products, (2) the penetration rate of computer and the Internet, and (3) the number of IT application personnel with a certain education level and the consumer group with substantial income and demand for information consumption.

(1) Low popularity rate of the telephone. In 1998, the popularity rate of the telephone went over 51.7% in seven industrially developed countries, such as the US, Canada, Japan, Germany, France, the UK, and Italy; at the end of 2002

in China, however, the popularity rate of telephone only was 33.74% (4.7%, 8.11%, 13%, and 20% respectively in 1995, 1997, 1999, and 2000). Furthermore, the charge rate for a fixed-line phone and mobile phones made up 5–8% of resident incomes, much higher than the average international level of 1–2%, restricting the actual growth in demand of telephone traffic.

(2) Low per capita possession of computers. In 1998, 100 people in seven developed countries, owned 17 personal computers, some even had up to 38 computers in the United States; by the end of 2000 in China, however, the in-depth utilization rate of personal computers was only 6%; the popularity rate of the home computer was 20% in developed countries, and only about 10% in China.

(3) Low utilization rate of the Internet. While the number of the Internet subscribers grows quickly in China (59.10 million by December 31, 2002), they make up less than 5% of the total population, close to the proportion of global subscribers in the world's population. As compared with developed countries, however, there is still a big difference; for example, the number of American subscribers exceeds 100 million, about 50% of the world's total, because one third or half of the Americans above 16 years old are users of the Internet. In addition, the spending of nearly RMB200 Yuan per month per subscriber for surfing the Internet in China has imposed restrictions on network applications by existing enterprises or individual users and on the further popularization of the Internet.

(4) E-government just started in China. More than 7,200 government sectors built websites to facilitate online office and approval; however, day-to-day business is manually handled at all levels of government sectors, and there is only general information but few online services available on government websites. According to statistics in March 2001, the webpage content of e-government affairs made up only 0.2% of total pages on government websites, leading to a sharp contrast with some developed countries. For example, the US government has initiated an OA system to deal with e-government affairs; the central government of Japan and the secondary government sectors have set up Management Information System and Decision Support System to support their main business. The British Government information website now is able to provide rapid all-weather information services for the public, with the websites of 60% of government agencies opened or under construction; 41% of the public got access to government's services on government websites in 2002. The Singapore government began in 2002 to provide more than 1,000 online service items for the public so that ordinary people at home could come in contact with the government.

(5) E-commerce remains in its primary stage. According to the global trend of e-commerce development, the sales volume of global e-commerce business amounted to US$1.2 billion in 1994, it more than doubled up to US$2.6 billion in 1997, and got as high as US$50 billion in 1998. It is predicted that the trading volume of global e-commerce business will rise from

US$300 billion in 2000 to US$6–7 trillion during 2004 and 2005, accounting for 8–10% of total volume of global trade. In the United States, for example, the trading volume of business-to-business e-commerce exceeded US$1 trillion in 2003; whereas in the whole Asia, the trading volume of e-commerce business was estimated close to US$1 trillion in 2005.

In China, the e-commerce business started late, developed slowly, and currently remains in discussion about the maturity of technical means and standard specifications for security, confidentiality, certification, and relevant laws; as result, there are few practical applications of e-commerce. Based on the calculation of trading volume, China's e-commerce business now stays at a level only 0.23% of the United States, which is a primary stage in general.[4] In 2001, there were 1,345 B2B websites in China, with only 667 sites in effective and continuous operation, accounting for 49.6%, and 1,196 professional websites, with about 595 sites in effective and continuous operation, accounting for 49.7%. The operation of B2C websites seemed poorer; in 2001, there were 2,056 B2C websites in China, but only 569 sites operated effectively and continuously, accounting for 32%, due to small variety, high cost distribution, long time delivery, inconvenient returns, and unsatisfactory services for commodities available on websites. Only 10% of online transactions were paid for.

According to the 2001 Report of International Data Center (IDC), the trading volume of China's e-commerce business was RMB6 billion and 15 billion respectively in 2001 and 2002, and would be RMB30 billion and 70 billion respectively in 2003 and 2004. Because the mainstream mode of online shopping in China is limited to business to customer (B2C) rather than business to business (B2B), it is unlikely for wholesale e-commerce transactions to take shape in a short term. This might be caused by an immature market; an imperfect spot market and visible market; poor business credit; heavy arrears; an unsupported information system, logistics system, payment system, and institutional assurance; and a vast majority of enterprises lacking the sense of urgency in e-commerce development, etc.[5]

C. Poor ability in comprehensive application of information technology

In *China's Information Ability Research Report* submitted by International Statistical Information Center of National Bureau of Statistics in 1999, which presents a comparison of information ability in 28 countries including China by 30 indicators of four categories, such as the ability to utilize information technology and relevant equipment, the ability to develop and utilize information resources, informationization talent and population quality, and State support for the development of information industry, the results show that the United States scored the highest with 71.76 points, followed by Japan with 69.97 points; China scored 6.17 points, the last but one in 28 countries (See Table 1.7.1).

According to Table 1.7.1, China ranks the 27th in 28 countries and lies at the primary stage of informationization. According to Table 1.7.2, developed

Table 1.7.1 Aggregate Level Ranking of Information Ability in 28 Countries

Ranking	Country	Points scored	Ranking	Country	Points scored
1	US	71.76	15	Poland	21.57
2	Japan	69.97	16	Mexico	17.43
3	Australia	65.59	17	South Africa	17.11
4	Canada	59.40	18	Brazil	15.34
5	Singapore	57.07	19	Romania	12.92
6	Netherlands	54.06	20	Turkey	12.71
7	UK	53.45	21	Philippines	11.54
8	Germany	53.25	22	Egypt	10.64
9	New Zealand	52.32	23	India	9.28
10	France	49.26	24	Indonesia	8.46
11	South Korea	40.23	25	Thailand	8.34
12	Italy	34.71	26	Sri Lanka	8.19
13	Spain	33.75	27	China	6.17
14	Russia	26.21	28	Pakistan	5.28

Source: Zheng Jingping and Yang Jingying, *China Information Almanac* (2001), China Information Almanac Press, 2002 edition.

Table 1.7.2 Comparison of All Countries' Ability to Utilize Information Technology and Information Equipment

Ranking	Country	Points scored	Ranking	Country	Points scored
1	US	92.88	12	Spain	33.92
2	Australia	80.41	13	South Korea	33.56
3	Japan	66.73	14	Poland	20.02
4	New Zealand	63.35	15	Russia	16.83
5	Canada	60.42	16	Brazil	13.59
6	UK	57.96	17	Turkey	13.55
7	Germany	53.77	18	Mexico	10.94
8	Netherlands	53.62	19	South Africa	10.11
9	Singapore	52.12	20	Thailand	9.53
10	France	46.78	21	China	9.39
11	Italy	38.07	22	Indonesia	8.66

Source: Zheng Jingping and Yang Jingying, *China Information Almanac* (2001), China Information Almanac Press, 2002 edition.

countries and new industrialized countries have scored more than 30 points in utilization of information technology and information equipment; countries that scored more than 60 points include the United States, Australia, Japan, New Zealand, and Canada; China scored only 9.39 points, falling far behind developed countries and some developing ones.

It is Chinese enterprises' inability to utilize information technology that led to a big difference between China and developed countries. In the United States, major enterprises tried a large-scale and comprehensive utilization of information technology as early as two decades ago; today, 60% of small enterprises, 80% of medium enterprises, and above 90% of large enterprises carry out business activities by way of the Internet. It is also estimated that nearly 70% of American enterprises and 50% of European enterprises have fulfilled their business tasks on the Internet. The US Government even made a directive decision: any enterprise that failed to take advantage of e-business and supply chain technology would lose the title as a preferred supplier by 2004. In China, however, quite a few of enterprises know little about information technology, much less the applications. By the end of 2002, according to statistical results, there were 217,000 enterprises registered on the Internet, including 20–25% of large- and medium-sized enterprises; of 10 million small- and medium-sized enterprises registered in the Industrial and Commercial Administration, less than 10% have some information technology equipment. Quite a few enterprises that have carried out information construction fail to make the best of information technology in improving professional ability and efficiency of operation. In regard to the application of information technology systems, less than 3% of domestic enterprises have adopted ERP system,[6] and less than 10% adopted a computer-aided design system, an office automation system, and an information management system, much less the degree of informationization in production process. According to relevant analysis, China falls at least four decades behind the United States in terms of computer application.[7]

D. Unbalanced development

China is faced with prominent problems of unbalanced development during information construction, such as uneven development between eastern and western regions, between large- and medium-sized cities and small cities and rural regions, and between large-sized enterprises and SMEs. This section highlights the digital gap between the eastern region and the western region concerning the imbalanced economic structure relevant to informationization, which is a bottleneck problem that restricts the process of China's informationization and industrial modernization. According to a joint investigation conducted by China Internet Network Information Center (CNNIC), China's Center for Information Industry Development (CCID), and Nanjing Research Base for National Information Resources Management in June 2001, there is a huge difference in possession of information resources between Beijing, Shanghai, Guangdong, and 10 provinces/cities in the middle and western regions. For example, the number of Internet users, websites, and web pages in Beijing, Shanghai, and Guangdong makes up 45%, 46.6%, and 54.4% of the national total, but the number in 10 provinces/cities in the middle and western regions makes up only 8%, 6.6%, and 3.8% respectively.

From *The 11th Statistics on China Internet Network Development* published by CNNIC one and a half years later (January 2003), the number of websites in 10 provinces/cities/districts in western regions accounts for only 7.3% of national total websites, or 8.6% even with Inner Mongolia and Guangxi included, but the proportion is 42.7% in Beijing and 45.6% in Shanghai (see Table 1.7.3). The number of Internet users in 10 western provinces/cities/districts accounts for only 15.7% of national total, or 18.9% even with Inner Mongolia and Guangxi included (see Table 1.7.4).

According to Table 1.7.3, by Dec 31, 2002, there were 371,600 WWW websites in China. The regional distribution of WWW websites fits with regional distribution of WWW websites in previous investigations; the

Table 1.7.3 Distribution of WWW Websites in Provinces/Cities at the End of 2002

Province/city	Number of websites	Percentage (%)	Province/city	Number of websites	Percentage (%)
Beijing	75,066	20.2	Chongqing	3,206	0.9
Shanghai	70,192	18.9	Shaanxi	3,132	0.8
Guangdong	39,667	10.7	Guangxi	3,082	0.8
Zhejiang	31,216	8.4	Yunnan	2,959	0.8
Jiangsu	29,202	7.9	Jilin	2,682	0.7
Shandong	16,740	4.5	Inner Mongolia	2,014	0.5
Fujian	13,690	3.7	Jiangxi	1,971	0.5
Liaoning	12,567	3.4	Shanxi	1,959	0.5
Sichuan	11,557	3.1	Xinjiang	1,711	0.5
Hubei	8,567	2.3	Hainan	1,399	0.4
Hebei	8,037	2.2	Gansu	1,333	0.4
Henan	6,216	1.7	Guizhou	1,093	0.3
Hunan	5,697	1.5	Tibet	947	0.3
Tianjin	4,843	1.3	Ningxia	691	0.2
Anhui	4,568	1.2	Qinghai	316	0.1
Heilongjiang	3,769	1.0			

Source: *The 11th Statistics on China Internet Network Development*, January 2003, www.cnnic.net.cn. The statistics cover the number of websites opened in Mainland China, exclusive of Hong Kong, Taiwan, and Macau.

Table 1.7.4 Regional Distribution of China's Internet Users at the End of 2002

Guangdong	Shandong	Liaoning	Hunan	Tianjin	Anhui	Inner Mongolia	Qinghai
9.5%	6.5%	4.8%	2.9%	2.3%	1.9%	1.2%	0.3%
Jiangsu	Zhenjiang	Fujian	Henan	Shaanxi	Yunnan	Gansu	Ningxia
8.1%	5.5%	3.8%	2.8%	2.2%	1.7%	1.2%	0.3%
Shanghai	Hubei	Heilongjiang	Chongqing	Jiangxi	Shanxi	Guizhou	Tibet
7.1%	5.4%	3.8%	2.5%	2.0%	1.6%	0.8%	0.1%
Beijing	Sichuan	Hebei	Jilin	Guangxi	Xinjiang	Hainan	
6.6%	5.2%	3.7%	2.4%	2.0%	1.4%	0.4%	

number of websites in North China, East China, and South China accounts about 85% while the proportion in Northeast, Southwest and Northwest is quite small (see Fig. 1.7.1). By Dec 31, 2002, the total number of Internet users in China was 59.1 million persons, the distribution of which is illustrated in Table 1.7.4. According to the regional distribution of Internet users in previous investigations (see Fig. 1.7.2), the number of Internet users in Northeast, Southwest, and Northwest makes up less than 30% of total number of users nationwide (the proportion of users in other regions than North China is on the rise).

The difference between the eastern region and the western region in economic development and cultural progress together with the huge difference in possession of information resources has directly led to a huge gap between the eastern region and the western region in application of information technology. According to the results of research and calculation conducted on index system of total index of e-commerce by International Statistical Information Center of the National Bureau of Statistics and China Internet Institute (CII), the total index of e-commerce throughout the country is 51.47. From the regional distribution, provinces ranking high are located in the eastern region, with the top five including Beijing (57.1), Guangdong (54.6), Shandong (51.09), Shanghai (48.24), and Liaoning (47.97). Provinces in the western region have scored less than 30 points. Other investigations have also drawn the same conclusion:

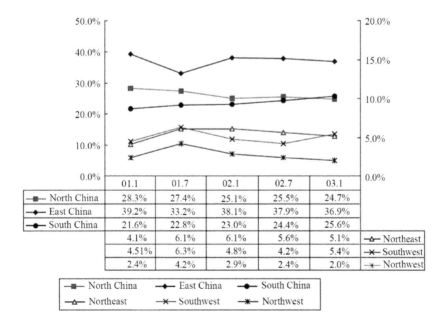

	01.1	01.7	02.1	02.7	03.1	
North China	28.3%	27.4%	25.1%	25.5%	24.7%	
East China	39.2%	33.2%	38.1%	37.9%	36.9%	
South China	21.6%	22.8%	23.0%	24.4%	25.6%	
	4.1%	6.1%	6.1%	5.6%	5.1%	Northeast
	4.51%	6.3%	4.8%	4.2%	5.4%	Southwest
	2.4%	4.2%	2.9%	2.4%	2.0%	Northwest

North China   East China   South China
Northeast   Southwest   Northwest

Fig. 1.7.1 Regional Distribution of WWW Sites in Previous Investigations

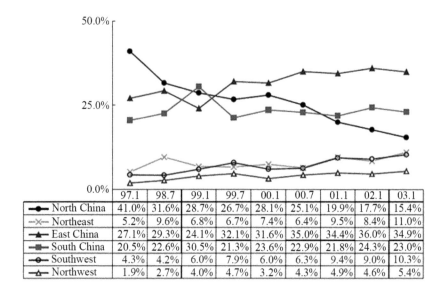

	97.1	98.7	99.1	99.7	00.1	00.7	01.1	02.1	03.1
North China	41.0%	31.6%	28.7%	26.7%	28.1%	25.1%	19.9%	17.7%	15.4%
Northeast	5.2%	9.6%	6.8%	6.7%	7.4%	6.4%	9.5%	8.4%	11.0%
East China	27.1%	29.3%	24.1%	32.1%	31.6%	35.0%	34.4%	36.0%	34.9%
South China	20.5%	22.6%	30.5%	21.3%	23.6%	22.9%	21.8%	24.3%	23.0%
Southwest	4.3%	4.2%	6.0%	7.9%	6.0%	6.3%	9.4%	9.0%	10.3%
Northwest	1.9%	2.7%	4.0%	4.7%	3.2%	4.3%	4.9%	4.6%	5.4%

Fig 1.7.2 Regional Distribution of Internet Users in Previous Investigations

a huge digital gap exists between the eastern region and the western region, which can hardly be narrowed in a short time.

In addition to the digital gap between different regions, we can also find various problems concerning the unbalanced economic structure that have much to do with the informationization between economically developed and less-developed regions/cities, between industries with different competitiveness and size, and between individuals with different educational backgrounds, which constitutes the bottleneck in the process of China's informationization and industrial modernization. In order to use informationization to promote industrial modernization, we must be fully aware of the serious problem of the digital gap between the eastern and western regions; get rid of the erroneous idea that "informationization is a game designed for the strong"; take into consideration all areas in the eastern and western regions, including economically developed and less-developed areas, and all hidden dangers of an unbalanced economic structure; take the opportunity of informationization to eliminate social and economic gap between the first mover and late mover; get rid of the shackles of dual economic structure; and try to promote a positive interaction, interpenetrating, and synergetic development of informationization and industrial modernization in China. This is what is defined in the statement that informationization is used to promote industrial modernization, and also is of due and overall strategic significance to China's economic growth and sustainable development of society.

E. Laggard key information technology and information product despite large quantity and rapid growth rate of information industry

Over the past dozen years, China's information industry, which features strong market demand, high income elasticity, and high industrial relevancy, has been growing at a rate two to three times the rate of GDP growth and has become a leading industry of national economy and a new source of economic growth.

(1) Remarkable progress is made in the construction of the information infrastructure, including the first largest telephone network in the world. After the number of fixed-line telephone subscribers exceeded 100 million in January 1999, the number of fixed-line telephone and mobile telephone subscribers exceeded 420 million and the network size ranked the first in the world at the end of 2002.
(2) In 2002, the industrial added value of China's information industry amounted to RMB572.6 billion, the proportion of which in the GDP rose from 2.3% in 1997 to the current 5.7%, including RMB274.6 billion in communication industry, which made up 2.7% of the GDP, and RMB298.0 billion in electronic information products manufacturing industry, which made up 3% of the GDP.
(3) In 2002, the sales revenue of the electronic information products manufacturing industry throughout the year exceeded RMB1.4 trillion, which accounted for about 11% of the world's total sales volume and ranked the third in the world, second only to the United States and Japan.
(4) In 2002, China's export sales of electronic information products exceeded US$92.5 billion, accounting for about 30% of total export in China and contributing 46% to export growth. This industry has become the largest one in China that depends on utilization of foreign investment and export.

China's information industry begins to take shape, assumes a good development momentum, and increases its effect on domestic economic growth. From the division and competition pattern of information industries in the world, however, China's manufacturers are more competent in manufacturing products with low added value and technical content, such as PC, hardware, display and communication terminals, than in independent R&D and supply of products with high technical content, such as server and router. The lack of key information technology and independent innovation of high-end information products in industry chain has increasingly become a bottleneck for upgrading the technical level, optimizing the industrial structure, and enhancing the international competitiveness of China's information industry.

China now can hardly rival the world's advanced level since the key information technology depends largely on introduction from outside and the technical R&D ability is a far cry from foreign advanced level. Some developed countries grasp in hands the core technologies, such as large-scale integrated circuit chip design and manufacture, high-speed large capacity hard disk, ultrahigh speed parallel cluster computer technology, system software, Internet technology, and synchronous digital hierarchy as an investment into the information industry. The average proportion of R&D expenditure invested by China's information technology enterprises is less than 1% of their sales volume; whereas, the proportion of large enterprises in developed countries is usually up to 7–9%. In terms of the proportion of technology industrialization, the commercialization rate of electronic technology achievements in China is only 15% while it is usually 75% in developed countries. Take the integrated circuit for an example. While the production of integrated circuit chips in China has increased from 1.3 billion in 1997 to 8.5 billion and China is technically capable of design, development, and production of 0.18 micron chips, 70% of China's chips remain at the import and imitation stage since China's technological level falls more than 10 years behind countries including the United States and Japan, a difference up to two to three stages of development. Besides, the domestic integrated circuit chips take up only 20% shares on home market, with most of them on low-end market.

In the world electronic information products market in 1998, the production and sales of the United States, Japan, and European Union occupied 70% of the total volume, but China accounted for only 3.5%. The same year, China's sales volume of electronic information products was RMB286.24 billion, equivalent to only 44% of IBM's USD78.51 billion. In 1998, the sales revenue of China's electronic information products was 1.41% of the GDP, but in the United States and European countries, it was 3%. In 1999, the United States took the first place in product value of six fields such as computer and peripherals, control and instruments, medical and industrial electronics, radio communication and radar, telecom equipment, and fundamental classes, while Japan topped in fields such as office equipment and consumer electronics. Both occupied over 50% of the world's total product value of electronic products apart from consumer electronic products.[8]

According to Table 1.7.5: China's product value of computer and peripherals is only 17.0% of the United States and 25.4% of Japan, that of office equipment is only 31.3% of the United States and 30.5% of Japan, that of control and instruments is only 3.8% of the United States and 19.2% of Japan, that of medical and industrial electronic equipment is only 5.7% of the United States, that of radio communication and radar is only 5.9% of the United States, that of telecom equipment only is 10.5% of the United States and 24.2% of Japan, and that of fundamental electronic products is only 16.7% and 17.2% of the United States.

Since the year of 2000, the rapid growth of China's electronic information manufacturing has changed the aforesaid competitive landscape. As compared with powerful countries of information industry in the world, however, the backward situation of China's core technology in independent intellectual property rights indicates that China is a big country of the information industry with certain advantages in manufacturing quantity and has a lack of competitiveness in leading technologies of the leading information product field. This

Table 1.7.5 Comparison of Electronic Products in China, the US, and Japan in 1999

Item Product	Product value (US$)			Percentage in world's total of electronic products (%)		
	US	Japan	China	US	Japan	China
Computer & peripherals	835.3	559.7	142.00	27.24	18.25	4.63
Office equipment	49.7	51.0	15.56	27.53	28.25	8.62
Control & instruments	372.23	73.21	14.00	45.2	8.89	1.70
Medical & industrial electronics	166.45		9.4	43.3		2.44
Radio communication & radar	578.41		34.0	42.7		2.51
Telecom equipment	383.56	165.24	40.0	35.58	15.33	3.71
Consumer electronic product		167.91	144.60		19.4	16.7
Fundamental electronic products	747.09	721.71	125.0	25.9	25.0	4.33

Source: Sorted out from *The Yearbook of World Electronic Data* (2000 and 2001).

means that China is still inadequate to comprehensively equip its information construction with domestic information technology and products, which will result in problems such as high cost, long periods, and high maintenance cost of information construction in all fields of the national economy and further affect China's industrial modernization process.

F. Weak foundation of informationization

Based on an investigation in the exploitation and utilization of information resources, the information personnel training mechanism, the criteria for information technology and relevant policy and law system, China still has a very weak foundation for informationization. This situation is not consistent with the needs of China's national economy and social development for information construction and is also out of place with China's position and image as a big, developing country. With a wide range of strong influences on long-term development, the fundamental problems concerning information construction in China have become critical ones that must be tackled in the process where "informationization is used to promote industrial modernization".

(1) Low degree of information resources sharing and low rate of exploitation and utilization of information resources. With huge investment and rapid development since the 1990s, the main problems facing many of China's enterprises and government agencies now have less to do with communication network, computer selection, and website construction,

but have more to do with transforming decentralized and isolated information resources into networked information resources and by integrating "information islands" to achieve the quick circulation and sharing of information resources.

Due to the fragmented management system of social economy and the imbalanced development of informationization, a uniform information resources market has not yet formed in China, thus resulting in unsatisfactory exploitation, utilization, and sharing of information resources in all aspects of the national economy. In the field of economic operation, the effective sharing, exploitation, and utilization of information resources seem impossible among economic management and service departments such as industry and commerce, tax authority, banks, merchandise inspection, customs, foreign exchanges, transportation, telecommunication, insurance, and quality supervision under restrictions of sector monopoly, regional blockade, and infrastructure. In this case, problems such as increasing transaction costs, decreasing operation benefits, and inappropriately allocating resources become so urgent that they must be tackled immediately.

(2) Lack of a systematic mechanism for information personnel training. Now there is no such a mechanism in China. Nor is there a systematic guarantee system in China for college undergraduates majoring in information technology to carry out a social practice or internship and for graduates to receive training and re-educational programs. According to an estimate of capability to utilize information technology and information equipment in 28 countries and regions, China comes at the bottom in information personnel and their quality, falling far behind the developed countries and the Four Asian Tigers and even behind such developing countries as Brazil and Pakistan.

According to statistics by a relevant authority, the number of computer software experts and engineering technicians makes up only 12.5% and 6.25% of persons employed in the information industry in China, much lower in employment of the whole society; whereas in developed countries, the number of skilled workforce generally employed in the information industry makes up more than 50% of the labor force in the whole society. According to statistics by another authority, only about 150,000 software developers are urgently needed in China; only 48,000 information talents are produced per year in China; and computer doctoral graduates are outnumbered by archaeology doctoral graduates each year. Particularly, China is in urgent need of technical personnel and managerial personnel in the field of information security.

Lack of information technicians or shortage of technical force is one of the difficult problems hindering the promotion of information construction by the majority of IT application sectors, enterprises, and social organization (especially the small- and medium-sized organizations) in China. According to an investigation, two thirds of China's key enterprises admitted a shortage of information talents.

(3) Criteria, relevant laws, regulations, and policy systems for information technology have not been established. The establishment and improvement of a standard system for information technology is a prerequisite for informationization and industrial modernization. Without a mature, standard system, it will not be possible to realize an economic scale with industrial mass production, share information resources, and achieve a compatible system, or form a benign cycle where informationization is used to promote industrial modernization.

Information construction also requires a complete set of laws, regulations, and policy-supporting systems. Take the e-commerce development for an example, the government must provide a substantial legal system to ensure that both parties involved in an e-commercial transaction will abide by common rules for business activities, which includes the legality of an e-signature and other identity recognition program; the protection of intellectual property; the protection of trademark right and domain names; the protection of business and personal privacy; the validity of electronic contract; the effective specifications for electronic documents, etc.

China has lagged in development of criteria, laws, regulations, and policy systems for information technology. The lack of unified planning, the imperfect preventive measures and means as well as an immature credit system make it difficult to obtain evidence and verify various problems and disputes occurring in the process of information activities, including the lack of mandatory measures for imported information technologies and their Chinese instructions, the lack of effective legal and technical preventive means for computer and cybercrimes, etc. Obviously, this immature institutional environment can hardly create a necessary, orderly, social, economic, and technical environment for the process where "informationization is used to promote industrial modernization".

3. A strategic choice of using informationization to promote industrial modernization

In order to implement the spirits of the 16th CPC National Congress and accomplish the strategic deployment of promoting industrialization with informationization and boosting industrial modernization, we will try to carry out the following activities that have strategic significance.

A. Strengthen the strategic plan to use informationization to promote industrialization and boost industrial modernization

According to the realistic situation of China, longitudinally, there is a synchronous and crosswise development of industrialization and informationization, and horizontally, there is an imbalance in regional development. The intricate foundation and the urgent situation[9] require China to adopt the potent State will to implement the strategy of "using informationization to boost industrialization and promote industrial modernization".

The Chinese Government has realized the importance of strengthening strategic planning and guidance in this process. In the future, we need to work out overall planning and implementation plans for promoting industrial modernization with informationization. All sectors and regions are required to raise their awareness of this strategy from a comprehensive height, and to develop and fulfill corresponding objectives by combining this strategy with the promotion of industrialization, with the upgrading of industrial structure, with the expansion of domestic demands and promotion of sustainable economic growth, with the response to challenges facing entry into the WTO and deepening the reform of systems, and with the construction of a well-off society and acceleration of modernization process.

B. Give priority to the development of the information industry

The priority development of information industry aims to do the following: in about ten years in the future, build China's information industry from the present industrial pattern that focuses on manufacturing of electronic information products into a pattern that allows balanced development and benign interaction among information product manufacturing, software and information service industry; achieve a RMB10 trillion general scale of information industry, about 40% of the general scale of national economy; enable domestic enterprises to provide 80–90% necessary technology and product equipment for information construction in all fields of national economy; and make it possible that the sales volume of main electronic information products makes up 20–30% of the global sales revenue.

(1) Seize the opportunity of international industrial transfer to accelerate development of electronic information products manufacturing. By incorporating China's long-term development of information industry into a global IT industrial pattern, we will seize the opportunity that the developed countries are substantially transferring production manufacturing into Asian countries, especially into the eastern coastal regions in China, and grasp the international opportunity of China's entry into the WTO and bidding for the Olympic Games to formulate and implement the open policies, attract international capitals and build China into an internationally important manufacturing base and R&D base for electronic information products so as to constantly consolidate China's competitive position of electronic information products manufacturing in the world dividing system of information industry and promote upgrading from the low end to the high end in the world industrial chain.

(2) Implement the State Council's No. 18 document *Several Policies to Encourage Development of Soft and Integrate Circuit Industries*. The integrated circuit and software are key and fundamental to the information industry. By means of introduction, assimilation, absorption, and innovation, we need to produce key software and integrated circuit products that are necessary to China's information construction, that can reflect Chinese characteristics, and that have independent intellectual property rights.

(3) Substantially promote the development of the information service industry. The information service industry is an important industrial system to implement and support the strategy that "uses informationization to boost industrial modernization". It will be of great significance in fields such as social development, economic growth, information security, national defense technology, cultural education, and international exchanges. Various measures must be taken to promote the information service industry in China so that its scale and level will be close to or reach up to the international advanced level.

(4) Accelerate development of information security industry to safeguard the national information security. We need to independently develop, innovate, and industrialize key technologies and products concerning information and security of national economy, and have scale production capability. We also need to accelerate research and formulation of special policies for government procurement, specify the localization ratio of information system in critical sectors, and gradually change the situation of substantial dependence on imports or foreign technologies.

C. *Popularize IT applications in industrial areas to accelerate the transformation of traditional industries*

As China now lies in the middle stage of industrialization, traditional industries such as raw materials, chemistry, machinery, and textile are dominating the industrial economy. According to relevant data, the traditional industries in a general sense make up two thirds of all enterprises and 87% of the GDP, and a large number of handicraft enterprises have not been subject to technical transformation.[10] Among these traditional enterprises, many have a high consumption of energy and raw materials, resulting in a high unit product cost, low technical and equipment level, poor R&D ability, poor quality product, low technical content and value added, and low labor productivity. The comprehensive utilization rate of energy resources is only about 32% in China, more than 10 percentage points lower than developed countries; the energy consumption per 10 thousand Yuan of the Chinese GDP quadruples that of developed countries, and the energy consumption per unit is 30–90% higher than that of developed countries; the industrial emission of pollutants is tenfold that of the developed countries; the manufacturing technology and equipment level of China's machinery industry is 15–20 years behind developed countries; and the number of CNC machine tools makes up only 2.8% of domestic metal cutting machine tools in China, but the proportion was 30% in 1987 in Japan and 54% in 1990 in Germany. The product technology remains low in China, e.g. the number of electromechanical products that reach up to the advanced level of foreign countries in the 1980s and early 1990s makes up only about 40%, and the number of those that reach up to the world's contemporary level makes up less than 5%. The specialization level of China's enterprises remains low, e.g. the specialization level of China's machinery industry is only 15–30%; whereas in the United States, Japan, and some western European countries, this index has reached up to 75–95%. China's enterprises have low ability to develop new products. It is estimated that, in the year of 2000, the new product contribution rate of China's manufacturing industry to the GDP was only about 5.9%, with the development cycle of new products being 12–24 months, the average life cycle of leading products being 10.5 months, and the degree of localization of typical products technology being 43%; whereas in the United States, the four indices of similar enterprises were 52%, 3–6 months, 3 years, and 98.4% respectively. In addition, there is bigger gap in labor productivity between China and other countries in the world. In 1996, the labor productivity of machinery industry in China was US\$2,200 per person per year, several tenfold behind the developed countries.[11]

The reasons for the above differences may be diverse, but an important reason is that the work that uses information technology to transform traditional industries has lagged behind. Information technology features strong relevancy, permeability, and promotion as well as high value added and a large input-output. The International Telecommunication Union estimated that the national income per capita of a country will increase 3% per 1% investment increased in communication construction. IT applications have also made great changes in labor structure. Take the proportion between physical labor and mental labor for an example. The proportion was 9:1 at the early stage of mechanization and 6:4 at the stage of semi-mechanization, but it dropped to 1:9[12] at the stage of information-based automation. Some of the developed countries therefore have emphasized the use of information technology in the transformation of tradition industries. As early as in the 1950s, American enterprises made use of computer technology for product design and production process control in traditional industries, and adopted numerical control technology for the transformation of machine tools and industrial equipment. In the 1970s, they used computer technology (CAX) for the large-scale transformation of production systems. In the 1980s, they used CIM technology to upgrade the production mode. In the 1990s, they used CIC technology to upgrade their mode of business operation. By the end of the twentieth century, the developed countries had completed upgrading the control of design, manufacturing, and production processes in traditional industries. Of course, this transformation and upgrading did not stop. In 1995, the German Government issued the *2000 Framework Scheme for Manufacturing Technology* to define the six key researches concerning Germany manufacturing development in the 21st century, and decided to provide financial aids in huge amounts for SMEs that did not have sufficient funds for independent research and development. Three of the seven key researches aided were directly related to information technology (IT-based modular development technology to shorten the cycle of new products development, computer-controlled 3D rapid processing technique of physical samples, and information technology in manufacturing process), and the other four were indirectly related to information technology.

The acceleration of the transformation of traditional industries aims to make the contribution rate of IT input, IT popularizing rate, and information technology to national economy up to or close to or overtake the level in developed countries. This means that China's IT input will make up 2–3% of total social investment, the IT popularizing rate up to 50%, and the contribution rate of information technology to national economy up to one-third.

In the whole industrial field, information technology will be widely used to improve industrial equipment and promote the upgrading of industrial products; economic means will be taken to both accelerate the IT transformation of key equipment manufacturing and to promote and deepen applications of information technologies and intelligent tools such as CAD/CAM, CIMS, dedicated chips, and embedded software; and the self-supply and matching capacity of integrated optical, mechanical and electrical equipment, and large complete-set equipment will be enhanced to facilitate upgrading the industrial equipment, further improve automation and intelligentization in the whole industry, save energy, reduce consumption, prevent pollution, and raise labor productivity.

In specific industry sectors, the advanced information technology will be utilized to upgrade traditional products such as machinery, metallurgy, chemical industry, textile, building materials, and household appliances so as to strengthen research, development, and innovation of technologies; improve design and technological level; accelerate development of generic technology, key technology, and matching technology; increase the variety of industrial products; improve quality; enhance the ability to develop and process industrial products; promote a combination of information products and tradition products; and increase the IT value added in products. Information technology will be applied into production and operation management to modify the management method, improve management efficiency, reduce operation cost, and enhance enterprises' market competitiveness.

We will promote the adjustment of the technical and industrial structure in the old industrial base, give active support to IT transformations in the old industrial base, and strive to foster new advantageous industry and enterprises by making good use of its solid foundation and talents.

In addition, we will popularize information technology in public utilities such as energy, transportation, and telecommunication as well as in such fields as commercial circulation, science, education and culture, community services, municipal administration, and government administrative management in order to coordinate with the informationization of the national economy and provide supporting services and environment for the process that uses informationization to promote industrial modernization.

D. Accelerate the process of informationization in enterprises

First, we need to raise awareness, renew ideas, work out relevant policies and measures, encourage and guide enterprises in all fields to suit practical situations of the trade they are involved in, carefully choose the key contents of information construction, and increase investment into information construction.

Second, we need to improve the market competition mechanism, guide enterprises to make overall planning for short-, medium-, and long-term information construction so as to solve practical problems. We also need to promote information construction and encourage the introduction of advanced management ideas in enterprises, with efforts focused on the reform, reorganization, upgrading, and better management as well as specific jobs concerning basic management of enterprises.

Third and finally, we need to normalize information consultation and service market for enterprises. We need to produce a group of high-level and creditworthy information service organizations and improve social ability to provide information services for enterprises by accreditation of information while consulting organization qualifications, administration and appraisal of vocational qualifications of information consultants, as well as by information disclosure.

E. Strengthen national management of information resources and promote effective exploitation and utilization

First, we need to raise awareness of information; make uniform national policies for information resources and strengthen national overall planning and management of information activities, information resources, as well as exploitation and utilization of these resources; and constantly enhance national planning functions for information infrastructure and information resources management network.

Second, we need to create or improve the national information resources system, strengthen government's management of information resources, constantly improve the relationship between provider and user of government information resources, and guide all fields, especially comprehensive large information agencies (including those under all ministries and committees and libraries in colleges and universities), in the exploitation and utilization of information resources so as to increase the level of information resources utilization by all society and achieve the synergetic development of the country, society, economy, and culture.

Third, we need to constantly improve the social information environment, further open information resources to the outside world, promote the marketization of information resources, break up regional and sectoral segmentation, encourage free competition in the information market, especially encourage social forces to take an active part in the commercial development of information resources, separate the production of information resources from information services, and encourage enterprises to increase value added information services based on information users' needs.

Fourth and finally, we need to strengthen our ability to protect, early warn, discover, and respond to the security of information resources network in China in order to safeguard national information security and information sovereignty.

F. Allow information to play a full role in balancing regional economic development

First, we need to give full play to the roles of information in balancing regional economic development. For this purpose, we must intensify efforts on "poverty alleviation via information-based services", constantly raise awareness of the importance of informationization in the eastern economically backward regions as well as central and western regions, coordinate allocation of information construction funds in different regions, and make reasonable distribution and optimal combination of information resources throughout the country.

Second, we need to speed up information infrastructure construction in economically backward regions.

Third, we need to encourage local government and key industrial enterprises in economically backward regions to make selective applications of information technology, and strengthen application demonstration.

Fourth, we recommend that the process of "using informationization to promote industrialization and industrial modernization" be combined with the "western development" strategy, and that a work plan be formulated to fill the digital gap between eastern and western regions and achieve great-leap-forward development in the central and western regions.

Fifth and finally, we need to pay attention to improving the educational level and population quality in the central and western regions. We will also highlight the cultivation, exploitation, and utilization of information personnel.

G. Accelerate construction of IT criteria and relevant legal system

First, we need to strengthen the supervision of the information industry and the construction of supporting legal systems in order to create a market environment for fair play, and to prevent and crack down computer crimes and cybercrimes.

Second, we need to speed up legislation research of IT applications to provide legal security for the popularization of information technology and its applications. The departments concerned need to produce a general technical policy for IT applications and work with major enterprises in all industries to develop related technical policy, define IT content criteria for products and technologies in certain trade, encourage extensive IT applications, compulsorily eliminate or restrict technologies with high energy consumption as well as those products and technologies below technical standard. Considering that actual situations may vary, each region or sector needs to formulate a technical policy for the region or the trade, specifying the direction, goal, and criteria of IT applications. We need to encourage eligible trade and enterprises to strengthen efforts on IT applications and raise the proportion of IT in the technical content of the trade.

Third, we need to specify that information resources are protected by laws as other resources are. We will also build or improve the management standard, technical criteria, and policy and law system for the national administration of information resources. Particularly, we will develop a scientific and feasible catalog system and exchange system for national information resources, and define a uniform framework and technical criteria for constructing information resources.

Fourth, we need to accelerate research and the formulation of a national informationization standard system that suits the need of China's information-based development, and accelerate the formulation and improvement of a technical standard system and legal system for e-commerce, protection of intellectual property rights, government procurement, information security, information resources, and integration of three networks (telecommunication, Internet, and broadcasting network).

Fifth, we need to accelerate research and formulation of technical standards concerning State security and significant technical systems and to encourage the development of IT standards and system with independent intellectual property rights and the development of IT product standards conforming to international practice.

Sixth and finally, we need to take an active part in and facilitate negotiation and formulation of the international convention on information development.

H. Strengthen IT education and promote cultivation and effective applications of IT personnel

First, we need to thoroughly implement the *Key Informationization Special Planning during the 10th Five-Year Plan of National Economy and Social Development* issued by the national leading group for information construction; set up a special fund and increase investment into education to expand the interdisciplinary talents training scale, popularize IT knowledge in the whole society, and enhance people's ability to apply information technology; guide the various existing schools to actively promote computer and network education, set up compulsory courses such as computer and network technology rudiments in primary and secondary schools, increase new faculties in institutions of higher learning, and adjust curriculum settings to speed up the cultivation of IT personnel; strengthen IT training for in-service teachers and other staff and public servants to improve jobholders' quality; and encourage domestic IT and information management personnel to go abroad and learn advanced information technology and managerial experiences.

Second, we need to encourage private capitals into information talent education and training institutions of different forms and at various levels, especially the vocational education and technical training and skill training institutions, to produce a complete information personnel training system.

Third and finally, we need to facilitate effective utilization and rational mobility of IT personnel; encourage all provinces, municipalities, and all fields to formulate policies and measures for cultivation, use, and retainment of high-quality technicians and managerial personnel as well as returnees studying abroad; and improve incentive mechanisms such as IT, management, and intellectual property contributed as investment or share options.

I. Create an integrated environment for using informationization to promote industrialization and industrial modernization

First, we need to provide solid financial support for the process of using informationization to promote industrial modernization in aspects of finance, taxation, and investment.

Second, we need to further strengthen planning for the basic, inter-disciplinary, and comprehensive information systems, such as e-government affairs system, personal data query system, enterprise credit query system, and community public services system, etc.

Third and finally, we need to adapt to the development trend of information construction; set up communication and cooperation mechanisms between different sectors and regions to break up original barriers therein; encourage private capitals into the information industry to facilitate amalgamation and cross competition of information industries; and promote free mobility, sharing, and comprehensive utilization of the information infrastructure, information resources, and information personnel of all fields in society.

(This is the author's sub-report for *Research on China's Industrial Modernization* (A), a major research project under the Chinese Academy of Social Sciences, 2004)

Notes

1 Li Jiwen, Informationization and Strategic Adjustment of China's Industrial Structure, *China Economic Times*, September 28, 2002.
2 Song Jian, Manufacturing and Modernization, *Guangming Daily*, September 26, 2002.
3 Lv Zheng, Permeable and Merging Relationship between Knowledge Economy and Agricultural Economy and Industrial Economy, *Guangming Daily*, October 17, 2000.
4 Yang Weidong, *Current Situation and Development of Global and China's E-Commerce*, April 4, 2002, http://www.chinaren.com

5 Li Xinxin, Problems in the Process of China's Using Informationization to Promote Industrialization and Policy Recommendations, *Review of Economic Research*, volume 86, 2001.

6 CCID, *Research Report on China Enterprise Informationization (2001)*, October 2001.

7 Li Xinxin, Problems in the Process of China's Using Informationization to Promote Industrialization and Policy Recommendations, *Review of Economic Research*, volume 86, 2001

8 *China's Industrial Development Report 2002*, Beijing, China: Economic Management Press, 2002 edition, p. 181.

9 Bao Ran and Hai Bian, China's Declaration of Information Age: Written after the 2nd Meeting of the National Information-based Leading Group, *China Computer World*, volume 26, July 25, 2002.

10 Hu Guoliang, On Development of Traditional Industries in the New Economic Age, *Modern Economic Research*, volume 11, 2000.

11 Institute of Industrial Economy, Chinese Academy of Social Sciences, *China's Industrial Development Report (2002)*, Beijing, China: Economic Management Press, 2003 edition, p. 168.

12 Zhou Zhenhua, Informationization Transforms Traditional Industries: Basic Connotation and Implementation Mechanism, *Tianjin Social Sciences*, volume 6, 2000.

8   Advice on the establishment of the north economic zone along the Beibu Gulf

1. An urgent task: accelerating the process of industrialization in Guangxi

In recent years, the Party Committee and government of the Guangxi Autonomous Region highlighted the industrial development to accomplish the strategy of "boosting Guilin's economy with industry". This is a correct and necessary approach to Guangxi's economic development and modernization. It is proven by the process of economic development in all countries and regions all over the world that modernization is impossible without industrialization. Similarly, Guangxi's modernization relies on the development of its industries. Two decades have passed since the high-speed advancement of industrialization throughout China, so it is urgent to accelerate the industrializing process in Guangxi.

Despite the fast development of Guangxi's industry since the economic reform and opening up in 1978, Guangxi has a small economic aggregate and low economic growth due to a weak economic base; therefore, a broad gap exists as compared with the national level of economic growth and the growth level in other advanced regions. In 2004, the total output value of Guangxi was RMB332.0 billion Yuan, per capita GDP about RMB7,196 Yuan, and the three industries were proportioned at 24.4:38.8:36.8; in contrast, China's GDP the same year was RMB13.6515 trillion Yuan, per capita GDP about RMB10,319 Yuan, and the three industries were proportioned at 15.2:52.9:31.9. Obviously, Guangxi falls behind the national average. In terms of the industrialization process, Guangxi remains in a transition period from the initial stage to middle stage of industrialization while other regions have entered the middle stage, which indicates that Guangxi falls behind the national average level, specifically including the following areas: first, high added value of the primary industry – in 2004, it made up 24.4% of Guangxi's GDP, nearly 10 percentage points higher than the national average; second, low rate of urbanization – in 2004, it was only 31.7%, about 10 percentage points lower than the national average 41.8%; finally, Guangxi's industrialization level is apparently lower than that in advanced regions – if the industrialization level is measured by the ratio between added value of agriculture and added value of industry, the ratio in

2003 was 1:1.29 in Guangxi, 1:5.12 in Guangdong, and 1:3.10 in Fujian; this means that the rate of industrialization in Guangxi in 2003 was only 22.5% of Guangdong and 37.1% of Fujian. It is thus obvious that Guangxi's industrialization has a long way to go and that "boosting Guilin's economy with industry" is of great strategic significance.

In 2005, the strategy "boosting Guilin's economy with industry" was materialized as the industrial development pattern of "three points and one plane" at the 3rd Session of the 10th Guangxi People's Congress. The three points refer to Liuzhou's old industry base being reliant on manufacturing industry, Baise's new industry base being reliant on aluminum industry, and Guilin's industry base being reliant on new technological industries, and one plane means modern industry base being reliant on the Nanning, Beihai, Qinzhou, and Fangcheng Port coastal economic zone. It is believed that this is realistic, but the emphasis is placed on the construction of the Guangxi Beibu Gulf Economic Zone.

2. The Beibu Gulf economic zone suggested being included into the national 11th five-year plan

The Beibu Gulf Economic Zone encompasses three cities: Beihai, Qinzhou, and Fangcheng Port, and extends northwards to the Nanning area. We suggest incorporating the Beibu Gulf Economic Zone into the national 11th Five-Year Plan so that it will not only become the growth pole of Guangxi's economic development but also become an important economic growth pole for China. Our suggestion is based on the following:

First, the Beibu Gulf Economic zone is the only coastal area in China that has not been incorporated into the national development planning. All the coastlines in China, from Bohai Sea Rim and the Yangtze River Delta to Pearl River Delta, have become the important national economic growth zones. Recently, Fujian's planning for the construction of the Western Taiwan straits Economic Zone was recognized by the State. The northern Beibu Gulf area is the only coastal area in West China that has not been incorporated into the national development planning. Today, with implementation of the develop-the-west strategy, we have no reasons to exclude the northern Beibu Gulf area as an important and independent economic development zone from the national development planning. We need to facilitate rapid economic development in this area and make it a new economic growth pole in Guangxi and even in the country as well as a clearing point during the implementation of the develop-the-west strategy.

Second, the Beibu Gulf Economic Zone is an ideal economic circle where medium- and large-sized cities neighboring each other ensure convenient transportation because they are mutually complementary and common in character. The distance from Beihai, Qinzhou, and Fangcheng to Nanning is less than 100km, linked by expressways. These cities have much in common: e.g. all of them lie in the same stage of industrial development; development of industry depends on port; three of them have ports that handle products of raw resource materials. In addition, each of the cities has its distinct features: e.g. Nanning has stronger general strengths; Beihai is well-known for tourism; Qinzhou has abundant industrial land resources; and Fangcheng has the largest port. With these commonalities and particularities, the area is endowed with the natural conditions for an economic circle.

Third, promoting rapid economic development in the northern Beibu Gulf area is inevitable to effectively utilize coastal location advantages. In 2004, the per capita GDP of Beihai, Qinzhou, and Fangcheng was RMB10,989 Yuan, 5,131 Yuan, and 10,662 Yuan respectively; that of Beihai and Fangcheng was slightly higher than the national average, and that of Qinzhou was much lower. The same year, the proportion of the three industries in Beihai, Qinzhou, and Fangcheng were approximately 27.9:29.8:42.3, 32:34:34, and 25.9:37:37.1 respectively, indicating that the three cities have not entered the middle stage of industrialization in terms of industrial structure and fall behind the national average. This is obviously ill-suited to the position of coastal cities, and we can even say that the location advantage of economic development in the coastal area is wasted. Currently, the economic development in eastern coastal regions has entered a period in which the quantitative growth of industries is turning to the improvement of industrial quality. If rapid economic growth cannot be achieved in the northern Beibu Gulf area, the gap with eastern coastal regions will be widened.

Fourth, accelerating the economic development in the northern Beibu Gulf area is inevitably required by the development of the China-ASEAN Free Trade Area. According to international experiences, the development of a large free trade area usually requires support from a highly developed economic center; otherwise, its cohesive and emissive force will be reduced. For this reason, if the northern Beibu Gulf area cannot become a highly developed economic zone but merely a main port in southwestern area or a traffic hub in the Southwest China, South China, and ASEAN markets, then the influence of China-ASEAN Free Trade Area will weaken in Guangxi and even the whole southwestern region of China.

Fifth, the northern Beibu Gulf area is equipped with the conditions for rapid development of resource industry: (1) location close to origins of resources (including Middle East, Africa, Southeast Asia, India, Australia, etc.) and stable market demands of petroleum and steel materials in three southwestern provinces; (2) excellent port cluster, complete facilities of roads and railways, sufficient land and fresh water for resource industry; and (3) transition from initial stage to intermediate stage of industrialization paving the way for rapid industrialization.

Sixth and finally, now there is a golden opportunity for the rapid economic development in the northern Beibu Gulf area. China's industrial development is currently based on heavy chemical industry that demands a huge quantity of resources, especially petroleum, petrochemical, and steel products. For several years in the future, the import of raw resource materials such as crude oil and iron ore will increase in China, providing a good opportunity for the northern Beibu Gulf area to develop coastal resource-based industries, such as petroleum, petrochemical, and steel and electric power by utilizing foreign resources.

3. Development strategy and recent priorities of the Beibu Gulf economic zone

The development strategy of the northern Beibu Gulf area can be summarized as "developing an industrial cluster, building a hub port, constructing integrated logistics, and achieving a leap forward in economic development".

Specifically, the current priorities involve the following: first, make plans for the economic development in the northern Beibu Gulf area, and try to incorporate the plan into the State planning in order to attract State, private, and foreign investment; second, accelerate infrastructure construction based on port; apart from efforts on north-to-south design of traffic routes, give careful consideration to the route leading to Guangdong with the purpose of forming a railway transport line around the Beibu Gulf; third, choose appropriate leading industries – on the one hand, give continuous support to leading industries such as energy, steel, petrochemical, grain and oil processing, wood pulp paper, on the other, pay increasing attention to hi-tech industries as well as farm products and the marine industry by making good use of subtropical agricultural and marine resources, in addition, give close attention to the supporting capacity of industrial development to form an industrial cluster; and fourth, strengthen the construction of a logistics-based service system. If we facilitate modern logistics through industrial development, the latter will in turn provide effective support for industrial development.

The aforesaid is just a tentative idea. More intensive studies are needed for the economic development in the Beibu Gulf Economic Zone.

(This article is the policy advice for Guangxi proposed after investigation by CAS members and experts during the "Western Trip Activity" organized by the Organization Department of the CPC Central Committee in May 2005)

9 Balance the urban and rural development in the new industrialization process

It was put forward in the *16th CPC National Congress Report* that China would have basically realized industrialization in the first 20 years of this century. This is a grand but arduous task. Considering China's national situation and the epochal characteristics, China will neither follow the traditional industrialization path of developed countries nor take the road of industrialization in times of planned economy. To open up a new road of industrialization, China needs to deal well with the relation between industrialization and informationization, the relation between industrialization and modernization, the relation between industrialization and urbanization, the relation between industrialization and job enlargement, the relation between industrialization and marketization reform, the relation between industrialization and ecological environmental protection, and the relation between China's industrialization and economic globalization. How to balance the urban and rural development is a major issue that requires focused research and an immediate solution.

We need to balance the relationship between rural industrialization and agricultural industrialization and mechanization. Rapid development of township enterprises is an evitable choice for accelerating rural industrialization. In 2002, the added value of RMB3.18 trillion Yuan realized by township enterprises accounted for 31% of the GDP; the industrial added value was RMB2.2 trillion Yuan, occupying 46.15% of the national added value; and there were 132.85 million employees in township enterprises, occupying 26.8% of the national total rural labor force. The development of township enterprises, which facilitated the transfer of a huge amount of the rural labor force into non-agricultural industries and promoted the emergence and development of a large number of small towns, has paved the way for rural industrialization. We need to promote reorganization, restructuring, technical progress, and improved quality of township enterprises. We also need to encourage them to combine their development with agricultural industrialization, to regard agricultural products processing as the main business, and to drive development and upgrading of agricultural industrialization by boosting deep processing of agricultural products. We need to steadily promote the process of agricultural mechanization in order to alleviate farmers' labor intensity and raise labor productivity.

We need to balance urban and rural employment. China's population makes up 21% of the world population and labor resources make up 26% of the world; however, China's natural and capital resources are less than 10% of the world's total. In cities and towns in China, about 10 million newly-increased labor forces enter the labor market every year, and as many as 24 million persons need to be employed or re-employed. Meanwhile, about 150 million rural surplus labor forces need to be migrated. The issue of employment is a difficult task challenging us for a long time. In the process of industrialization, we need to take into overall consideration both the urban employment and migration of rural surplus labor forces. Various discriminative policies must be eliminated. While we are developing hi-tech industries, carrying out technical innovation, and transforming traditional industries by new technology, new equipment, and new process, we also need to increase jobs. While we are promoting the development of such industries as knowledge-intensive hi-tech industries, capital and technology-intensive heavy chemical industries, and equipment manufacturing industries in order to upgrade the industrial structure and raise the industrial modernization level, we also need to encourage the development of labor-intensive industries so as to give full play to China's comparative advantages in abundant labor resources and low labor cost, expand exports, and provide more jobs. While adjusting the industrial structure, we need to develop the tertiary industry. At the present stage, 170,000 jobs are created per percentage point increased in the output value of the secondary industry, but 850,000 jobs are created per percentage point increased in the output value of the tertiary industry. In 2002, the number of employed persons in the tertiary industry made up 28.6% of all employed persons, much lower than the 60–75% in developed countries, and lower than the 40–50% in some developing countries. Despite tremendous space, the development of the tertiary industry can absorb more labor forces. When adjusting the ownership structure and organizational structure of the enterprises, we need to encourage the development of private enterprises. Of employed persons in cities and towns in 2001, as against in 1991, the public-owned economies laid off 53.61 million persons, and private-owned economies increased 118 million persons. When we emphasize development of large enterprises and large business groups, we also need to encourage the development of SMEs, especially the township enterprises that have provided 80% of the new jobs in recent years.

We need to balance the relationship between developing large- and medium-sized cities and developing small towns. China now lies in the middle stage of industrialization. With the development of industrialization, the process of urbanization will accelerate constantly and an increasing number of rural populations will transfer into cities. There are three approaches to improving the urbanization level: first, with the development of industrialization, more rural populations will rush into cities, especially the large cities and mega-cities; second, some new, large- and medium-sized cities will emerge in the process of industrialization; and finally, a large number of new, small cities will absorb a large amount of the population migrating from rural areas.

The urbanization in developed countries is mainly accomplished via the first two approaches. In China, there is no doubt that quite a few rural populations will transfer into megalopolises and large- and medium-sized cities as the industrialization level improves, but it is unlikely that all rural population will dwell in large- and medium-sized cities. China's small enterprises, township enterprises in particular, are well developed; most of them are located in small towns and can absorb a large number of rural labor forces that are more or less related to land. Therefore, it is not advisable that China follow the traditional road of urbanization in developed countries; instead, it should open up a new road to urbanization with Chinese characteristics, which focuses on the development of small towns.

We need to balance the relationship between urban and rural social development by increasing investment into rural education, culture, health, and social relief, and by encouraging and supporting the development of rural social security causes, so as to narrow the gap between urban and rural social development.

We need to balance the relationship between urban-rural economic development and ecological environment protection. Neither urban nor rural economic development will be accomplished at the cost of environmental pollution. We must stick to a sustainable development strategy; pay close attention to protection, restoration, and reconstruction of the rural ecological environment while controlling urban environmental pollution; accelerate the construction of the natural forest protection area, wildlife protection area, and natural protection area; increase investment into the conversion of farmland into forests and desertification control; speed up the construction of a forest and eco-agricultural protection system; and prevent against the pollution of water resources as well as the abuse and waste of land resources and mineral resources.

(Published in *People's Daily*, Oct 28, 2003)

10 Suggestions and opinions on the construction of the Western Taiwan Straits economic zone

As the conjunctive point between the Chinese mainland, Taiwan, and Hong Kong and between the Yangtze River Delta and Pearl River Delta, Fujian Province has unique location advantages. The Western Taiwan Straits Economic Zone, proposed by the Fujian provincial Party Committee and government, is creative and feasible because it features opening up, coordinated development, and all-round prosperity.

1. Brief evaluation of the construction outline of the Western Taiwan Straits economic zone

Starting from the year of 2004, according to the *Construction Outline*, the economic zone will comprise three development stages, a three-tier regional layout, seven supporting systems, and three objectives.

Three development stages: initially forming stage (2004–2010), developing stage (2011–2015), and comprehensively rising stage (after 2016).

Three-tier regional layout: coastal economic cluster area, inland economic development area, and peripheral economic cooperation area.

Seven supporting systems: strongly competitive industrial supporting system, modern infrastructure supporting system, integrated urban supporting system, people-oriented social development supporting system, export-oriented opening up supporting system, unified and open market supporting system, and sustainable ecology supporting system.

Three overall objectives: apart from specific objectives for each of three development stages, the Outline also put forward three overall objectives for the construction of the Western Taiwan Straits Economic Zone: building the economic zone into an important growth pole of Chinese economy; into an important zone for economic and trade cooperation, scientific, technical, and cultural exchanges between Chinese mainland, Taiwan, and Hong Kong; and into an important base that can promote the reunification of China.

The *Construction Outline* also specifies some critical economic and social indices.

In general, the Outline looks at Fujian's development in the view of economic globalization and regional coordinated development, defines Fujian's position in the view of national overall situation of development, and allocates productive force in the view of overall planning for the whole Fujian Province. Proper understanding of the connotation and denotation of the Western Taiwan Straits Economic Zone is conducive to Fujian's development and prosperity, to linking the Yangtze River Delta and Pearl River Delta, to implementing the Central Government's policy for Taiwan, and to reunifying China.

(1) The outline reflects requirements of "Five balances" and scientific outlook on development

The Outline proposes "construction of the Western Taiwan Straits Economic Zone that features opening up, coordinated development and all-round prosperity", which is clearly targeted and operable because it completely reflects the "five balances" specified by the Central Government, reflects the requirements of the scientific outlook on development, reflects requirements of coordinated development and all-round development, and also materializes these requirements.

(2) Break the limits of administrative division to develop the economic zone

The Western Taiwan Straits Prosperity Belt in the southeastern coastal areas, extending from Fuzhou to Zhangzhou proposed by Fujian in 1995, aimed at a "strategic rise of an administrative district", but the Western Taiwan Straits Economic Zone, an economic plate covering Fujian and its surrounding areas, aims at a "strategic rise of an economic zone" that extends from Fujian to economically coordinated areas including eastern Guangdong, southern Zhejiang, and southern Jiangxi. The "belt" is upgraded to the "zone", indicating that Fujian has deepened its awareness of the regional position, and that the Western Taiwan Straits Economic Zone has shaken off the yoke of administrative-district economy, abandoned the old idea of a "strategic rise of an administrative district", and chosen the development route of a "strategic rise of an economic zone" focusing on inter-provincial links and regional integration. With a strategic vision for long-term integrated development, this idea aims to promote reasonable mobility of economic resources and trans-regional economic cooperation in order to enhance the overall competitiveness of the region.

This original and trans-regional planning fits in well with the law of regional economic development; links the Western Taiwan Straits Economic Zone to the two economic regions – "the Yangtze River Delta and Pearl River Delta" – that are most powerful and fastest growing in China; links the zone to inland provinces with abundant resources and remarkable advantages; promotes overall prosperity in the coastal areas in the eastern part of China and economic interaction in eastern, middle, and western part of China; consolidates the relationship between the Chinese mainland and Taiwan, Hong Kong, and Macau; receives the industrial transfer from the east coast of the Taiwan Province to realize complementary resources; strengthens economic communication and technical exchanges with other countries, especially the developed ones, to improve the zone's capability to absorb, digest, generate, and innovate, so as to make the Western Taiwan Straits Economic Zone powerful enough to cooperate or compete with other economic zones in the eastern part of China and become a window to the outside world in the southeast that radiates to Jiangxi, Hubei, Hunan, southern Zhejiang, and eastern Guangdong.

(3)   Give play to the regional advantages and Taiwanese advantages in Fujian

As the junction point between the Chinese mainland, Taiwan, Hong Kong, the Yangtze River Delta, and Pearl River Delta, Fujian has unique regional advantages: it adjoins the Yangtze River Delta on the north, Taiwan Province on the east, the Pearl River Delta on the south, and Jiangxi Province on the west; it has a coastline that is the second longest one in China (3,324km); it owns abundant marine resources and port resources; and it possesses 22 large harbors and 367 quay berths (46 above 10 thousand tons). Fujian is also the second largest hometown of overseas Chinese in China; more than 10 million Fujian natives live abroad in more than 100 countries and regions, and 80% of Taiwan compatriots have their native place in Fujian. There are six kinds of relationships between Fujian and Taiwan, such as close blood relationship, long historic relationship, deep cultural relationship, homologous language, similar spiritual relationship, and custom relationship. These relationships create congenital conditions for the integration of economic zone. In terms of geographical conditions, Fujian and Taiwan are separated by a strait and have been exchanging with each other quite often. Recently, Xiamen has become the third channel for personal exchanges between the Mainland and Taiwan, next to Hong Kong and Macau. The special relation with Taiwan makes Fujian the first place of investment made by Taiwan merchants in the Mainland. Currently, there are six investment zones for Taiwan merchants and more than 7,700 Taiwan-funded projects in Fujian, accumulatively attracting more than US$10 billion funds from Taiwan. In recent years, the investment from Taiwan businessmen and the investment already put in Fujian are on the rise, indicating Fujian's unique attraction.

Apart from favorable location and human harmony, the Western Taiwan Straits Economic Zone is initiated at the right time because Taiwan's economy currently continues falling in sharp contrast with the rapid growth in the Mainland. At this time, the Western Taiwan Straits Economic Zone proposed by Fujian will attract more Taiwan merchants' investment and will quickly transform Fujian's geographic advantages and Taiwanese advantages into regional economic advantages and industrial amalgamation advantages.

(4)   Coordinate with the national development plan

According to the outline of the national 10th Five-Year Plan, the national economic growth will be promoted by such economic regions as the Bohai Rim, Yangtze River Delta, southeastern Fujian, and Pearl River Delta. The Western Taiwan Straits Economic Zone has extended and developed the concept of southeastern Fujian region. As it looks at Taiwan across the Strait, adjoins Hong Kong and Macau, and links the Yangtze River Delta on the north and the Pearl River Delta on the south, this economic zone is a regional economic unit in Chinese southeastern coastal regions that has its own features and unique advantages, and also is an integral part of the national regional development strategy. When the southeastern Fujian is expanded into the Western Taiwan Straits Economic Zone, three economic zones – the Yangtze River Delta, the Western Taiwan Straits Economic Zone, and the Pearl River Delta – will join as one for further development so as to consolidate resources in eastern economic plates and complement each other's advantages; promote industrial linkage, market linkage, and infrastructure linkage; achieve complementary advantages, expansion of hinterland, and enhancement of strengths; and allow better play to three economic zones in national economic growth. In addition, acceleration construction of the Western Taiwan Straits Economic Zone and placing Fujian in a higher and broader open situation will not only promote the development of the economic circle around the Taiwan Strait but also consolidate the overall economic strength of Chinese southeastern coastal regions and raise its ability to participate in regional economic cooperation in East Asia and even in the world arena.

2. Several suggestions for improving the *construction outline*

(1) Play the "Cross-strait" trump: strengthen economic relations and win public support

According to the *Construction Outline*, building the Western Taiwan Straits Economic Zone is conducive to China's reunification; in other words, the economic zone should be based on the Strait, but how to make the best of the Strait needs to be further studied. Facts have proven that the guideline of strengthening economic relations, offering tangible benefits to Taiwan businessmen, increasing the cost of the "independence of Taiwan", and decomposing Taiwan independence forces is a successful strategy. We must stick to this guideline and realize that economic relations serve only as a bridge, but what matters is the public support. In addition to strengthening economic relations between Fujian and Taiwan, we need also to deal with Taiwan businessmen's ideological condition so that they identify with the Chinese nation's history, ethnics, and culture. Specifically, the government should try to raise working efficiency; create a just, open, honest, and highly efficient image; and enhance institutional competitiveness; while dealing well with unified front work at the governmental level, the Party and the government should encourage the development of civil organizations, enlarge civil exchanges, and enhance the charisma of culture and kinship.

(2) Play the "Internal integration" trump: break the limits of the old system and longitudinally integrate coastal economic clusters

The Western Taiwan Straits should attract economic radiations from the Eastern Taiwan Straits, but the key lies in construction of the Western Taiwan

Straits itself into an open economic zone and then attract more investments from Taiwan and other places. The construction of the Western Taiwan Straits Economic Zone should currently focus on the consolidation of coastal economic clusters and then spread to inland economically developed regions and peripheral economically coordinated regions. The key to the consolidation of coastal economic clusters is to break internal administrative divisions. Due to the existing management system and administrative divisions, the development of coastal economic clusters is confined to each administrative division; the isolated point advantage can hardly be transformed into a congregate group advantage, let alone the formation of an organic unity of economic development. We should seize the opportunity of building the Western Taiwan Straits Economic Zone to break up the institutional obstacle that hinders industrial cooperation and regional exchanges, and create a unified, open, and grand market. To achieve this purpose, we should first unify development strategies of each region under the framework of the Western Taiwan Straits Economic Zone to form a unified planning, define the position of each region, and minimize internal friction so that all development strategies and plans in the zone will move together rather than converge at a focal point, and then gradually adjust low-level repetition of the industrial structure in the zone and make unified planning for large infrastructure construction. In a short term, we can strengthen the polarization of the coastal economic clusters; but in a medium and long term, we need to spread their economic radiations.

(3) Play the "External integration" trump: define regional advantages and promote adjustment of industrial structure

The Western Taiwan Straits Economic Zone gains the foothold by its unique location contiguous to the Yangtze River Delta on the north, to the Pearl River Delta on the south, to Taiwan on the east across the Strait, to Hong Kong and Macau, and to Chinese inland on the west. It serves as a fulcrum or a pivot that can lever coastal economic plates in the east and receive industrial transfer from the Eastern Taiwan Straits regions. Selection of industries will be essential to the economic zone. Some leading, supporting, and fundamental industries are suggested in the *Construction Outline*, such as electronic information, mechanical equipment (including automobile, shipbuilding, and engineering machines manufacturing), and petrochemical industry. This kind of industrial structure is somewhat isomorphic to that in the Yangtze River Delta and Pearl River Delta zones, more substitutable than complementary, and more competitive than cooperative, but it's difficult to form active diffusion and benign interaction; besides, strategic security needs consideration in petrochemical industry. Therefore, we need to identify the local advantages, give priority to the development of industries with comparative advantages and strong complementarities, and achieve a transition from comparative advantages to competitive advantages.

(4) Play the "sustainable development" trump: promote the development of intensive economy and saving economy

Chinese economy is obviously getting more extensive, so much so that it maintains rapid growth via a huge amount of investment and consumption of resources. The input–output ratio of the developed countries is 1:1, the world's average is 2.9:1, but it is 5:1 in China. Though China has abundant resources, the per capita possession of resources is much lower than the world's average; particularly, for resources that are essential to human survival and are of great importance to China's industrialization, such as fresh water, arable land, and forests, the per capita possession in China is one-fourth, one-third, and one-sixth of the world's average respectively; the per capita energy reserve and potential value of mineral resources makes up only one-half of the world's average; the bulk mineral resources, except coal, can hardly meet the domestic needs; in addition, there is enormous consumption and serious waste of resources in China. In 2003, China's GDP at current exchange rates made up 3.8% of the world's GDP, but the consumption of steel, coal, and cement amounted to 36%, 30%, and 55% respectively of the world's total output in 2001. China's energy consumption per unit of output value was three to four times that of developed countries; the average utilization rate of energy resources was only 30%, 10–20 percentage points lower than developed countries; the unit water use of main products was more than 500 times that of developed countries; the repetitive use rate of industrial water was 3.5–4 times lower than that of developed countries; the utilization rate of timber was only 40–45%, and the comprehensive utilization rate was only one-eighth of that in developed countries; the arable land area reduced by 2.11 million *mu* per year on average during the 8th Five-Year Plan; and the comprehensive utilization rate of slag, coal ash, gangue, and petrochemical residues was only 83.7%, 47%, and 45% respectively. This development mode has come to an end. In recent years, the economic development is increasingly restricted by resources and environmental factors. The only approach to China's economic development in the future will be a sustainable, intensive, and saving economy. To make a success of the Western Taiwan Straits Economic Zone, we must give top priority to development of intensive and saving economy.

(This article was a speech delivered by the author at the symposium of "Construction of the Western Taiwan Straits Economic Zone" in October 2003)

11 Speed up the construction of the economic zone at the middle reaches of the Yangtze River in order to plan the regional economic development as a whole

At the 3rd Plenary Session of the 16th CPC Central Committee, planning regional economic development as a whole was regarded as an essential requirement for improvement of the socialist market economy system in China, which is of great importance to coping with the unbalanced development in the eastern and western regions as well as the eastern and middle regions. To solve this problem, we must allow full play to the middle region. Therefore, I have been constantly paying active attention and holding a positive attitude to the conception of constructing the Wuhan-centered Middle Reaches Economic Zone of the Yangtze River because I firmly believe that the Yangtze River Economic Belt will flourish once the Middle Reaches Economic Zone is established, and that China's modernization will come true at the rise of Central China.

First, accelerating construction of the Yangtze River Middle Reaches Economic Zone is conducive to the coordinated development of the Yangtze River Basin economy. The entire Yangtze River Economic Belt is divided into three economic zones, i.e. Chongqing-centered Upper Reaches Economic Zone, Wuhan-centered Middle Reaches Economic Zone, and Shanghai-centered Lower Reaches Economic Zone. The Lower Reaches Economic Zone has already become an essential part of China's economic development thanks to Shanghai. The Upper Reaches Economic Zone develops well and promises well owing to the national develop-the-west strategy and Chongqing municipality. Notwithstanding the great achievements since the economic reform and opening up to the outside world, the Middle Reaches Economic Zone relatively lags way behind due to constraints such as outmoded ideology, outdated systems and mechanisms, and a non-optimized allocation of elements. To tackle these problems, the construction of the Yangtze River Middle Reaches Economic Zone must be accelerated to realize the coordinated development of the Yangtze River Basin economy.

Second, accelerating construction of the Yangtze River Middle Reaches Economic Zone helps play its role of "linking the eastern and western regions as well as the northern and southern regions". In the eastern regions of China, rapid economic development has taken the lead in realizing modernization since the economic reform and opening up in 1978. In the western regions, investment has increased and infrastructure has improved ever since the implementation of the "develop-the-west" strategy and policy. However, it seems that little attention has been paid to the economic development in the middle regions. According to the law of economic development, the middle regions should not have been skipped in the east-to-west process of development. In other words, the development and prosperity of the western regions would be impossible without the development and prosperity of the middle regions, and China's modernization would not be realized without a modernized middle region. The middle reach of the Yangtze River is viewed as an important economic development region in Central China because it plays the role of a strategic fulcrum in the development of China's regional economy that links the eastern and western regions as well as the northern and southern regions. A balanced and complete structure of China's regional overall layout will form as a result of rational mobility and allocation of factors including development of the Yangtze River Middle Reaches Economic Zone.

Third, accelerating the construction of Yangtze River Middle Reaches Economic Zone will help form a new growth pole of economic development in China. The central region is one that has the largest potential of economic development. It is likely that the Wuhan-centered Yangtze River Middle Reaches Economic Zone would be a new growth pole for China's economic development. Wuhan, the largest economic center in Central China, is a strategic place where many north-to-south and east-to-west traffic lines meet, so called "the thoroughfare of nine provinces". This area is characterized by abundant natural resources, especially fresh water, and broad marketplace; by developed technology and education, e.g. Wuhan is deemed as the third largest center for science and education and the second largest intelligence concentrated area in China; and by a solid foundation for development of industries, e.g. as one of the old industrial bases in China, Wuhan has the complete range of industrial categories, including four pillar industries such as steel, automobile, machinery, and hi-tech industries. The natural conditions, capital amount, market capacity, and infrastructure in this have created the basic conditions for it to become the center of regional economy or a growth pole in the future.

Fourth, accelerating the construction of Yangtze River Middle Reaches Economic Zone is helpful to the revitalization of the old industrial bases. The State Government has put on the agenda the revitalization of old industrial bases in Wuhan, Huangshi, and Ezhou where dominant traditional industries include metallurgy, machinery, chemical industry, building materials, and textile that made great contributions to the country but need to be transformed today. Wuhan has the basic conditions for revitalizing old industrial bases and for developing hi-tech industries due to its S&T human resources, comprehensive S&T ability, and a good industrial base.

To accelerate the construction of Yangtze River Middle Reaches Economic Zone, governments at all levels need to free their minds, change ideas, reach a consensus, and enhance cooperation. For quite some time, the construction of the national economy has been carried out by administrative divisions in China, with each division creating its own system for overall development.

As the reform and opening up policy deepens, this provincial regionalism and antiquated idea still exist, though they have been changed to some extent; in addition, there are serious phenomena of industrial monopoly and regional blockade in contradiction with the construction of the uniform socialist market economy system and with the trend of regionalization and integration of the global economy. We must thus set up a win–win or multi-win concept to establish regional cooperation mechanism following the principle of mutual benefit and development on the basis of resources. In the process of building the Yangtze River Middle Reaches Economic Zone, we will realize linkage development and common prosperity in a region to maximize regional benefits.

It is of great importance to make regional planning for centric cities, especially the development planning and strategy of Wuhan. As a centric city, Wuhan plays an irreplaceable role in the construction of the Yangtze River Middle Reaches Economic Zone. For this end, we must build a new Wuhan in accordance with the overall objectives and requirements of the economic zone by creating new concepts and new strategies. More specifically, we should improve the functions of Wuhan as a centric city to allow a play to radiation and the promotion roles of Wuhan and facilitate the coordinated development of Wuhan with peripheral cities and regions; optimize the urban spatial layout of Wuhan and promote the adjustment and optimization of the industrial spatial layout and functions in accordance with the requirements of the coordinated development of the economic society to raise comprehensive service capacity of Wuhan; strengthen the infrastructure construction of high quality and high level modern public utilities such as the urban road network, communication networks, power supply networks, water supply and drainage networks, and the gas supply network; transform and renovate old cities to improve the city-town system and expand the urban space; strengthen efforts of environmental governance and promote ecological engineering construction of urban gardens and forest planting to build the eco-city that embraces rivers or lakes and thus becomes suitable to living; improve the investment environment in the region; enhance the ability to attract both internal and external; and strengthen efforts on improvement of soft environment as well as on hard environment (including traffic, communication, water supply, power supply, etc.), e.g. improve and normalize all preferential to create a good legal environment, streamline the government, normalize governmental behaviors, increase work efficiency, strengthen credit education, standardize behaviors of market entities, and regulate market order.

Accelerating the process of industrialization and urbanization is one of the important measures to promote the construction of the Yangtze River Middle Reaches Economic Zone. By 2020, preliminary industrialization will have been realized in China. In order to achieve this goal, the process of industrialization must speed up from now on, especially the rural industry and private enterprises; namely, the pace of rural industrialization will be accelerated. Industrialization has kept pace with urbanization. The present urbanization rate of China is only 38%, but the world's average is 47%. When urbanization is realized by 2020, the planned urbanization rate will be 57%, and the urban population will be 800–900 million, with about 15 million additional per year. According to the history of urbanization in developed countries, urbanization was carried out in several big cities at the initial stage; with growing population in small cities, the rate of urbanization increased as well. Urbanization in the future will be boosted by megalopolis or large cities, which will facilitate the urbanization of the medium- and small-sized cities. In other words, regional economies will be divided in large cities and megalopolis to accommodate the rural population and agricultural labor forces.

The construction of the Yangtze River Middle Reaches Economic Zone needs supports from the State Government. The State supports include the following: first, preferential policy support for finance, taxation, State-owned enterprise reform, disbursement of social insurance fund, revitalization of old industrial bases, science and technology education and other social undertakings; and then funds and project support for infrastructure construction, technical reform, revitalization of old industrial bases, and construction of new large projects. Though the construction of the Yangtze River Middle Reaches Economic Zone depends largely on local governments at all levels, it will not work without State support, which has been proved by practices in all economic zones since the economic reform and opening up. For this reason, the economic zone must be proactive to gain the State support in order not to miss out on such a good opportunity for further development.

(This is the speech delivered by the author at the symposium on "Accelerating Construction of the Yangtze River Middle Reaches Economic Zone" in May 2003)

12 Deepen the reform to provide a system guarantee for the revitalization of the old industrial bases including those in the northeastern region

During the 1st and 2nd Five-Year Plans and subsequent large-scale construction over years, some old industrial bases were established in regions including the northeast and based on such heavy industries as steel, heavy equipment manufacturing, machine tools, automobile, shipbuilding, and energy. They laid the foundation for industrialization in China and played important roles in China's economic development. Since the economic reform and opening up in 1978, however, the development of the northeast old industrial base has encountered many difficulties, e.g. increasingly acute institutional and structural contradictions, strategic adjustment of state-owned economies, reform and transformation of state-owned enterprises, and the high pressure of laid-off workers and unemployment. To change this situation, the Central Government made a significant, strategic decision on the revitalization of old industrial bases including the northeastern one, following the decision on Western Development. This is of great importance to the exploiting the huge potential of these old industrial bases, planning the coordinated development of the regional economy as a whole, constructing a new growth pole of Chinese economy, and building a well-off society in an all-round way.

Apart from policy and investment supports from the Central Government, the revitalization of old industrial bases including those in the northeastern region requires a system guarantee provided by deepening the reform and improving socialist market economy system because it can ensure the creation and application of a new mechanism and new impetus, stimulate initiatives and creativity, and enhance the self-development ability of the old industrial bases. To revitalize the old industrial bases, therefore, we must implement the Decisions of the 3rd Plenary Session of the 16th CPC Central Committee and improve the socialist market economy system following the principle of "five overall plans" and "five persistences". The reform and improvement should aim at five aspects of the socialist market economy system, i.e. enterprise system, market system, distribution system, social security system, and government regulation and control.

Considering the large proportion, wide distribution, heavy social burden, and inflexible mechanism of state-owned enterprises in the old industrial bases, we must continue with the strategic adjustment and the layout adjustment of these enterprises, we must set up a reasonable entry/exit mechanism for state-owned capitals, and we must optimize the allocation of state-owned assets. We must also deepen reform of the state-owned enterprises so that they become production management organizations that can make their own management decisions, assume sole responsibility for their own profits or losses, and achieve self-development and self-discipline. For the state-owned large- and medium-sized enterprises, they can go public, attract foreign capital, and allow participation of private capitals to accelerate corporation reform, diversify investors, strengthen reform of internal management system, set up standard legal person governance structure, develop a number of large business groups that have prominent main businesses, high management level and strong competitive ability and operate across regions, trade, ownerships, and countries. They should develop a mixed ownership economy so that the stockholding system becomes the major form of public ownership, improve and develop policies and regulations of private enterprises to create fair environment, and promote and positively guide the development of non-public economy.

Though the government's support is essential to revitalizing the old industrial bases, we will not follow the development pattern and method of the planned economic system; instead, we must respect the objective laws of economic development so that the market can play a fundamental role in resources allocation. For this purpose, we must promote market-oriented reform, improve the market system, break regional blockade, open up and further develop and perfect the commodity market; accelerate the development and cultivation of the market for factors such as capital, land, technology, and labor force; improve the formation mechanism of production factors price; encourage and facilitate the capitalization of production factors; eradicate system obstacles that restrict rational flow and optimal allocation of product factors; improve rules for market competition, rectify the market order, safeguard legitimate rights and interests of all market entities, and effectively supervise behaviors of market entities and intermediary organizations; strengthen credit education and legal education; and accelerate the creation of a unified, open, competitive, and orderly market system.

Deepening the reform of distribution system. We need to set up a diversified distribution system with distribution according to work as the main form, work out policies and regulations for the distribution of production factors according to contribution, absorb foreign capital and private capital, and attract technical personnel and management personnel so that investors' enthusiasm can be aroused. In addition, we need to reorganize and standardize the distribution order to safeguard legal income and confiscate illegal income, and we need to strengthen the regulation of income distribution to control over-high income and protect low income groups so that the gap between social members' income can be narrowed.

Improving the social security system. There are many surplus workers, retired workers and laid-off workers in the old industrial bases. During social and economic development, we must enlarge employment, improve employment policies, and perfect the business and employment environment. We need to both speed up the pace of reform of social security system, and set up and improve the social security system suitable to socialist market economy. In addition, we should learn from the pilot reform of enterprise pension insurance in the Liaoning Province, increase the proportion of social pension insurance and fund the personal accounts; improve the unemployment insurance system and re-employment system by creating an unemployed persons management system and re-employment service network at four levels, including the urban government, district, street office, and community in the large- and medium-sized cities; promote the reform of urban medical system; expand the coverage of social insurance and increase the collection rate of social security contributions; and set up and improve the subsistence allowances for the urban residents and other social relief systems, for which governmental finances at all levels should increase the expenses to ensure sufficient source of funds.

Deepening the reform of the administrative system and transforming government functions. For this end, we need to streamline governmental organs and personnel, define the functions of each organ, and set up a rigid responsibility system; deepen reform of administrative approval system, standardize governmental behaviors, and advocate administration by law; strengthen service consciousness and service functions; change the style of work and raise work efficiency; strengthen the construction of a clean government; and set up an honest image. Local government is required to give priority to the improvement of the investment environment, improve and standardize all preferential policies, and create an ideal legal environment.

(Published in *People's Daily*, Nov 27, 2003)

13 Several problems of China's Western Development

Western China comprises 12 provinces, municipalities, and autonomous regions, such as Shaanxi, Gansu, Qinghai, Ningxia, and Xinjiang in the northwest, and Sichuan, Chongqing, Yunnan, Guizhou, and Tibet in the southwest, along with Guangxi and Inner Mongolia, covers an area of about 6.6 million square kilometers, taking up 68.7% of China's territory, has a population of 351.87 million, accounting for 28.5% of China's total population.

The Western Development strategy is an important part of Deng Xiaoping's strategic thought of China's modernization construction. As early as in 1988, Deng once said: "With a population of 200 million, the coastal area should speed up opening to the outside world to achieve priority development and promote better development inland. It really matters to overall development of the whole country. The inland should take it into serious consideration. Once the conditions have matured, the coastal region is required to help inland regions with economic development. This is our overall plan. The coastal regions must obey it."[1] The Phase II strategic objectives of China's modernization construction were materialized at the end of the 20th century, and now we are on the way to the Phase III strategic objectives. At this critical moment, the Western Development strategy was initiated. It is of great practical significance and profound historic significance to the expansion of domestic demand, economic growth, social stability, national unity, frontier consolidation, coordinated development between eastern and western regions, and the final achievement of common prosperity.

1. Background for the Western Development strategy

The Western Development strategic decision was made at the Central Economic Working Conference in 1999. The historical background is as follows.

(A) Economic and social development gap widening between the eastern and western regions

Since the founding of the People's Republic of China in 1949, especially since the economic reform and opening up to the outside world in 1978, substantial progress has been achieved in China's economic development, particularly in the eastern coastal regions. The gap of economic development thus began to widen between the coastal regions and the mid–western regions. In 1999, the per capita GNP, the urban per capita disposable income, and the rural per capita net income were RMB10,102 Yuan, 7,034 Yuan, and 2,994 Yuan respectively in the eastern regions, but only 4,294 Yuan, 5,260 Yuan, and 1,673 Yuan respectively in the western 12 provinces/regions/municipalities, accounting for 42%, 74%, and 56% of those in the eastern regions (see Fig. 1.13.1).

The major economic indicators in the western region fall behind the eastern region and far behind the national average and the middle region. In 1999, the national per capita GNP, the urban per capita disposable income and the rural per capita disposable income were RMB6,546 Yuan, 5,854 Yuan, and 2,210 Yuan respectively, but the three indicators of the 12 provinces in the western region accounted for 65%, 90%, and 76% respectively of the national average (see Fig. 1.13.2).

Of the 12 provinces/regions/municipalities in the western region, if measured by per capita GDP, only Xinjiang reached up to the national average but the rest only made up about 60% of the national average; if measured by the per capita disposable income of urban residents, only Chongqing, Yunnan, and Tibet exceeded the national average and the rest were lower than the national average; if measured by the per capita disposable income of rural residents, all western regions were lower than the national average, with seven provinces/regions less than 70% of the national average, including Yunnan, Guizhou, Tibet, Shaanxi, Gansu, Qinghai, and Xinjiang (see Table 1.13.1).

As the economic development in the western region falls behind that in the eastern and middle regions, poor population is centralized in the western regions. In 1999, the rural poor population was 24.122 million, including 16.441 million in western provinces, accounting for 48.18% of the total poor population in the country.

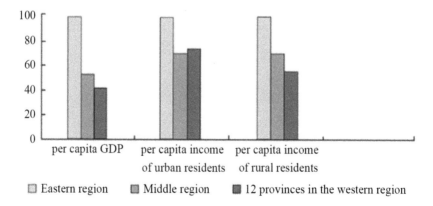

Fig. 1.13.1 Income Gap between the Eastern and Middle Regions and 12 Provinces in the Western Region

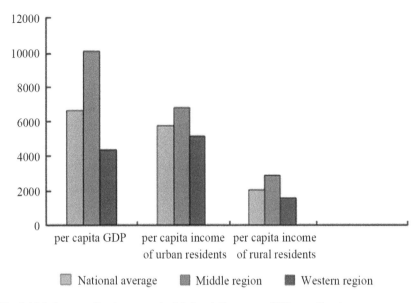

Fig. 1.13.2 Income Gap between the National, Eastern, and Western Regions

Table 1.13.1 Comparison of Major Economic Indicators between Western Provinces and National Average

Indicator Region	Per capita GNP		Per capita income of urban residents		Per capita income of urban residents	
	Absolute amount (Yuan)	Percentage of national average (%)	Absolute amount (Yuan)	Percentage of national average (%)	Absolute amount (Yuan)	Percentage of national average (%)
National average	6,546	100	5,854.02	100	2,210.34	100
Chongqing	4,852	74.1	5,895.97	100.7	1,736.63	78.6
Sichuan	4,356	69.3	5,477.89	93.6	1,843.47	72.1
Guizhou	2,463	37.6	4,934.02	84.3	1,363.07	61.7
Yunnan	4,444	67.9	6,178.68	105.5	1,437.63	65.0
Tibet	4,125	63.0	6,908.67	118.0	1,309.46	59.2
Shaanxi	4,107	62.7	4,654.06	79.5	1,455.86	65.9
Gansu	3,595	54.9	4,475.23	76.4	1,357.28	61.4
Qinghai	4,707	71.9	4,703.44	80.3	1,466.67	66.3
Ningxia	4,477	68.4	4,472.91	76.4	1,754.15	79.4
Xinjiang	6,653	101.6	5,319.76	90.9	1,473.17	66.6
Inner Mongolia	4,264	65.1	5,619.54	96.0	2,003.93	90.6
Guangxi	5,400	82.5	5,169.54	88.3	2048.33	92.7

Source: Based on data available in *China Statistical Yearbook* (2000).

Due to the underdeveloped economy, the infrastructures in the western regions, such as education, health, culture, communication, and transportation, lag behind the eastern regions (see Table 1.13.2, Table 1.13.3 and Table 1.13.4).

(B) Requirement for expanding domestic demand

Since the middle 1990s, the shortage of commodities has been eradicated in the Chinese economy, but relative surplus of commodities has emerged periodically. First, a large number of enterprises ran under production capacity due

Table 1.13.2 Comparison of Major Social Development Indicators between National Average and Western Provinces

Indicator Regions	Education years per capita	Number of college students per ten thousand persons	Number of libraries per million persons	Number of culture galleries per million persons	Number of doctors per thousand persons	Number of ward beds per thousand persons	Popularity rate of telephones (%)
National average	7.18	27.65	2.20	2.30	1.67	2.51	7.00
Chongqing	6.88	27.19	1.37	1.40	1.43	2.15	5.04
Sichuan	6.66	17.89	1.51	2.00	1.51	2.23	3.30
Guizhou	6.08	11.63	2.40	2.29	1.21	1.58	2.18
Yunnan	5.82	15.05	3.51	3.03	1.46	2.23	4.54
Tibet	2.95	13.68	0.39	18.75	1.95	2.52	2.34
Shaanxi	7.14	41.40	3.12	3.07	1.77	2.67	5.06
Gansu	6.35	21.44	3.58	3.26	1.53	2.32	3.78
Qinghai	5.97	17.28	7.45	8.24	1.96	4.31	4.43
Ningxia	6.66	21.03	3.87	4.05	1.84	2.39	6.97
Xinjiang	7.94	26.74	4.45	5.19	2.48	3.78	6.84
Inner Mongolia	7.35	18.11	4.57	4.40	2.33	2.81	5.35
Guangxi	6.84	16.57	2.46	2.08	1.29	1.81	3.39

Source: Based on data available in *China Statistical Yearbook* (2000).

Table 1.13.3 Infrastructure Coverage of Administrative Villages in Eastern Regions and Western Regions (%)

Region	Villages with electricity	Villages with postal service	Villages with telephone services	Villages with accessible roads	Villages with running water
National	97.4	91.6	48.4	88.7	17.7
Eastern	102.1	100.8	75.8	93.1	33.5
Western	89.5	75.6	19.3	79.8	9.2

Source: Rural investigation task force of the National Bureau of Statistics, *China Rural Statistics Yearbook* (2000), p.173.

Note: Calculated by the number of administrative village committees.

Table 1.13.4 Infrastructure Coverage of Rural Townships in Eastern Regions and Western Regions (%)

Items Region	Water supply station	Bus station	Power station	Installed capacity of telephones	Computerized telephone
National	20.7	33.2	22.7	93.4	84.2
Eastern	32.3	41.6	21.8	99.1	97.3
Western	8.2	32.7	24.6	87.9	70.1

Source: Rural investigation task force of the National Bureau of Statistics, *China Rural Statistics Yearbook* (2000), p.177.

to industrial overcapacity. From the middle 1990s, an overwhelming majority of China's industrial sectors witnessed a serious surplus of production capacity. According to an investigation on production capacity of 80 main industrial products, there were 28 products with a capacity utilization rate below 60%, accounting for 35%, and quite a few of them had a capacity utilization rate around 50%. Then, there was an oversupply of commodities in the market. According to an investigation of 440 industrial products in the second half of 1999, 383 products were oversupplied, accounting for 87% of total products investigated; 57 products maintained a balance between supply and demand, accounting for 13%; and none of them had ever come short. There was also relative surplus of agricultural products, resulting in a decline in prices, a reduction of income despite rising output, and the slow growth of farmer's income for consecutive years. At the end of the 1990s, the deficiency of effective domestic demand became a restricting factor for the continuous, rapid growth of the Chinese economy. In this case, a considerable part of the domestic capital, technology, and labor forces need to seek for new production fields, new markets, and new development space. Due to the vast territory and abundant natural resources, the western regions will anticipate huge investment opportunities, huge market potential, and development potential. The Western Development can absorb a large amount of investment to increase people's income and fuel domestic demand.

(C) Requirement for unity of nationalities

As a multiethnic country, China has 56 nationalities, more than 80% of which are minorities distributed in the western region, including five national autonomous regions and 27 of 30 national autonomous prefectures. In this sense, the Western Development will facilitate the economic development of minority areas, which is of great significance to the unity and common prosperity of nationalities as well as the stabilization of frontier areas.

(D) Inevitable trend of opening up to the outside world

China's open-door policy was initiated in eastern coastal region. Over the past decades, a considerable amount of foreign investment (including from

Hong Kong, Taiwan, and Macau) has been drawn into coastal regions through location advantage and market advantage and preferential policy. According to statistical data, the total capital amount of foreign capital investment utilized in the coastal region made up 87.83% of the total foreign investment through-out the country by the end of 1998, but the amount utilized in the western region accounted only for 3.28%. Over two decades of reform and opening up, great development has been achieved and people's living level improved in the coastal region; however, the labor cost is on the rise and the competi-tive advantage weakens to some extent. Some industries will be transferred to inland areas. It is thus evitable for the western regions to accelerate opening to the outside world. To attract foreign investment, the western regions need to make use of preferential policies and good environment.

In addition, after over 50 years' construction, especially over two decades' reform and opening up, the comprehensive national power of China has been enhanced and people's living level has reached up to the well-off level; at this moment, the Government has the ability to increase investment into the west-ern regions. These are the basic conditions for the implementation of the West-ern Development strategy.

2. Focal points and progress of Western Development

As an ambitious systematic engineering and also an arduous historic mission, the implementation of the Western Development requires long-term effort. In the future 5–10 years, breakthroughs will be achieved in infrastructure con-struction and eco-environment protection and construction; substantial pro-gress will be made in technology and education, characteristic economy and competitive industries; some major infrastructure projects concerning water conservancy, transportation, energy resources, and communication in the west-ern region will be completed; the backward infrastructure situation will be improved for the sake of ecological construction and environmental govern-ance in major river basins, in the restraint of deteriorating the eco-environment in key areas, and in the prevention and control of pollution; the market com-petitiveness of advantageous agricultural products, mineral resources produc-tion, and tourism will be improved to accelerate the transition from resource advantage to economic advantage; the advanced applicable technology will be widely used in key development areas, the nine-year compulsory education system popularized, and talent team expanded; the subsistence problem of the rural, impoverished population will be basically solved and people's living qual-ity raised to the well-off level. By the middle of the 21st century, a new western region will emerge, featuring economic prosperity, social progress, peaceful life, united nationalities, beautiful mountains and rivers, as well as wealthy people.

The strategy of Western Development was implemented quite well in the first two years of 2000 and 2001. The social fixed investment in 12 western provinces/regions/municipalities amounted to RMB611.1 billion Yuan in 2000 and 734.3 billion Yuan in 2001, increasing 15% and 19% respectively over the previous year, higher than the national average of 9.3% and 13.7% and also higher than average growth rate in the eastern and middle regions. In 2000, the construction fund invested into the western region by the government finance totaled RMB70 billion Yuan, including RMB43 billion Yuan of public debt. In 2001, the construction fund exceeded RMB80 billion Yuan, including addition of 60 billion of public debt. Over two years, more than 20 key projects were initiated by the State in the western regions; total investment amounted to RMB400 billion Yuan, with 70 billion already in place. The GDP of the western 12 provinces/regions/municipalities grew about 8.5% due to increasing investment and consumer demand, obviously higher than previous years and higher than the national average growth rate.

From the present to the near future, our priorities will be as follows:

(A) Accelerate infrastructure construction

With an emphasis on road construction, infrastructure includes railways, airports, and natural gas trunk pipelines; power grids; communications; broadcast and television; and water conservancy (with priority given to rational exploitation and economical utilization of water resources). A series of big projects under construction comprise the following: Qinghai-Tibet railway, west-to-east electricity transmission, west-to-east gas transmission, national main trunk roads, key water-control project in upper reaches of the Yangtze River and the Yellow River, and reconstruction of rural transportation, electric power, and communication facilities. As of the end of 2001, an investment of more than RMB1 billion Yuan has been put into Qinghai-Tibet railway project; for west-to-east electricity transmission project, the construction of two batches of projects and several large power stations has commenced; for west-to-east gas transmission project, the preliminary work of pipeline project from Tarim Basin to the Yangtze River Delta went smoothly, and five junction projects kicked off simultaneously in early 2002; the construction of trunk roads sped up, so more than 20,000 km of highway mileage was built in western regions over the past two years; the key water-control project in upper reaches of the Yangtze River and the Yellow River went quite well, works that have kicked off including Zipingpu on the Minjiang River in Sichuan, Shapotou on the Yellow River in Ningxia, Baise on the Youjiang River in Guangxi, and Nierji in Inner Mongolia. Thanks to the Western Development strategy, people in the western regions now see their dreams come true.

(B) Strengthen protection of eco-environment and natural forest

During the implementation of projects, the protection of eco-environment and natural forest was carried out following the principle of "reforesting marginal arable land, closing hillside to facilitate forestation, using food supply as a form of relief, and entering contracts with individuals" to convert sloping cropland into forest in steps as planned, the grain subsidy and seedlings for which are provided free of charge by the government. As of the end of 2001, the pilot reforestation converted 1.24 million hectares of cropland and 1.09 million hectares of wasteland into forests, totaling 2.33 million hectares afforested. The natural forest protection project in 2001 completed the forestation of 430,000 hectares, the air seeding forestation of 1.02 million hectares, and the artificial plantation of 180,000 hectares. In 2002, an additional 2.27 million hectares of cropland and 2.66 million hectares of wasteland will be converted into forests.

(C) Adjust economic structure and open up to the outside world

The western region has witnessed the rapid development of a characteristic economy, the growing varieties of characteristic agricultural products such as cotton, quality fruits, and meats; the robust exploitation of resources such as hydraulic power, natural gas, non-ferrous metal, sylvinite, and rare earth; the increasing investment into tourism infrastructure; and the accelerated construction of hi-tech industrial bases in Xi'an and Yanglin in Shaanxi as well as in Chengdu and Mianyang in Sichuan. The effort in transformation, restructuring, reform of enterprises in the western region was also consolidated. Over the past two years, 275 projects of technical transformation were supported by soft loans from the State Government; more than 420 bankrupt enterprises were annexed; and about RMB27 billion Yuan of bad and doubtful debts in banks were cancelled. In the western region, the development of non-public enterprises paced up and absorbed the increasing amount of investment both at home and abroad.

(D) Carry out scientific education

In the western poverty-stricken counties, construction works include vocational education centers, infrastructure in colleges and universities, campus networks, and modern distance education poverty alleviation demonstrations in primary and secondary schools. The State Government has strengthened support for talent projects in the western region by assigning a large number of excellent young cadres from the Central State organs to work as part-time officials in the western region. In turn, an increasing number of local cadres were selected from western regions and minorities to practice in the Central State organs or eastern regions: about 6,000 local cadres trained in 2001. The national technological funds were mainly used to support works such as a comprehensive control of eco-environment, a comprehensive utilization of resources, the industrialization of agriculture, the enhancement and commercialization of superior resources, and the industrialization of modern–traditional Chinese medicine.

3. Several basic relationships during the Western Development

The Western Development is a complicated systematic project that requires unified leadership, planning, and staged implementation. In the process of development, we need to generate new ideas, new thoughts, and new strategies. For this purpose, we must deal well with the following relationships:

(A) Relationship between development and eco-environment protection

The western region lies in the upper reaches of the Yangtze River, the Yellow River, and the Pearl River, where the national ecological protective barrier has been created. Development contradicts protection of ecological environment. No longer will economic development be achieved in sacrifice of ecological environment. The word "development" in the Western Development means more of a coordinated development of the economic and social environment than an economic growth, i.e. development in a sustainable way. The protection of the ecological environment must be incorporated into the range of development. To protect water resources in the western region and prevent environmental pollution, we must prohibit felling natural forests and implement protective works of natural forests in upper reaches of the Yangtze River and the Yellow River, prohibit destroying forests and grass to reclaim wasteland, return sloping farmland to forests or grasslands in a planned and stepped way, recover vegetation in desertification areas, and combine grain for forest/grass and poverty relief work, which can improve the eco-environment and living conditions in poverty-stricken regions and also can help effectively overcome poverty and become better off.

(B) Relationship between government support and market mechanism

The implementation of the Western Development certainly requires support from the government, especially from the Central Government; however, we will not follow the traditional economic development pattern; instead, we must respect the objective economic law and allow market mechanism to play its role. In the past, the State put sufficient investment in the western region but achieved little; to a large extent, this is because the investment was the product of the government's action to promote industrialization rather than the result of market regulation that emphasized social private capital. In the future, we must change our concept from government promotion to market regulation so that the market can play its fundamental roles in resource allocation. As far as the western region is concerned, the "dependent mentality" must change to a cultivation of capital market to attract various social private capitals, especially from eastern regions and foreign countries, into local industrialization. As far as the Central Government is concerned, in addition to providing support for infrastructure construction, education, and environmental protection the western regions, it needs to work out investment-encouraging policies to encourage both internal and external capitals into Western Development. Individual production project will depend largely on social private capitals. Even for some public infrastructure projects, such as roads and bridges, private investment is also welcome.

(C) Relationship between natural resources and human resources

The western region is an abundant region of natural resources, including petroleum, natural gas, minerals, land, and water conservancy, which has always been the unique superiority of economic development in the western region. Over years, however, the superiority is not fully developed, i.e. resource superiority has not been transformed into economic superiority. In contrast, the eastern regions have witnessed rapid economic development even without resource superiority, because they have the talent superiority. This indicates that regional development depends more on other superiorities (human resources in particular) than resource superiority. In the western region, there is a sharp contrast between the abundant supply of natural resources and shortage of talent resources. According to statistical data, there is obviously an insufficient supply of talents in the western region, and the existing talent team remains unstable. For an example, per 10 thousand laborers in the western region, there are only 92 persons with a degree above a technical secondary school or job title above junior level, less than 1/10 of persons in the eastern region. In a long run, a shortage of talents will be the main factor restricting resource superiority. Therefore, we must emphasize the cultivation and use of talents, must change the past development pattern that ignores human factors, and must give priority to the use, development, and introduction of talents.

(D) Relationship between public economy and private economy

By comparing the economic structure in the eastern and western regions, the State-owned economic entities make up a smaller proportion than non-State-owned ones such as private enterprises, foreign-funded enterprises, and township enterprises in the eastern region; the case is quite different in the western region where the State-owned economy prevails. As a whole, the non-State-owned ones make up less than 50% of economic aggregate in the western region, even less than 25% in Xinjiang and Qinghai. According to statistical data, since the 1990s, the annual output of township enterprises in the eastern coastal regions has accounted for over 70% of the local GDP; in the western regions, however, the output made up less than 30% of the local GDP. Therefore, the development difference of township enterprises in different regions has become the main cause that widens the regional economic gap. Facts have proved that the regional economy grows fast with the rapid development of its non-State-owned economies, especially the township enterprises. The economic gap between the eastern region and the western region is dependent on the development of a non-State-owned economy rather than on the development of Stated-owned economies. Consequently, the key to accelerating economic development in the western regions is to accelerate the development of non-State-owned economies, especially the township enterprises. In the western regions, the support for township enterprises should be combined with employment enlargement, market acti-vation, technical innovation, construction of small towns, and promotion of industrial growth.

(This was the author's speech delivered at the 4th Sino-Russian Econo-mists' Forum in June 2002)

Note

1 *Selected Works of Deng Xiaoping* (Vol. III), Deng Xiaoping, Beijing: People's Publishing House, 1993 edition, pp. 277–278.

14 The development and utilization of energy and environmental protection in China

China leads the world in energy reserves and is also the second largest energy producing country and consuming country in the world. The development and utilization of energy resources, on the one hand, promotes economic development; but on the other, it causes serious environmental problems. Since the middle 1990s, China has virtually solved the "energy shortage" problem that existed for a long time and restricted economic development, and realized the primary balance of total energy supply as the energy structure increased constantly, the elastic coefficient of energy production and consumption appeared to be decreasing, and the efficiency of energy utilization improved continuously. Meanwhile, people raised their awareness of environmental protection, they gave close attention to and achieved great progress in environment protection activities, and a virtuous cycle was formed in the development and utilization of energy and economic development.

1. Current situation of energy development and utilization in China

China possesses abundant and diverse energy resources, and leads the world in total energy supply. From a long-range perspective, China's gross reserve of primary energy resources is 4 trillion tons of standard coal. With a large population, however, China's per capita possession of energy resources is far lower than the world average. In 1990, China's per capita proved coal reserve was 147 tons, 41.4% of the world average; per capita proved petroleum reserve was 2.9 tons, 11% of the world average; per capita proved natural gas reserve was 4% of the world average; and the per capita proved available hydropower resource was lower than the world average. In terms of per capita consumption of energy resources in 1994, the world average was 1,433kg oil equivalent, the developed countries 5,066kg oil equivalent, and China about 670kg oil equivalent. In 1997, China's per capita possession of installed capacity was 0.21kW and the per capita electricity consumption was 900kWh, amounting to only one-third of the world average. The development and utilization of energy resources in China were characterized by the following:

First, coal is used as the main energy; the energy is developed and utilized insufficiently. In China, the proved coal reserve makes up over 90% of total primary resources such as coal, petroleum, natural gas, hydraulic energy, and nuclear energy. Coal takes a dominant position in China's energy production and consumption and accounted for over 90% of total resources before the 1960s, over 80% in the 1970s, and about 75% since the 1980s; the production and consumption of other resources grew rapidly, but they took a subordinate position. In 1995, the total production of energy resources in the world amounted to 123 trillion tons of standard coal, with the proportions of solid energy, liquid energy, gas energy, hydraulic energy, and nuclear energy being 28.3%, 38.4%, 23.5%, and 9.8% respectively. During the transition of the world's major energy from coal to oil gas, China remains one of the few countries fueled by coal.

Second, the total energy consumption increases constantly, and the efficiency of energy utilization stays low. With the expansion of the economic scale, China's energy consumption appears to be in an uptrend. From 1957 to 1989, the total energy consumption in China increased from 96.44 million tons of standard coal to 969.34 million tons of standard coal, rising by nine times. From 1989 to 1999, it increased from 963.94 million tons of standard coal to 1.22 billion tons of standard coal, rising by 26%. Under the influence of capital, technology, and energy prices, the efficiency of energy utilization in China was much lower than in developed countries. The comprehensive utilization of energy was 32%, and the total efficiency of the energy system was 9.3%, about 50% of that in the developed countries. In 1994, China's energy consumption per unit of GDP (ton of standard coal/thousand US dollars) was 14.4, 11.3, 10.6, 8.8, 8.3, 7.2, 4.6, and 4.2 times that of Switzerland, Italy, Japan, France, Germany, the UK, the US, and Canada respectively.

Third and finally, energy consumption depends largely on domestic supply, environmental pollution deteriorates, and the supply of high-quality energy is insufficient. China's economic development is based mainly on domestic energy production and supply, and the energy technical equipment relies on domestic supply. Before the mid-1990s, China's self-sufficiency rate of energy resources exceeded 98%. With the rising energy consumption, the energy structure based on coal led to serious urban air pollution; excessive consumption of biomass energy gave rise to ecological damage, thus resulting in increasing pressure on ecological environment. According to the World Bank, China's economic loss caused by air and water pollution made up about 3–8% of China's GDP. Even some Chinese scholars argued that China's economic loss due to environment disruption accounted for 10% of China's GDP.

2. Environmental impact on development and utilization of China's energy

The environment problems caused by energy activities are very complicated: the production or utilization of energy is the main factor influencing regional environment problems such as air pollution, acid rain, and forest reduction as well as the global environment problems such as climatic change and ozone layer depletion. Being a big producer and consumer of energy resources, as well as a country that uses coal as its main energy, China is now encountering serious environmental problems due to excessive exploitation and utilization of energy resources. In the future, we will inevitably discharge some pollutants during economic development and increase energy consumption; therefore, China will face serious ecological and environmental problems.

The energy environment problems facing China are typical in developing countries and have impacts on human health and the sustainable development of the social economy, mainly including the following: urban air pollution caused by burning coal, ecological damage caused by excessive consumption of biomass energy, indoor air pollution caused by household burning coal, and carbon dioxide emission. There is also water pollution and solid waste pollution. We will further emphasize air pollution during the development and utilization of energy resources.

The increasing carbon dioxide concentration in the atmosphere and the global warming due to the greenhouse effect will exert a significant impact on the surrounding areas and global economic and social development. The carbon dioxide released during the utilization of energy resources in China accounts for about 80% of the total emission of greenhouse gases. According to data estimated by the US Energy Information Administration in 1997, the global carbon emission due to burning fossil fuel was 6.241 billion tons in 1995; China contributed to 821 million tons, 13.2% of the global emission, next only to 1.424 billion tons of the United States. Since the 1980s, China's carbon emission growing rate has been far higher than the world average as a result of a dramatic increase in coal consumption. From 1990 to 1995, new carbon emission of 196 million tons was added in China, accounting for 85.6% of the total carbon emission newly added in the world.

According to our estimate, a fundamental change has occurred in the uptrend of carbon emission in China since 1996. Before 1996, China's annual carbon emission increased substantially. After 1996, however, it dropped from 908.549 million tons in 1996 to 890.1934 million tons in 1997, 844.7721 million tons in 1998, and down to 773.9058 million tons in 1999. There were two reasons for the decline: first, the total energy consumption of China dropped from 1,389.48 million tons of standard coal in 1996 to 1,381.73 million tons of standard coal, 1,322.14 million tons of standard coal in 1998 and down to 1,220 million tons of standard coal in 1999; then, China's energy consumption structure changed. Due to considerable difference in carbon dioxide emission factors of coal, oil and natural gas (0.725, 0.583, and 0.409 respectively), the declining consumption of coal will reduce the total carbon emission. Since the 1990s, the coal consumption appeared in a downtrend in China's energy consumption structure, and the downtrend accelerated after 1996. The proportion of annual coal consumption dropped by less than 1 percentage point before 1996; however, it dropped by more than 2.5 percentage points after 1996.

In 1998, China's carbon dioxide emission was 20.90 million tons, ranking first in the world, 85% of which was exhausted by coal burning. In 1995, the emission was 23.70 million tons (including township industry), 33.2% exhausted by coal-fired power stations, 34.4% by industrial boilers, 11.4% by industrial kilns, 11.8% by household cookers, and 9.2% by others. According to the monitoring findings in 88 cities, the daily mean carbon emission ranges between 2 and $424mcg/m^3$ every year; it is $81mcg/m^3$ in northern cities and $80 mcg/m^3$ in southern cities. There are 48 cities exceeding the standard, such as Chongqing, Guiyang, Yichang, and Yibin in the south, and TaiYuan, Zibo, Datong, Qingdao, and Luoyang in the north. In recent years, the total carbon dioxide emission of China has dropped from 23.70 million tons in 1995 to 20.90 million tons in 1998. In addition, the annual average concentration of urban carbon dioxide also dropped from $80mcg/m^3$ in 1995 to $56mcg/m^3$ in 1998.

NO_x and some NO_2 are generated by nitrogen and oxygen interacting in the air at the time of fuel burning. In developed countries, the NO_x is mainly generated by vehicle exhaust, but in China, it is generated mainly by coal-burning facilities, such as in metropolises like Beijing and Guangzhou where automobiles are the main source. NO_x also preludes acid rain. In recent years, China's NO_x pollution in the urban atmosphere has worsened. According to monitoring findings in 88 cities, NO_x was the first of pollutants in winter in Beijing and Guangzhou in 1995. Recently, the annual average of NO_x concentration in cities has dropped from $47mcg/m^3$ in 1995 to $37mcg/m^3$ in 1998. Furthermore, the annual average of NO_x in northern cities is on the decline; on the average, however, it is much higher than that in southern cities.

In China, NO_x pollution shows a tendency to deteriorate with sharp increase of vehicle exhaust, notwithstanding China's coal-based energy structure and coal-burning pollution at present. The daily average value exceeds the standard in all large cities; NO_x became the first of pollutants in Guangzhou in 1992; in the late "8th Five-Year Plan", the over standard rate of NO_x daily average approached 50% in Beijing. NO_x pollution maintains a high level in cities such as Lanzhou, Zhengzhou, Dalian, Shanghai, Chengdu, Shenyang, Anshan, TaiYuan, Chongqing, and Shenzhen; in some of these cities, coal-burning air pollution is changing into air pollution of vehicle exhaust (i.e. photochemical smog). Apart from a mass of CO, NO_x, and NMHC gases, the vehicle exhausts also include Pb and polycrylic aromatic hydrocarbon (PAH) particles. CO and NO_x hinder oxygen delivery in the human body; Pb curbs child development and thus leads to liver dysfunction; PAH can have carcinogenic effect in the human body. Vehicle exhausts do much harm to pedestrians, especially to traffic police. In addition, when exposed to sunlight, gases like CO, NO_x, and NMHC exhausted by vehicles can react in the air to generate photochemical secondary pollution that may extend and do more harm to human health and the environment.

In some big cities, pollution by lead in the atmosphere has deteriorated. In 1995, motor gasoline discharged 303 tons of lead into the atmosphere in Guangzhou, one-fifth of the total discharge throughout the country; the mean concentration of lead in atmosphere increased from $0.097mcg/m^3$ in 1988 to $0.113mcg/m^3$ in 1995, resulting in a serious impairment to human health.

More than 90% of the lead in the atmosphere comes from motor vehicles. Now leaded gasoline is used by most vehicles. The lead content is very high in this kind of gasoline, e.g. #90 gasoline contains 0.22–0.45g lead per liter, 1.8–4.6 times higher than 0.08g of the international standard.

In 1995, China's soot emission was 17.44 million tons (including township industries), about 70% of which was exhausted by coal burning. According to monitoring findings in 87 cities, the soot emission of 45 cities exceeded the national standard Grade II, and Beijing, Tianjin, Shanghai, Chongqing, Shenyang, Jinan, and TaiYuan were among cities with the most severe soot pollution in the world. According to monitoring findings in recent years, China's soot emission has been under control. Though the coal consumption appeared in a fast uptrend, the soot emission dropped slightly from 17.44 million tons in 1995 to 14.52 million tons in 1998. However, the soot emission in more than half of the cities exceeded the national standard Grade II, and TSP concentration in big cities went far beyond the national standard.

The soot, sulfide, nitric oxide, carbon monoxide, and other pollutants generated by air pollution have a direct impact on human health, giving rise to incidences of respiratory diseases such as lung cancer, pulmonary heart disease, asthma, and chronic tracheitis. According to calculations by the Environment Research Center of the Chinese Academy of Social Sciences, the health loss (both direct and indirect) of the urban population incurred by air pollution in China in 1993 amounted to about RMB7.8 billion Yuan (price in the current year); the impact of some air pollutants, such as acid rain and greenhouse effect, may spread to the whole region or even the entire globe.

Acid rain impairs the human body, and also damages the ecological environment due to the long-term negative effect of soil acidification. In China, the ecological systems vulnerable to acid rain comprise evergreen forests in the southern subtropical zone, the high-latitude tundra in Tibet and Qinghai, the coniferous forests in Northeast as well as Southwest and East China. In Southern China, especially in Sichuan, Guizhou, Guangxi, and Hunan, there is high sulfide emission due to the consumption of high-sulfur coal; particularly in the peripheral of Chongqing, the annual acid precipitation is already $11,000mg/m^2$ higher than critical value. It is estimated that the annual loss of crops and forests in China due to acid rain amounted to about US$5 billion (the World Bank, the Big Blue). In 1995, China's emission of carbon dioxide in defined control zone of acid rain and carbon dioxide made up 89% of the country's total emission; the economic loss incurred by carbon dioxide and acrid rain reached up to RMB116.5 billion Yuan (crops, forests, and human health). This loss will increase unless countermeasures are taken immediately.

3. Rational utilization of energy resources and protection of eco-environment

Not until the middle 20th century did mankind realize the global ecological and environmental pollution caused by the long-term inappropriate production and consumption during economic and social development, by the excessive consumption of natural resources in the process of global industrialization, and by the production mode that discharges masses of pollutants and the living style that consumes too much. The pollution impedes economic development and improvement of people's living quality, and further threatens human survival and evolution in the future.

As a big producer and consumer of energy resources as well as a country that uses coal as its main energy source, China now is encountered with serious environmental problems due to excessive development and utilization of energy resources. With national economic development, the environmental pollution caused by energy consumption will become more and more serious. In the process of economic development, China cannot follow the path of developed countries, i.e. governance of pollution is preceded by pollution itself. Instead, China should work out new solutions to environment protection that fit in well with its actual conditions.

(A) Saving energy – an essential task for China in the long future

With a large population, China is relatively short of energy resources. As Chinese economy develops and people's living quality improves, the annual per capita consumption of energy will increase year by year; however, the relative shortage of conventional energy resources such as petroleum and natural gas will be a factor hindering China's economic and social sustainability.

Despite the current balance between production and consumption of energy resources in China, the gap between energy supply and demand will widen in the future. It was predicted that China would be 80% short of energy in 2010 and about 24% in 2040, providing we apply advanced technology to save energy and accelerate development, and we utilize renewable energy resources and optimize the allocation of energy resources under market forces.

Considering the downtrend of energy consumption in recent years and the current energy-saving measures in China as well as the 2.8% of the average annual growth of energy consumption in the future years (given the growth rate of the GDP is 7% and the elastic coefficient of energy consumption is 0.4), the total energy consumption in 2001, 2005, 2010, 2015, and 2040 will be 1.44 billion, 1.65 billion, 1.89 billion, 2.17 billion, and 4.34 billion tons of standard coal respectively. Given the growth rate mentioned above, the total energy consumption of China by 2040 will exceed experts' predicted value (up to about 3 billion tons of standard coal in the year of 2040, predicted by experts from the Chinese Academy of Engineering). For this reason, the average annual growth rate of energy consumption must slow in China and down to zero in 2040. It is thus clear that the development of the national economy and improvement of people's living quality must be based on the efficient utilization of energy resources.

Since the 1980s, remarkable progress has been achieved in China's energy-saving activities. From 1981 to 1999, Chinese economy witnessed a rapid growth (average annual growth rate of 9.7%), but the growth rate of energy consumption (4.6%) was much lower than the economic growth rate. Over the past two decades, an accumulative amount of 950 million tons of standard coal was saved in China, as measured against the GDP; the energy consumption per unit of GDP dropped about 60%; the energy-saving rate moved up to 4.5%, equivalent to reducing the emission of 12 million tons of dust, 250 million tons of ash residue, 19 million tons of sulfur dioxide, and 420 million tons of carbon dioxide. Apart from saving energy, China also discovered an effective approach to protecting the environment and reducing the emission of greenhouse gases.

Even so, there is still a huge space of energy-saving potential in China. First, the product energy consumption remains high. In China, the energy consumption per unit product of main energy-using products is 25–90% higher than developed countries, and the weighted average higher by about 40%. There is a difference of one to four times between the minimum and the maximum of energy consumption per unit product of domestic enterprises. According to an analysis of 15 energy-saving enterprises, the energy saved through technical measures is about 100 million tons of standard coal. Second, the energy consumption per unit output value remains high. China is one of the countries in the world that has high energy consumption per unit output value. The higher the energy consumption per output value, the lower the output value generated per energy consumption. The GDP generated per kilogram of standard coal is US$0.36 in China, but it is US$5.58 in Japan, US$3.24 in France, US$1.56 in South Korea, and US$0.72 in India; the world average is US$1.86, so Japan is 15.5 times, France is 9 times, the world average is 5.2 times, South Korea is 4.3 times, and even India is twice that of China (note: uncomparable factors were considered, such as exchange rate, energy structure, and climatic condition). It is estimated that China's recent energy-saving potential of energy consumption per national economic output value has reached about 300 million tons of standard coal after the implementation of such measures as adjusting the industrial structure, adjusting the product structure, reducing the proportion of enterprises with high energy consumption, increasing the proportion of products with high value added, and optimizing household energy consumption. During the 10th Five-Year Plan, China's total energy-saving potential is about 400 million tons of standard coal; by 2015, it will be about 900 million tons of standard coal.

During the 10th Five-Year Plan, the annual average growth rate of China's GDP is planned at about 7.0%. If the elastic coefficient of energy consumption ranges between 0.38 and 0.42 and the annual average energy-saving rate ranges between 4.0% and 4.4%, the total energy saved will reach up to 300–360 million tons of standard coal (note: this is accumulative energy saved month over month, about 100–150 million of which is achieved via fixed asset investment and technical progress, and the remaining amount is achieved via structure adjustment; so the fixed-ratio energy saved will reach up to 330–400 million tons of standard coal). The energy consumption per 10 thousand Yuan GDP has been reduced to 2.3–2.5 tons of standard coal; the energy consumption per 10 thousand Yuan GDP has been reduced to 3.35–3.45 tons of standard coal (calculated by fixed price in 1990). Some shortage of energy supply can be supplemented by imported energy sources. The efficiency and benefit of energy utilization should be increased constantly, up to 36% in 2005, with 4 percentage points increased over that in 1997. The energy consumption of the main energy-using products should also be reduced year over year, down 5–10 percentage points in 2005; the energy consumption per 10 thousand Yuan output value should be reduced to 15–17% in 2005.

(B) Developing clean coal technology (CCT)

For a considerably long time in the future, coal will remain the major energy in China. The development and utilization of coal now have an enormous impact on environment. So the development of clean coal technology will be of great strategic significance to the development of energy resources in China.

In China, considerable R&D and promotion work was carried out on how to improve the utilization rate of coal and how to minimize environment pollution. In 1995, the State Council set up a State Leading Group for Promotion and Planning of Clean Coal Technology. *The 9th Five-Year Plan and 2010 Development Outline for China's Clean Coal Technology* was formulated by the group and approved by the State Council in June 1997.

The framework of China's clean coal technology plan covers four fields (coal processing, high efficiency and clean combustion of coal, coal conversion, pollution emission control, and waste disposal) and involves 14 technologies: coal washing, coal briquette, coal water slurry; CFB (circulating fluidized bed), PFB (pressurized fluidized bed), and IGCC (integrated gasification combined) power generation technologies; coal gasification, coal liquefaction, and fuel cells; and flue gas purification, fly ash comprehensive utilization, development and utilization of coal-bed methane, comprehensive utilization of coal gangue and slime water, industrial boilers, and kilns.

The development of clean coal technology in China aims to "improve efficiency of coal utilization, reduce environment pollution and promote economic development". As the research, demonstration, and promotion of clean coal technology involves a wide range as well as high technical difficulty and huge investment, the development of clean coal technology in China begins with the mastery of some clean coal technologies suitable to China's practical condition and with the recognition of some international advanced technologies in this regard. From 2001 to 2010, the final consumption structure of coal will be optimized; the main fields that utilize clean coal technologies will approach the international advanced level and will be widely applied.

(C) Developing clean energy resources including natural gas

As high-quality clean fuel and essential chemical raw material, natural gas has become one of the three backbone energy resources in the world. China's natural gas industry has maintained a stable development trend continuously. Since 1983, the output of natural gas grows at a rate between 4% and 6% for most of years; the output reached up to 22.3 billion cubic meters in 1998. China has solid resource conditions for the development of the natural gas industry. According to the results of the second round evaluation of China's oil-gas resources, the total resource of China's conventional natural gas amounted to 38 trillion cubic meters. Judging by the current technical level and experience, the proved geological reserve of natural gas is about 13.2 trillion cubic meters. It is estimated that the proved reserve of China's natural gas will be close to 6% in 2000. This proportion keeps rising in recent years. China's natural gas resources are mainly distributed in the middle, western, and offshore regions; more than 80% of natural gas resources are centralized in Tarim Basin, Sichuan, Shaanxi, Gansu, Ningxia, Zunghar Basin, Qaidam Basin, Songliao Basin, and the southeast sea areas.

The development of the natural gas industry in China is restricted to some extent by the gas consumption structure due to the lagging resource exploration, inefficient utilization of natural gas resources, and imperfect supporting policies. With the social progress and economic development in China, the natural gas will inevitably become the major energy, so accelerating the development and utilization of natural gas is one of the important measures to ease the contradiction between the supply and demand of energy resources and optimize the energy structure. China has considered the development and utilization of natural gas essential to optimizing the energy structure and upgrading the petroleum industry in the 21st century. The exploitation and production of natural gas will peak in the new century. The proved reserve of China's natural gas resources will maintain an annual average growth rate of about 120 billion cubic meters. The first 5–10 years in the 21st century will be a period in which the natural gas development will accelerate, the proved reserve will increase, the construction of the gas transmission pipeline will pace up (including the west-to-east natural gas transmission project), and the gas consumption market will improve.

(D) Accelerating the development and utilization of renewable energy resources

China's renewable energy resources are abundant, but are developed and utilized at a low rate. The exploitable installed capacity of water energy is 378 million kW, and the annual electricity production is 1.92 trillion kWh, ranking the first in the world; however, the installed hydro–power capacity is 65.074 million kW, and the utilization rate of water energy is 10% only, lower than 11.5% – the average utilization rate of water resources in developing countries. The solar energy is found on two-thirds of China's territory, and the annual radiation exceeds $600,000J/cm^2$; the solar energy absorbed by the earth's surface per year is roughly equivalent to energy of 17 trillion tons of standard coal. The exploitable wind energy is about 1.6 billion kW; the exploitable wind energy is about 250 million kW; the installed capacity of wind energy power generation is

223,600 kW (the world's was total up to 9.6 million kW in 1998); the possible reserve of geothermal resources is 1,371.1 billion tons of standard coal, and the proved reserve is 328.3 billion tons of standard coal (about 5,800 MW available for high temperature power generation, about 200 billion tons of standard coal to be directly used for medium- and low-temperature power generation; the geothermal energy is developed and utilized at a low rate, with the quantity realized equivalent to 2 million tons of standard coal). The biomass energy resources are also abundant: the resource quantity of agricultural wastes including straws is equivalent to 310 million tons of standard coal per year, and that of fuel wood is equivalent to 130 million tons of standard coal, plus bio-organic municipal wastes, the total quantity of resources exceeds 650 million tons of standard coal. Other exploitable resources, such as marine energy, amounts up to 440 million kW (including 110 million kW of tidal sand energy, 18 million kW of tidal current energy, 30 million kW of marine current energy, 23 million kW of wave energy, 150 million kW of temperature difference energy, and 110 million kW of salinity gradient energy).

In the future decade, the development of China's renewable energy resources will aim to improve conversion efficiency, reduce production cost, increase its proportion in energy structure, make breakthroughs in new technologies and new processes, realize the large-scale modern production of mature technologies introduced either at home or from abroad, establish a comparatively perfect production system and service system, and ensure actual consumption up to 390 million tons of standard coal (including the traditional utilization method and quantity of biomass energy) to facilitate environmental protection and the sustainable development of national economy. To realize the above-mentioned objectives, the development and utilization of China's renewable energy resources will have to accomplish a primary task, i.e. selecting a group of key technologies for R&D that will be of great value to national economy and ecological environment in the first decade of the 21st century, priorities of which will be the pilot demonstration of these technologies and the transformation of scientific achievements so as to promote industrialized and commercialized production and popularization and application.

(Published in *World Technology Equipment and Trade Magazine*, Issue 2, 2001)

Part 2

On deepening the reform

1 Deepening the economic system reform and constructing the mature marketing economy

In January 2012, our Institute was assigned by the Central Government to undertake a Research Project of Deepening the Economic System Reform. Chen KuiYuan, the president of the Institute, decided to set up a research group that was comprised of top scientific research professionals, the backbone of the industry. I was appointed the group leader.

After the research group was established, we began sorting out all the problems to be addressed under this project before the Spring Festival 2013, we organized group members to review all important documents in regard to economic system reform since the 14th National Congress, and we collated some main ideas and propositions about deepening the economic system reform. In addition, we framed a detailed research outline, allocated jobs inside the research group, decided the place to research, and defined the schedule.

From February 5th to the middle of February, the research group conducted an investigation in the Guangdong, Anhui, and Zhejiang provinces, and organized a panel discussion to solicit opinions and suggestions from leaders of these provinces and Guangzhou, Hefei, and Wenzhou cities as well as leaders of enterprises and theoretical circle.

Sometime later we came back to Beijing, we worked out five sub-reports that eventually formed the general report. We also organized two small symposiums inside the group and invited some experts and scholars both inside and outside the Institute. At the symposium, modifications to the report contributed a lot to the finalization of the report after four revisions. In early March, the study report was finalized.

According to the research group, in the future 5 to 10 years, the objective and primary task of China's deepening the economic system reform will be constructing a mature socialist market economy system. This is the core judgment and the main title of our research results.

With the task accomplished, the research group spent more than half a year enriching relevant information and data and improving theories, carried out a comprehensive analysis of strategic challenges facing the construction of a mature socialist market economy system in China, and defined the countermeasures. What is presented to readers now is the result of our extended studies, which is composed of three parts.

1. China sets about constructing the mature socialist market economy

Since the economic reform and opening up to the outside world, China has been sticking to market-oriented reform. At the 14th National Congress of the Communist Party of China (CPC), the objective of the economic system reform was defined expressly as constructing the socialist market economy system; the basic framework was depicted at the 3rd Plenary Session of the 14th Central Committee of the CPC. Over years of reform thereafter and by the end of the 20th century, the framework of the socialist market economy system has formed. In the 21st century, the 16th National Congress of the CPC Central Committee concluded a resolution aimed to improve the socialist market economy system; the 3rd Plenary Session of the 16th Central Committee of the CPC made special arrangements for the construction of a perfect socialist market economy system as well as a more vibrant and open economic system, which specified a series of tasks with regard to deepening reform.

Over three decades' reform and opening up to the outside world, China has completed the significant transition from a traditional, planned economy to a socialist market economy, and also established a solid foundation for the socialist market economy system. However, there are still some deep-seated institutional obstacles hindering the improvement and formation of the socialist market economy system. Due to severe pressure from the transformation and upgrading of the economic development pattern along with the complicated situation that interlaces interest relations with social conflicts, deepening reform is confronted with new challenges. Deng Xiaoping's South Tour Speech in 1992 pointed out: "I'm afraid that a complete set of mature and finalized systems will be formulated in next thirty years. But the guidelines and policies will be finalized under these systems".[1] Deng pointed to the year 2020 as the one by which the socialist market economy system will have matured and finalized. Deng's anticipation is roughly in line with the reform and opening process, as well as the situation and tasks in such a process. In the future decade, therefore, China's improving the socialist market economy system will advance toward constructing a mature socialist market economy system. Upon the completion of the construction, the socialist market economy system needs to be improved constantly.

A mature socialist market economy system is an economic system capable of self-regulation, self-improvement, and self-evolution as characterized by the following seven points:

First, the micro-foundation is vitalized after the basic socialist economic system has finalized. The basic economic system in the primary stage of socialism keeps public ownership as the mainstay of the economy and allows diverse forms of ownership to develop side by side. On this basis, the diverse forms of ownership economy will be entitled to equal use of production factors, equal participation in market competition, and equal legal protection, and will be put under supervision. Within the state-owned economy, all economies will have a property rights structure, where the state-owned capital is allowed to flow in or out while the non-state-owned capital is allowed to participate in transaction with state-owned capital. A mixed economy pattern based on a joint stock system will be formed through the transformation and upgrading of the private economy as well as penetration and merger of state-owned capital and various non-state-owned capitals. The state-owned enterprises will hence become the legal entity and competition entity adaptable to the market. The private economy and the state-owned economy will jointly constitute the foundation of the socialist market economy.

Second, the formation of the modern market system allows the market to play its basic roles in resource allocation. The developed commodities and production factors market will facilitate the formation of market-oriented factor pricing mechanism. The perfect market access and exit mechanism will help break trade monopolies and regional blockades to realize free mobility and competition of commodities and factors across the country.

Third, the market economy system that rules by law will be formed by a perfect legal system suitable to the socialist market. The basic property system will be improved under the market economy condition to protect social organizations and citizens' legal properties against damage, and protect the equal rights of various property rights with different natures in market transactions. The contractual relations and credit relations will be further improved to ensure a normal social credit order.

Fourth, a service-oriented government has formed since its separation from the market. The government's responsibility scope is defined under the principle of minimizing governmental interventions in the management of enterprises, capitals, public service units, and market agencies. The government is required to play fundamental roles in providing top-quality public services and safeguarding the socialist equity and justice. In terms of economic regulation, both economic and legal means will be used for indirect regulation and control of economy. In terms of market supervision, monopolies will be fought against and market barriers removed to create and maintain an essential institutional environment for fair competition on the market. In terms of social management, the government will work with social organizations to safeguard social justice, order, and stability.

Fifth, the profit distribution pattern and social welfare system will fully reflect social equity and justice. The pattern of distribution according to work done will be combined with the distribution of production factors according to contributions. The production factors will be distributed on the basis of contributions to the formation of social wealth, and individual effort levels positively stimulated under equal opportunity and equal rules so as to motivate the enthusiasm and creativity of factor providers. The re-distribution regulatory mechanism will be perfected, the income distribution order standardized, and the social structure stabilized, so that the number of middle-income people will account for more than 60% of the total population.

Sixth, a harmonious civic society will eventually form provided that the social vitality is aroused and that full play is given to the creativity of social organizations and social members. For this end, all social organizations are encouraged to take part in making public policy and supplying public services so as to create a set of social self-governance rules by which all citizens are capable of self-management and self-service. A social order suitable to marketization will be established in response to the diversification of economic sectors and social forces.

Seventh and finally, a mutually coordinated and promoted new pattern of reform and opening up will eventually form. A set of equilibrium mechanisms that persist in opening up to the outside world and protect the national interests will be adopted to ensure advancement of the open-door policy to a higher level and ensure smooth interactive channels between reform and opening up. To construct a mature socialist market economy system, we need to consider the planning of strategies, paths, and dynamics of reform through overall innovation of all institutions: 1) reunite consensus on reform and enhance dynamics of reform, 2) give priority to top-level design and promotion, 3) respect pioneering spirits of enterprises, and 4) promote multilevel coordination of overall reform.

To strengthen top-level promotion and boost the coordination of reform, we need to set up a high-level, trans-department, and separately interested organization based on the overall planning of reform. The functions of the organization provide opinions and suggestions for the Central Government to make decisions on reform, guide reform activities of local government or department, coordinate reform agencies of all department and regions, supervise and check if local authorities or departments follow the Central Government's arrangement, and collect feedbacks about reform activities.

2. Accelerating reform of the government administrative management system is the key to constructing the socialist market economy system

The 5th Plenary Session of the 16th Central Committee of the CPC pointed out that the key to deepening the reform in an all-round way and improving the level of opening up to the outside world was to accelerate the reform of the administration system. The construction of a mature socialist market economy system in the future will require a coordinated and balanced relation between enterprises, markets, and government. In terms of the whole economic system reform process at present, great progress has been achieved in the reform of enterprises and markets, but the biggest problem is the reform of the administration system, because of which the reforms of key fields and key links remain stagnant, some even in regression. The problem must be repaired to make breakthroughs in the administration of system reform.

Strengthen efforts to promote large department system reform. Exploring a new administration system framework and optimizing the governmental organization structure will follow a streamlined, unified, and efficient principle. In the process of promoting large, department, system reform, the approval system will be considered when reducing, canceling, or merging organizations that directly engage or intervene in micro-economic activities and social affairs; in addition, organizations engaged in public services and social management will be strengthened and improved.

To tackle such problems as excessive centralization and the ineffective supervision of power and poor implementation, we need to innovate and improve the administration operating and set up a power structure by which the rights to make administrative decisions, to execute decisions, and to supervise can restrict and coordinate with each other so as to create an administrative system that features consistent power and responsibility, a reasonable division of labor, scientific decision, smooth implementation, and forceful supervision.

Restructuring and optimizing the government organization structure should follow the "overall planning linkage" principle, i.e. government agency reform linked with Party-masses reform, administrative organ reform linked with public service unit reform, Central Government reform linked with local government reform, and local government reform linked with the reform of government sectors at all levels. At the present stage, the linkage between the upper and lower government agencies seems particularly urgent.

The administration system reform should be combined with the transformation of government functions. Rather than simply merging, splitting, or streamlining, the move of large department system reform has to be premised by a scientific and reasonable definition of government functions. It will become merely formalistic if the administration system framework is downsized without the transformation of government functions.

The ultimate goal of all of the government's administrative activities is to maximize people's well-being at the least burden, i.e. an optimal combination of tax burden and public services. Focusing on economic construction does not necessarily mean that the governments at all levels are required to engage directly in production and management activities. Defining government functions will ensure that the market can operate in a way as it is expected to, so can the enterprises and the social organizations. The government will change from an all-inclusive system into a system that provides public services in a limited and effective way so that the market and social mechanism will play their leading roles in resource allocation and social ordering.

The basic idea of reform in public institutions is to diminish the number and size of such institutions. All public institutions that perform administrative functions will be put under management of the government, those engaged in production and operation activities will be transformed into enterprises, and the remaining institutions that carry out commonweal activities will be in the charge of the state government. For all commonweal institutions sponsored directly by governments at all levels, the nonprofit nature will remain unchanged and workers will be equally treated in remuneration and other benefits, and they will be provided with various necessary conditions for business development by public finance; however, these institutions will not be forced to create income on their own in order to afford employees' remuneration and benefits. Social forces are allowed and encouraged to participate in common-weal services, and social capitals are encouraged to go into non-profit social service organizations so as to create a new pattern for social services characterized by multi-subjects and multi-modes and are capable to provide widely-covered and multi-level social services for the masses.

Reforms will be strengthened in public institutions directly under the Central Government, especially in affiliated ministries and commissions. First, the income handover system will be set up in public institutions directly under the Central Government to ensure the separation between revenue and expenditure. Second, the nominal wages and income structure of public institutions under the Central Government will be integrated as early as possible to ensure equal treatment in the same city and at the same level as well as implement a differentiated merit pay system based on job performance. Third, the retirement systems will be consolidated in organizations under the Central Government to set up a unified pension system and a social insurances management agency for departments and units directly under the Central Government. Fourth, business units in public institutions will be separated and transformed into independent market entities. Fifth and finally, the research and consultation agencies of all departments will be consolidated into comprehensive research and decision-making consultation institutions so as to reduce the number and staff of public institutions and avoid departmentalization and low-level repetition of research results.

3. Constructing the socialist market economy system requires promoting the reform in key fields and links

The state-owned economy will be subject to strategic adjustment, and the reform in state-owned enterprises will be deepened. First, adjustment will be made in the entry and exit of state-owned capital. Second, the new state-owned enterprises system will be set up. The system should be very good to reflect the nature of the people so that all people can directly and substantially share the achievements of the development of state-owned enterprises. Third, the new round of reforms in monopolized industries will be initiated. Fourth and finally, the reform of a state-owned asset management system will be furthered. The government's state-owned asset contributor functions will be strengthened to improve the state-owned capital management budget, the income distribution and benefit appraisal of state-owned enterprises management, to enlarge the implementation scope of the state-owned capital management budget, to increase the hand-in proportion of the state-owned capital gains, and to include the gains into the public finance budget. The National People's Congress (NPC) will strengthen the budget review of state-owned enterprises and supervise the distribution and use of the gains.

Priorities will be given to the development of private economies. First, define the social attribute and development orientation of individual and private economies. Second, create conditions for the development of individual and private economies, provide financing support for small and micro enterprises, encourage private enterprises to raise funds directly from the capital market, support private capital to participate in development of bank and non-bank financial institutions, continue with structural tax reduction, and clear up and standardize charges from enterprises to relieve the tax and fees burden of small and micro enterprises. Third and finally, improve the overall qualities of individual and private economies.

The public finance systems will be set up and improved. First, transform the development pattern of finance and taxation, and successively eliminate the dual finance systems to ensure the publishing of financial systems. Second, improve the income distribution functions of finance and taxation systems. Third, adjust the structure of fiscal expenditure to improve people's livelihood. Fourth, maintain the integrity, scientificity, and solemnity of the budget. Fifth, accelerate the new round of reform in tax and fees system. Sixth and finally, define the powers and expenditure responsibility of governments at all levels, and ensure coordination between powers and expenditure responsibilities and financial resources.

The financial reform, opening up, and development will be promoted comprehensively. First, stick to the requirement that finance serves the real economies, and construct a multi-level, diverse, and moderately competitive financial service system to provide first-rate services for economic and social development. Second, accelerate the reform of financial market, improve the indirect regulatory mechanism of market, and gradually strengthen roles of price leverages such as interest rate and exchange rate. Third, strengthen and improve financial regulation to prevent systematic financial risks. Fourth and finally, accelerate the construction of a multi-level capital market system and a register system that is exercised in securities issuance, and we should accelerate the development of the bond market to provide diverse and multi-level financial services for enterprises of different scale, types, and stages.

(This is the Preface of the book *Construction of a Mature Market Economy System*, published by Economic Management Press in 2012)

Note

1 Deng Xiaoping, Talking Points in Wuchang, Shenzhen, Zhuhai and Shanghai, *Selected Works of Deng Xiaoping Vol. III*, Beijing, China: People's Publishing House, 1993, pp. 371–372.

2 Change the economic development form characterized with investment motivation, strengthen consumption

Changing the economic development form is a key task facing China's economic development in a very long period during and after the 12th Five-Year Plan. To change the development mode involves various problems; one of them is to change the government-led system and mechanism with investment motivation and strengthen consumption.

1. Investment motivation is the main feature of China's economic development

Since the economic reform and opening up to the outside world in 1978, the Chinese economy has maintained an annual average growth rate of nearly 10%. China's GDP has risen from the sixth place to the second; the total volume of foreign trade has risen from the seventh place to the second in the world; and the economic strength and comprehensive national power have improved substantially and made remarkable achievements. However, Chinese economy is also encountered with some underlying problems such as an extensive development mode, a severely unbalanced economic structure, and a low quality of economic growth.

With regard to the driving force of economic growth, the rapid growth rate of the Chinese economy is mainly stimulated by investment, which is the leading feature of the Chinese economic development mode. According to the composition of the GDP during the 11th Five-Year Plan, the proportion of investment in the GDP increased year over year, i.e. 50.9% in 2006 and up to 69.3% in 2010; the capital formation rate was 41.8% in 2006, and rose to 48.6% in 2010. According to the investment growth rate, the annual growth of investment in real terms was 21.9% during the 11th Five-Year Plan, much higher than the 11.2% of the GDP's growth rate. With regard to the contribution rate of investment to economic growth, it was 43.9% in 2006, 54.0% in 2010, and even up to 91.3% in 2009 (see Table 2.2.1).

As investment became the driving force to stimulate economic growth, the driving force of consumption has weakened. According to stimulation and contribution of three major demands to economic growth, during the 11th Five-Year Plan, the consumption demand contributed only 41.4% to economic growth per year on the average and also showed a declining trend, dropping from 40.0% in 2006 to 36.8% in 2010, down 3.2 percentage points (see Table 2.2.2).

Table 2.2.1 Proportion of Investment in GDP and Its Contribution to Economic Growth during the 11th Five-Year Plan

Year	Proportion of fixed assets investment in GDP (%)	Capital formation rate (%)	Growth rate of capital formation (%)	Contribution rate of capital formation to economic growth (%)	Percentage of economic growth stimulated (%)
2006	50.9	41.8	23.9	43.9	5.6
2007	51.7	41.7	24.8	42.7	6.1
2008	55.0	43.9	25.9	47.5	4.6
2009	65.9	47.5	30.0	91.3	8.4
2010	69.3	48.6	23.8	54.0	5.6

Source: *A Statistical Survey of China (2011)*, China Statistics Press 2011 edition.

Table 2.2.2 Contribution Rates of Three Major Demands to GDP Growth

Year	Final consumption		Capital formation		Net export	
	Contribution rate (%)	Percentage of economic growth stimulated (%)	Contribution rate (%)	Percentage of economic growth stimulated (%)	Contribution rate (%)	Percentage of economic growth stimulated (%)
2006	40.0	5.1	43.9	5.6	16.1	2.0
2007	39.2	5.6	42.7	6.1	18.1	2.5
2008	43.5	4.2	47.5	4.6	9.0	0.8
2009	47.6	4.4	91.3	8.4	−38.9	−3.6
2010	36.8	3.8	54.0	5.6	9.2	0.9

Source: *A Statistical Survey of China (2011)*, China Statistics Press 2011 edition.

In 2011, Chinese economy grew at 9.2% and the consumption contributed 51.6% to economic growth, increasing 14.8 percentage points in figures as compared to the year of 2010, but it did indicate that the structure of investment and consumption improved because it had something to do with the declining economic growth rate and the negative percentage of economic growth stimulated by export. With regard to the growth rate of the total retail sales of consumer goods, it grew 17.1% only, i.e. 11.6% in real terms, dropping 3.2 percentage points as compared to 2010, much lower than about 13% of the growth rate in normal years.

Investment plays a leading role in contribution to Chinese economic growth and a large part of investment is derived from direct and indirect investment of governments at all levels and from state-owned enterprises and public institutions, so investment is often used by governments as a means for macro-economic regulation and control. When the economic growth slows down, investment will be increased to stimulate economic growth; when the economy grows too fast, investment will be cut down to suppress economic growth. It seems that investment has become a sovereign remedy that is usually used by the government to regulate economic growth.

2. The development pattern with investment motivation is unsustainable

When the economic base is weak, it is certainly necessary to increase investment to lay a solid foundation for economic development; in the long run, however, the reliance on investment for economic growth will deform the economic structure and reduce the quality of economic growth, and also will be unsustainable.

First, it leads to severe unbalance between investment and consumption. During the 11th Five-Year Plan, the specific value of China's fixed asset investment and GDP was on a steady rise, e.g. 50.9% in 2006, 51.7% in 2007, 55.0% in 2008, 65.9% in 2009, and 69.3% in 2010, increasing 18.4 percentage points over that in 2006, with 4 percentage points raised per year on average. According to the formation rate of fixed assets, during the 11th Five-Year Plan, it was below 42% just in the first two years but increased quickly in the following three years, e.g. 43.9% in 2008, 47.5% in 2009, and 48.6% in 2010. In contrast, the citizen consumption rate was on a decline; in 2006, it was 36.9%, below 36% after 2007, and only 33.8% in 2010 (see Table 2.2.3).

From an in-depth perspective, the severe unbalance of investment and consumption structure squeezed resident income so much that the proportion of resident income in the GDP decreased year over year, that the national income distribution moved towards capital, and that the household income of residents made up less and less of the GDP (see Table 2.2.4). According to the rationale of macroeconomics, resident consumption is a function of resident income. This is why the proportion of resident consumption in the GDP has dropped in consecutive years, thus leading to an unbalanced proportion of investment and consumption.

Second, it leads to the unbalance of the industrial structure. At present, the internal structure of all industries in China is quite unreasonable, with the exception of the discordance of industrial structure in the primary, secondary, and tertiary industries. Take the manufacturing industry for an example: the

Table 2.2.3 Composition of Expenditure-based GDP during the 11th Five-Year Plan (%)

Year	Fixed asset investment/GDP	Capital formation rate	Citizen consumption rate	Urban residents consumption rate	Rural residents consumption rate
2006	50.9	41.8	36.9	27.4	9.6
2007	51.7	41.7	36.0	26.9	9.1
2008	55.0	43.9	35.1	26.4	8.7
2009	65.9	47.5	35.0	26.8	8.4
2010	69.3	48.6	33.8	26.0	7.8

Source: *A Statistical Survey of China (2011)*, China Statistics Press 2011 edition.

Table 2.2.4 Proportions of Gross Household Income of Urban and Rural Residents in GDP

Years	Household income of urban & rural residents	
	Gross income (100 million Yuan)	Proportion of GDP (%)
2001	51,798	47.2
2002	58,047	48.2
2003	64,526	47.5
2004	73,373	45.9
2005	83,247	45.0
2006	94,786	43.8
2007	113,190	42.6
2008	131,991	42.0
2009	146,322	42.9
2010	167,716	41.8

Source: Calculated according to per capita income and population of urban and rural residents in *A Statistical Survey of China (2011)*, China Statistics Press 2011 edition.

economic development pattern with investment motivation has led to a severe unbalance in proportion between the light industry and the heavy industry. At the beginning of the economic reform and opening up to the outside world, China's industrialization degree remained so low so that there was a serious shortage of manufactured goods for daily use as a result of a one-sided emphasis on the development of heavy industry instead of the light industry. At that time, priorities were given to adjusting the structure of the light and heavy industries. Over years of effort, the light industry's proportion in the manufacturing industry rose from 43% in 1978 to 47.4% in 1985. In the following dozens of years, the proportion of the light and heavy industries fluctuated around 50% but maintained a coordinated development trend. At the end of the 20th century, China's industrial structure featured heavy chemical industry. In the 10-year period from 1999 to 2008, the proportion of output value of the light industry descended from 41.9% to 28.9% but the heavy industry ascended from 58.1% to 71.1%, which maintained above 70% in the last three years, which is much higher than it was in the period before the economic reform and opening up. This change is directly associated with the investment-driven economic growth mode as well as with the development stage of industrialization. The large-scale and rapidly increasing investment has generated huge market demands for heavy industries such as steel and iron, cement, petrochemical, shipping, and energy resources. Some industries were encountered with serious overcapacity; for example, a heavy deficit was found in the steel and iron industry due to overcapacity and fierce competition. However, the brisk demand has also protected some enterprises with backward technology, a high consumption of raw materials, serious waste, low management levels, bad management, and severe environmental pollution, which added much to the difficulty in adjusting and upgrading the industrial structure.

Third, it overburdens the resources and environment. As investment was the key driving force to drive economic growth, more and more resources were consumed and many of them had to be outsourced. The dependence of resources including petroleum, iron ore, copper, and aluminum has exceeded 50% and is still rising, which gives rise to input inflation and exerts a tremendous impact on economic security.

The air, water, and land resources are increasingly polluted and damaged due to the rapid growth of economy, the huge consumption of resources, and the low cost of environmental nuisance. According to relevant data, about 30% of 411 surface water monitoring sections in the seven main water systems in China are rated as Class V inferior water quality; about half of the cities have witnessed serious pollution of groundwater, some of which even witnessed a phenomenon that "all rivers (if any) are running dry and all water (if any) is contaminated"; air pollution is so serious that China's carbon emission ranked the first in the world and that the air quality of 17.2% of the cities in China stayed below a Grade II national standard in 2010; according to preliminary statistics, serious land pollution involved about 120 million *mu* (approx. 8 million hectares) of land in China. A mass of investment was put into pollution treatment by the state, but it achieved little.

Fourth and finally, it reduces investment benefits. The investment effect coefficient reflects GDP increased per unit of fixed asset investment in a given period, which equals the additional amount of GDP divided by the amount of fixed asset investment. It is an import index to measure economic effects. In recent years, the investment effect coefficient is drastically inferior to the historical average and shows an obvious downtrend while fluctuating (see Table 2.2.5).

In 2009, the investment effect coefficient was 12.0%, the lowest in historical data, i.e. the GDP increased 12 million Yuan per hundred million Yuan of fixed asset investment, decreasing 33.20 million Yuan as against that in 1996. In addition, the investment efficiency dropped more obviously in years when investment was increased greatly, e.g. only 19.1 and 17.7 in 1998 and 1999 respectively, and only 12.0 and 21.7 in 2009 and 2010 respectively. This indicated that the production efficiency of capital inputs dropped with the increasing investment scale; in other words, the more investment, the lower the economic result. The

Table 2.2.5 Effect Coefficients of Fixed Asset Investment over the Years (%)

Year	Coefficient	Year	Coefficient	Year	Coefficient
1996	45.2	2001	28.1	2006	24.0
1997	31.3	2002	24.6	2007	36.0
1998	19.1	2003	27.9	2008	27.9
1999	17.7	2004	34.1	2009	12.0
2000	29.0	2005	26.1	2010	21.7

Source: Calculated according to *A Statistical Survey of China (2011)*, China Statistics Press 2011 edition.

investment benefit and quality were severely affected by the insufficient and ineffective utilization of part of the capital and by the low-level operation of investment capital.

3. Deepen reform to promote the change of economic development pattern

According to the analysis above, the development pattern with investment motivation has brought about many problems and is unsustainable. For this reason, we must deepen reform, change this development pattern, strengthen consumption, promote coordination between consumption, investment, and exports in China's economic development, and maintain a smooth, coordinated, and sustainable development of Chinese economy.

First, change the soft budget constraints of the government and state-owned enterprises and public institutions.

Strengthen the comprehensiveness, seriousness, and authoritativeness of government budget, and increase the openness and transparency. The government budget must cover all aspects and items under government revenue and outlay, and transit as soon as possible from the present formal nationwide budget management to a virtual, nationwide budget management; there must be managed objectives for legal deficits and all outstanding obligations, which will never be exceeded without approval by the National People's Congress (NPC); the use of financial surplus in the current year must be subject to approval by the NPC, unless it is used to offset the deficit or is transferred into a budget risk regulation fund or used to make up for a shortage of social insurance fund, and it will never be used to increase budget appropriation in principle; and neither the government nor the financial authority will be allowed to provide debt guarantee for any business entity. Once the budget is adopted at the NPC, the government and financial authority must implement it faithfully and will at no time adjust or alter it; the NPC shall spend more time and effort strengthening the approval and supervision of the budget; the transparency of budget and final accounts must be improved so that the budget performance comes under the intense scrutiny by the citizens and news media.

The state needs to strengthen budget management in the state-owned enterprises and public institutions, include revenues of state-owned enterprises into budget management and raise the proportion of revenues handed over to the treasury from the state-owned enterprises, strictly control the liability ratio of the state-owned enterprises, and prohibit the state-owned enterprises putting funds into industries with overcapacity or non-core business areas, especially into the non-entity economic fields. In recent years, the soft budget constraint problem is spreading into public institutions. For example, hundreds of billions of money (Yuan) was borrowed by colleges and universities, many of whom could hardly pay the interest, much less the principal. Similar cases are found in public institutions like hospitals. In truth, many entities meant not to repay the loan when they borrowed. Under the current financial system, the liability was totally transferred to the government. If the government is unwilling to help them out, bad and doubtful debts and potential financial risk will result. The direction of reform shows that full amount of financial allocation shall be executed for non-profit public institutions that must be established by the state; for profitable entities, revenue, and expenditure shall be separated for management. The profitable entities should manage within their means and avoid scale expansion or haphazard development.

Second, conscientiously carry out various policies of the Central Government for promoting the development of the private economy and accelerating development of private enterprises.

While controlling the scale of government investment, we need to deepen reform on monopolized industries; encourage and guide private investment into such fields as railway, petroleum, telecom, electric power, urban public utilities, and finance; create a fair and orderly competitive climate; increase investment returns; and enhance the endogenous power of Chinese economy.

Finally, accelerate the reform of the income distribution system to increase resident income and strengthen consumption.

In 2012, the difficulty in changing the negative contribution of exports to China's economic growth was due to flat economic growth and diminishing import demand reinforcing trade protectionism in developed countries. If the consumption demand is not strengthened, the economic growth will slow down drastically, e.g. at a rate below 8%, the voices for stimulating economic growth will be louder, and the government may loosen its control over investment and even formulate policies to encourage investment; consequently, the old economic development pattern with investment motivation will continue, the economic structure will be inevitably out of balance, and the quality of economic development will get worse and worse. We must be vigilant against this consequence.

According to data released in the first quarter of 2012, however, the growth rate of consumption was not as satisfying as expected. The total retail sales of consumer goods amounted to 4.9 trillion Yuan, increasing 14.8% year over year and 10.9% in real terms, 1.5 percentage points and 0.7 percentage points lower than that of the same period in 2011; the actual growth rate was lower than 11.6% in 2011 and about 13% in the past normal years. On this account, the most critical problem is whether we can change the economic growth pattern with investment motivation and stimulate consumption demands.

To strengthen consumption, we must accelerate the reform of the income distribution system and formulate the program for income distribution system reform; synchronize the resident income level with the economic development, increase the proportion of resident income in gross national income, and raise the proportion of workers' remuneration in the primary distribution; increase incomes of low-income groups, and build up the scale and proportion of middle-income population; continue improving the social security system, raising the pooling level of social insurances, and alleviating farmers' worries; accelerate construction of the long-term mechanism to expand consumption, optimize the consumption environment, increase, and improve policies to encourage and guide residents' reasonable consumption; actively promote reform on the equalization of basic public services; and endeavor to enhance the government's capability of public services.

(Published in *Reform of Economic System*, Issue 4, 2012)

3   The characteristics of the reform and opening up in China

The initiative of economic reform and opening up to the outside world in 1978 was one of the most significant, spectacular, and remarkable events since the 1970s. The 30-year period after the economic reform and opening up is a period with the most rapid social productivity development, the quickest rise of comprehensive national strength, the most benefits obtained by the people, and the most noteworthy enhancement of China's international standing, in which China completed the transition from a planned economy into a socialist market economy and from a big, agricultural country into a big, industrial country. Implemented under the socialist theory with Chinese characteristics, the initiative of economic reform, and opening up had distinctive characteristics. An in-depth study of China's reform and opening up will be of great significance to push forward the great undertaking at a new historical starting point.

1. The nature of reform is self-improvement and development

The initiative of reform and opening up was carried out according to the fundamental reality that China now is and will be at the primary stage of socialism for a long time, which has a dual implication: 1) China must stick to the socialist system and follow the socialist road; and 2) China now lies in the primary stage of socialism with an imperfect and immature socialist system, so the following generations are required to make efforts to solidify and develop the socialist system. As a "new and great revolution", the initiative of reform and opening up is the significant strategic measure to achieve this purpose. It did not mean to change China's socialist system, but to make productive relations more adaptable to productivity development and to make the superstructure more adaptable to the economic foundation so as to achieve self-improvement and the development of the socialist system.

2. The direction of reform is oriented to the market

China's reform began with execution of the household contract responsibility system in rural areas and the expansion of enterprise autonomy in urban areas. In 1982, the 12th National Congress of the CPC put forward the reform principle of a "planned economy supplemented by market regulation". In 1984, the 3rd Plenary Session of the 12th Central Committee defined the socialist economy as a "planned commodity economy". In 1987, the 13th National Congress of the CPC defined the new economic operation mechanism as "the market under state regulation and enterprises under market guidance". In 1992, the 14th National Congress of the CPC specified the objectives of the reform of the socialist market economy system. This process has affirmed the basic roles of market in resources allocation under the state macro-control, i.e. adhering to market orientation, strengthening roles of market mechanism, and eventually setting the objectives of the reform of the socialist market economy system.

3. The target model of reform is the socialist market economy

Based on the basic economic system by which the public ownership plays the leading role and the diverse forms of ownership develop side by side, the socialist market economy system is an organic combination of the market economy and socialism, for it features market economy and adheres to the socialist orientation. It is supported by five systems: enterprise system, market system, distribution system, social security system, and government macro-administration. It aims to 1) create the modern enterprise system that "clearly defines the property rights, the power and responsibility, the separation of enterprise from government administration and scientific management" so that the enterprises act as the main market players with independent management, self-development, self-discipline, and responsibility for their profit or loss; 2) develop a commodity market as well as a capital, land, labor force, technology, and management market so as to establish a unified and open market system with orderly competition; 3) create an effective market mechanism and give play to the fundamental roles of market in resources allocation; 4) implement the distribution system that is based on performance and supplemented with multiple distribution methods so as to combine efficiency with fairness; 5) gradually establish the social security system that covers both the urban and rural areas and set up a perfect social safety network; and 6) allow the government to use economic and legal means for economic regulation and control, or administrative means (where necessary), so as to maintain a steady, rapid, and healthy development of national economy. In addition, we need to learn lessons from reform experiences and establish the legal system that fits in well with the socialist market economy system.

4. The method of reform involves tackling the easiest problem first, deepening reform step by step, and progressively advancing the reform

China's reform has no precedent to go by or ready-made experiences for reference. As a big, developing country, China is vulnerable to reform risks.

In addition, the initiative of reform and opening up commenced under the destructive influence of the "Cultural Revolution" and extreme hardship of the national economy. Under such an environment and conditions, China's reform and opening up moved forward steadily as one is crossing a river, i.e. groping forward. Therefore, reforms with quick results preceded those with slow results; less difficult reforms preceded those with big difficulty; shallow-level reforms preceded deep-layer ones; reforms in competitive fields preceded those in monopolized industries; narrowing authorities of government agencies preceded reform in the administration system; and reform of economic system preceded reform of political, cultural, and social systems. For reforms with uncertainty, pilot reform came first, and then spread to other regions after summarizing the pilot experiences. This reform method has guaranteed the smooth progress of reform and opening up, and also avoided blunders and setbacks.

5. The overall plan for reform is to deal well with several vital relationships

Deal well with the relationship between rural reform and urban reform. China's reform began in rural areas. The household contract responsibility system initiated in rural areas since 1978 has greatly aroused farmer's enthusiasm in the cultivation of farmland; as a result, the shortage of grain was overcome immediately. The coupon system that had existed for years was abrogated throughout the country in 1993. This was a historical change. Not only has the rural reform provided sufficient food and non-staple food for cities, but it has also provided a mass of raw materials and surplus labor for urban reform and development. After the 3rd Plenary Session of the 12th Central Committee, the urban reform was put on the agenda, especially the industrial reform and development as well as the rapid progress of the industrialization process, which has created an economic foundation for "industry nurturing agriculture" and "cities supporting rural areas" and paved the way for deepening rural reform.

Deal well with the relationship between interest adjustment and innovation of mechanism and system. At the beginning of economic reform, whether the contract responsibility system was implemented in rural areas or the enterprise contract management and production responsibility system was implemented in urban areas, the focus was placed on interest adjustment, which aimed to adjust the distribution relationship between the state, enterprises, and individuals without radical changes in the planned economy system so as to arouse people's enthusiasm for economic reform and development. While it reduced the obstacles in reform and won over people's support for reform, the practice of expanding powers and transferring profits would not bring about revolutionary change in the planned economy system, nor would it sustain people's enthusiasm for long. As the reform deepens, the expansion of powers and transfer of profits will inevitably develop into the stage of mechanism and system innovation. In rural areas, the reform that empowers the long-term rights of land management and paid transfer of such rights to farmers has attempted to combine interest adjustment with system innovation. The reform of state-owned enterprises has entered the new stage of enterprise innovation and system innovation, thanks to the transition from a contract system into a shareholding system that aims at the corporate transformation through diversifying and decentralizing equities.

Deal well with the relationship between the reform of public owned enterprises and the development of non-public owned economies. The reform of ownership is promoted in two aspects: 1) the reform of state-owned and collective-owned enterprises aims to explore effective methods for the realization of public ownership, transform these enterprises into corporate enterprises, and achieve diversity of the ownership; and 2) vigorously developing non-public economies and make them an integral part of the socialist market economy. The reform of state-owned enterprises and the strategic adjustment of a state-owned economy have shortened the frontline, optimized the layout, and improved the quality of the state-owned economy, and also facilitated the development of private economy and mixed economy. The development of private economy has led to economic prosperity and created many jobs, but it also brought about competitive pressure and promoted reform of the state-owned and collective-owned enterprises.

Deal well with the relationship between internal reform and opening up to the outside world. China's economic reform and development created a favorable environment for foreign investment so that China has always come out on top in the introduction of foreign capital in the world. China's entry into WTO marked a new stage of both internal reform and opening up to the outside world. The open-door policy, on the one hand, urged us to accelerate reform and indicated that China's economic system and management method are in line with international convention, and on the other hand, enhanced China's rights of discourse when formulating international rules and raised China's competitiveness on the international arena.

Deal well with the relationship between reform, development, and stability. During the reform and opening up to the outside world, we have focused on economic construction and development. With the intention to emancipate and develop productivity, the reform can stimulate people's enthusiasm and creativity to provide a strong power for economic development, and also can provide a favorable mechanism and system guarantee for sound and fast development. As the basic premise of reform and development, this means making progress while maintaining stability. Neither the reform nor the development will be possible in case of social unrest. Therefore, attention should be paid to the relationship between the momentum of reform, the speed of development, and the degree acceptable to the society; they should be mutually coordinated.

6. The motivation of reform originates from the leadership of the party and government, the pioneering spirit of the people, and the roles of theoretical cycle

The Communist Party of China (CPC) is the core force to promote the reform and opening up to the outside world. China's initiative of reform and opening up was implemented under the leadership of the CPC. The Party's political authority and the government's administration created a good environment and safeguarded the continuous advancement of the reform and opening up.

The creativity of the social grassroots and the masses is the basic force to push forward the reform and opening up. Many reforms in China were initiated spontaneously by them and then were promoted to other regions in the country by the government after summarizing experiences, e.g. land contract management in Anhui, trial enlargement of enterprise autonomy in Sichuan, and shareholding system reform in Shanghai, Liaoning, etc. As forerunners and experimental fields of reform, some regions experimented with the creative development of the reform's tentative plan proposed by the Central Government. In Guangdong and Fujian, for example, pioneering activities were carried out during the introduction of foreign capitals, which accumulated experiences for nationwide promotion.

The theoretical cycle also is an essential force to promote the reform and opening up. By emancipation of their minds, theorists combined Marxism with China's practice; introduced foreign advanced management theories, methods, and means; absorbed beneficial achievements of modern economics; summarized historical experiences as well as new experiences and practice of the social grassroots and the masses during reform and opening up; conducted studies on new situations and new problems; made theoretical explanation of deepening reform and opening up; put forward many valuable suggestions; and played their roles as a think tank and brain trust.

7. The evaluation of reform measures, means, and achievements follows the criterion of "Three favorables"

The evaluation of reform measures, means and achievements using the criterion of "three favorables" is a piece of important experience of China's initiative of reform and opening up that has scored one victory after another after overcoming mountains of difficulties, and also it has embodied the scientific statement that "practice is the sole criterion for testing truth". The accomplishment of China's reform and opening up over 30 years has shaken the world, but there are still some shortcomings: inadequate overall coordination of reform and opening up activities; slow progress in reform of monopolized industries; insufficient transformation of government functions; lagging reform of the social management system; unresolved problems including identity and remuneration of hundreds of millions of rural migrant workers; backward production modes in rural areas as compared with rapid development of industrialization and urbanization; widening regional gap, urban–rural gap, and income gap; and excessive cost of resources and environment for rapid economic growth. It was inevitable that some problems and contradictions would occur during the unprecedented great movement of reform and opening up in China; the wheel of history rolls on in the process of overcoming these problems and contradictions. We will pay close attention to these problems and manage to get them resolved according to historical experiences. These problems are associated with reform and development, so they will be resolved only by following the criterion of the "three favorables", implementing a scientific outlook on development, deepening reform, and accelerating development.

(Published in *People's Daily*, November 17, 2008)

4 Implementing a scientific outlook on development and accelerating the reform of the social security fund operation and supervision system

Safe operation and maintenance and appreciation in value of the social insurance fund have a bearing on the fate of a nation and benefits the descendants. It is not only the material foundation and institutional carrier of social insurance, but also the institutional operation and institutional support and arrangement for safeguarding people's livelihood. The report of the 17th CPC National Congress pointed out that we will thoroughly apply the Scientific Outlook on Development, continue to emancipate the mind, persist in reform and opening up, pursue development in a scientific way, and promote social harmony to "strengthen the oversight and management of social security funds to maintain and increase their value". The basic experience of the 30 years of reform and opening up tells us that only under the Guideline of Scientific Outlook on Development can we establish an operation and regulatory system for social security funds in line with China's actual conditions and make due contributions to building a harmonious society.

1. Fully understanding the essence of a scientific outlook on development and respecting the operation law of the social security fund

A scientific outlook on development takes development as its essence; people first as its core; comprehensive, balanced, and sustainable development as its basic requirement; and overall consideration as its fundamental approach. The essence of a scientific outlook on development is of important guiding significance for establishing a sound operation and regulatory system for social security funds in China. To achieve the healthy development of the social security fund, it is necessary to establish a scientific investment operation system to maintain and increase the value of social security funds. In addition, we should mobilize various social resources to build a diversified funding system to expand the size of social funds. To reflect putting people first in the development of social security funds, we should first establish a scientific monitoring system to ensure that the safety of social security funds is paramount and the people will feel at ease. Just as what Premier Wen Jiabao said, "the social security fund is the high-voltage wire". Moreover, we should enhance the operational transparency of social security funds to the satisfaction of the people and form a consensus of the whole society so that social security funds will become a strong material foundation for social insurance and an institutional arrangement for safeguarding people's livelihood. To achieve the comprehensive and sustainable development of social security funds, we must expand the coverage of the social security system to increase the premium income. On the basis of ensuring the long-term actuarial balance of social security funds, we must fundamentally solve the sustainability of "contributory" social insurance funds and properly handle the dialectical relationship among security, liquidity, and appreciation, which should be of equal importance. We must make overall plans and take all factors into consideration in the development of social security funds. On the one hand, we must proceed from a long-term perspective and take into account the aging population trend in China. China entered the aging society as early as 2000 and the older population will peak around 2040, and the institutional arrangement of the operating system of social security funds must obey and adapt to this trend. On the other hand, we must make an overall arrangement and long-term consideration of all the pillars of the insurance system, including a pooling fund and a personal account fund of the basic insurance system, the corporate supplementary insurance fund of the second pillar and the "NSSF" operation management system with a strategic reserve nature.

The essence of the report of the 17th CPC National Congress and the Scientific Outlook on Development shows the right direction and sets the specific requirements for establishing, improving, and deepening the reform of China's social security fund operation and regulation system. Looking back into the past, we have made great achievements in the 30 years of reform and opening up. Looking forward to the future, we still face a long-term and arduous task and both opportunities and challenges in building a socialist social security fund operating system with Chinese characteristics.

2. Accelerating the legislation for the operation and regulation of social security fund with a scientific outlook on development as an overall direction

The report of the 17th CPC National Congress proposed to both "bring about a system which divides work in a rational way, fosters scientific decision-making, and ensures smooth enforcement and effective oversight" and build a service-oriented government. The social security fund operation and supervision system is the core content and most important part of the social insurance system. In building the social security fund operation and supervision system, "dividing work in a rational way" is to give full play to the role of audit supervision, financial supervision, social supervision, and supervision of banking, securities, insurance, and other functions and form a synergy supervision mechanism to jointly protect the safety of social security fund. "[F]ostering scientific decision-making" is to coordinate the subsystems of the social security system and establish a sound and scientific social security fund operation and investment system; "ensuring smooth enforcement" is to strengthen the building of the supervision team in the social security agencies at all levels and establish an effective top-down implementation system; "ensuring effective oversight" is to bring the social security fund supervision system to meet the basic requirements of the fund architecture system and vigorously strengthen the legislation to make social security fund supervision legalized, institutionalized, and standardized. The social security fund is the hub of the three fund flows of income, expenditure, and financial subsidies (fund surplus), so the social insurance fund supervision system, the social insurance system, and the agency system should constitute an inseparable trine social security system that is mutually promoting and coordinating.

In social insurance fund operation and supervision, we should supervise the social insurance funds according to the relevant laws and regulations. To ensure the safety of the funds, we must first enact the relevant law to realize the legalization of social security. From an international point of view, most countries have specific laws to regulate the supervision of social security funds and give the legal status and law enforcement power to the regulatory authorities.

Presently, the *Social Insurance Law* is being proposed. We should gradually establish a legal and regulatory framework for the supervision and management of social insurance funds based on the *Constitution* and the *Labor Law*, centering on the *Social Insurance Law* and supported by the *Regulations on Supervision of Social Security Funds, Measures for Administrative Supervision of Social Security Funds*, and other policy measures to guide and regulate the supervision of social insurance funds.

Social insurance fund operation and regulation legislation is very important. Based on the practices abroad, social insurance fund management legislation saw the most rapid developments in the recent decades. Since the 1990s, the global framework of the social insurance system has experienced the most important change since its creation. To adapt to the development trend characterized by the structural reform, the developed countries in America and Europe have established the multi-level social insurance system, adopted the partial accumulation mode, and introduced the personal account mechanism, showing different system innovation trends in the market-oriented development. For example, since the 1980s, the UK, Australia, the Netherlands, and Switzerland have taken a big step in the market-oriented legal regulation of social security funds, and the amount of social security fund assets has grown rapidly.

It is expected that the American and European countries will continue to strengthen the building of social security fund operation and regulation systems. In the meanwhile, Latin America, Eastern Europe, East Asia, and other emerging economies are also accelerating to strengthen the establishment of social security fund supervision systems. For example, due to the impact of the Chilean model, Peru, Mexico, Uruguay, and other Latin American countries and Poland, Hungary, the Czech Republic, and other Eastern European countries are accelerating to establish their competitive social insurance system and incorporate pension fund management companies, strictly enact laws and regulation and implement market-oriented operation, showing a growth trend faster than the United States and Europe, which plays an important role in stimulating and influencing other countries to implement a market-oriented reform of the social security fund. To meet the requirements and actual needs for a market-oriented reform of the social security fund, Japan, South Korea, and other East Asian countries have strengthened the operation and regulation system and adopted the market-oriented management mode emphasizing strict monitoring and restriction.

China should draw useful experience from foreign countries in establishing its social security fund operation and supervision system, and strengthen management, governance, and supervision. "Management" is to implement internal planning, organization, and control to achieve certain purposes; "governance" is to decompose functions and establish different agencies internally to achieve mutual restriction and balance and thus realize the organizational goals; "supervision" is to externally interfere with the fund management and governance structure to achieve certain goals according to appropriate authorization, including the formulation of laws and regulations beforehand and inspection in-process and afterwards. The three levels of social security fund operation and supervision have different emphases. "Management" mainly focuses on the operability and enforceability to achieve a strict enforcement of orders and prohibitions; "governance" emphasizes scientific and transparent decision-making to achieve good governance; "supervision" stresses formulation of regulation beforehand and inspection in-process and afterwards to achieve point-to-area management effect.

The purpose of making laws is to enforce them. After the laws are made, they should be strictly observed and enforced and law breakers should be punished, which is of particular importance. Laws and regulations must be strictly enforced to play their duel roles, achieve the purposes of law making, and truly regulate the supervision of social security funds. In the process of legislation for the supervision of social security funds, we should attach equal importance to law making and law enforcement, overcome the tendency to emphasize law making but ignore law enforcement, optimize the law enforcement environmental, and lay stress on law enforcement effect.

3. Establishing new ideas for social security fund operation and regulating the mechanism with a scientific outlook on development as guidance

The design concepts for the social security fund operation and regulation system abroad vary with different social security systems. But no matter what kind of system and model is adopted, China's social security fund operation and supervision system should reflect at least the four concepts of safety, responsibility, transparency, and participation.

The first is safety. Safety is the primary requirement for China's social security fund operation. Due to different financing modes of the social security systems in different countries, their risk tolerance levels are also different. In China's social security system combining social pooling with personal accounts, the risk tolerance level of pooled funds is different from that of personal account funds, so it is more complicated than the social security system of any other country and has a much stricter requirement for the safety of social security funds. In balancing safety and profitability, we would rather adopt the conservative investment strategy to ensure the safety of the social security fund. The primary task of building a harmonious society is to ensure the current payment ability of the social security system and to properly deal with the relationship between safety and liquidity.

The second is responsibility. In China's social security system combining social pooling with personal accounts, the responsibilities are mainly reflected in the fiscal responsibilities of pooled funds and the fiduciary responsibilities of personal account funds. Pooled funds assume the important responsibility of social mutual aid and have certain redistributive effects, and the state financial department should take some financial responsibilities. The account funds should assume the fiduciary responsibilities after being invested in the financial markets, including the government's fiduciary responsibilities for the insured persons. That is, before the insured person reaches the statutory retirement age, the balance of personal contributions is separated from the account holder, which is largely attributed to fiduciary factors, and the government agencies, as the trustees, should increase the yields, reduce administrative costs, and provide quality services to the public. The account funds with a strong nature of savings need a more mature capital market as their sound investment environment, and even the government should provide a portfolio to be selected by the account funds and a safe compensation mechanism when necessary.

The third is transparency. Transparency mainly involves two aspects. On the one hand, an annual reporting system should be established for social security funds according to good, international practice, including all information on the operating management structure, investment orientation, accounting and financial planning, open operation in the execution and reporting process of fund revenue, and expenditure and results of independent auditing of fund accounts. On the other hand, the level of retirement benefits should have good expectations so that the insured persons can rationally balance their lifetime consumption to create favorable conditions for the change of growth pattern.

The fourth is participation. Participation mainly refers to public participation in social security fund monitoring, which is both the necessary requirement for the social security fund regulation system and the inevitable result of building a harmonious society. Social security fund is a government-managed public good and a special public fund, therefore the extent of disclosure of important information on social security funds such as revenue and expenditure, costs, and future ability to pay is much higher than that of other general public funds. This requires broad participation of relevant stakeholders in an appropriate manner to acquire general social recognition and strong political support.

The above four design concepts for social security fund operation and supervision is an organic whole, each of which is to ensure the realization of the other three, and only by effectively combining the four design concepts can we achieve the ultimate goal of effective social security fund supervision.

4. Establishing the basic ideas for the social security fund operation and supervision system with a scientific outlook on development as criterion

As China's social security funds are mainly pooled at the county/city level, fund management is decentralized, the number of pooling units is up to more than 2,000, many adverse conditions exist for fund supervision and management, and there is a serious contradiction between the supervisory responsibilities and intensity of the central and local governments for fund management behaviors. This decentralized management has resulted in an increase in fund management level and in opportunities of local governments' illegal intervention. When the overall objective of social security funds is inconsistent or even conflicts with the goals of the local government, the government of the pooling area may abandon the goal of social insurance to ensure the realization of the goal of the local government. The central regulatory authority can only provide operational guidance to and has no jurisdiction over the local social security departments. In summary, China's social security fund supervision system has problems in the following three aspects.

First, the supervision system lacks legal support. Due to the lagging legislation for social security fund operation and regulation in China, there is no unified national legislative and institutional framework or constraint, there is no clear and defined regulation, and the responsibilities and functions of the regulatory authorities, administrative departments, and operators are unclear and overlapping. The laws enacted by the ministries and commissions tend to place undue emphasis on local interests, the phenomena of buck-passing and differing policies are very common, and some illegal and criminal acts such as misappropriation and diversion of social security funds can hardly be timely corrected and punished. The collection, management, operation, and payment of social security funds involve the labor and social security, finance, taxation, banks, post offices, hospitals, pharmacies, financial institutions, and other departments and institutions, with many management links and great difficulties in coordination. Any department or institution related to the funds may commit acts in violation of law or discipline, so fund supervision is an increasingly arduous task. This shows that legislation for social security fund supervision in China is lagging behind, the supervisory authorities and functions lack the support from the relevant laws and regulations, which has greatly affected the supervisory authoritativeness and effectiveness.

Second, the operation of social security funds is not open. At present, China's social security funds mostly find their way into negotiated bank deposits and government bonds. Under this "traditional" investment strategy, the financial, labor and social security, auditing, and other government departments will undoubtedly play the dominant role among the provincial-level regulatory authorities for social security funds. Although a limited number of business representatives, workers' representatives, experts, and professionals are absorbed, they can hardly play an independent role in actual operation. On the coordination of concrete matters, it is a common practice that social security fund supervision is treated as general public funds and still handled in accordance with the work procedures of government departments rather than as an integral part of the market. This is inimical to improving the yield rate of social security funds and the replacement rate of retirement income, to the sustainable development of social security funds, and to the prosperity and development of the capital market.

Third, institutions are not independent. Almost all provinces have established social security fund supervision authorities, but these authorities are generally not entirely separated from the administrative departments and operation agencies. There exists the phenomenon of "one identical institution under multiple different names", which will inevitably lead to unclear rights and responsibilities and limited supervision power. Supervisory functions exist in name only, and the administrative departments are in fact responsible for social security fund operation and supervision. That is, the leaders in charge of the provincial government are responsible for this task, and we have not yet formed a relatively independent, market-oriented, social security fund operation monitoring system.

Due to the problems in the above three aspects, social security fund operation and supervision in China is likely to be affected by the short-term behaviors of local government and departmental interests, social security funds are likely to be misappropriated and diverted to other purposes by local authorities, and so there exists management risks for social security funds.

According to China's actual conditions and international experience, we should take into consideration the following factors when establishing China's social security fund operation and regulation system:

(1) We should establish the social security fund operation and supervision system suitable for China's social security system combining social pooling with personal accounts based on the spirit of the 17th CPC National Congress and guided by a scientific outlook on development to form a sound regulatory system with clear responsibilities, full coverage, and strong regulation effect.

(2) We should establish the institutional framework for the social security fund operation and supervision system that matches the partially accumulated social insurance system, the social security fund management system, the social security fund investment operation mechanism, and the historical and cultural traditions in China.

(3) The social security fund operation and supervision system should meet the four objective requirements: supportable, powerful, effective, and rational. "Supportable" is to establish a sound legal system for fund supervision and improve the law enforcement capacity; "powerful" is to create a set of

advanced IT tools to improve the supervisory efficiency; "effective" is to explore ways to increase the value of the funds while protecting their safety and integrity; "rational" is to absorb the advanced experience of foreign countries.

(4) Social security funds in China should include a pooled fund, a personal account fund, a supplementary insurance fund, and a national social security fund. Among them, the pooled fund is mainly used for current benefit payments, and there are very strict safety and liquidity requirements for the fund; the supplementary insurance fund (mainly including enterprise annuity and occupational annuity) is accumulative and subject to the management of specialized institutions and complete market-oriented operation; the personal account fund is both a basic insurance fund and accumulative fund, which will gradually be invested in the capital markets; the national social security fund is the strategic reserve fund for the social security system in China; and the National Council for Social Security Fund is responsible for its management and investment operations. These four funds have different categories, so we should set different parameter requirements and take different operational and supervisory means for each.

(5) The social security fund operation and supervision system should consist of the four subsystems of beforehand supervision, in-process supervision, afterwards supervision, and on-site supervision. "Beforehand supervision" refers to prevention, forecasting, early warning, and other systems; "in-process supervision" mainly refers to the use of the supervisory system and measures to protect the healthy daily operation of the funds; "afterwards supervision" is mainly to investigate, punish, and redress illegal acts; "on-site supervision" is to carry out the inspection, training, and guidance of social security fund operation and supervision of social security funds in the operation in the entities or areas together with the audit, finance, and other related departments on a regular or irregular basis.

5. Facing new challenges and opportunities in social security fund operation and supervision from the perspective scientific outlook on development

According to the requirements of the Scientific Outlook on Development, to realize the goal of establishing the basic social security system covering both urban and rural areas by 2020 proposed at the 17th CPC National Congress, we are facing several challenges as follows in social security fund operation:

First, we should actively explore ways to establish a social security fund operation and management system in line with China's rapid economic growth. As we all know, China's five basic insurance funds totaled only RMB80 billion Yuan in 1998 and has currently exceeded 1.1 trillion Yuan, with an average annual growth of around 20%.[1] This is a result of both a wider coverage and sustained rapid economic growth. In the past 10 years, China was among the world's fastest growing economies with the economic growth rate of around

10%. Many economists predict that China will usher in a period of rapid economic growth, which will pose challenges to the operation and management system for the rapidly accumulated social security funds. In such a case, we should actively explore ways to establish a social security fund operation and management system to adapt to the expanding size of the social security fund. For example, we should improve the pooling level as soon as possible to prevent the "fragmentation" tendency of the social security fund operation and management system, continuously improve the level of centralized management, and strengthen its ability to "manage risks" and resist the risk of an aging population on the basis of enhancing the safety of the funds.

Second, we should actively explore ways to establish a social security fund investment management system in line with the social situation of the high average wage growth rate. Rapid economic growth has brought about the rapid growth of the average wage and improvement of people's living standards. For example, in the past 10 years, China's average wage of workers grew at a rate of more than 13.6% from 7,479 Yuan in 1998 to 24,932 Yuan in 2007. However, the rapid growth of the average wage brought a new problem to the social security fund investment and management system: how to improve the yield of social security fund and how to maximally avoid and prevent the "devaluation risk" caused by the rising CPI and other factors. Particularly, as the pilot program for fully funding personal accounts was carried out in 11 provinces, the personal accounts that have been fully funded currently have 80 billion Yuan,[2] which has posed a severe challenge to the investment management system for both personal accounts funds and pooled funds. It is a severe challenge to actively explore ways to establish a social security fund investment management system and improve the yield of social security funds.

Third, we should actively explore ways for the investment of the funds of different social insurance schemes. The five basic insurance schemes include pay-as-you-go, accumulated, defined benefit, and defined contribution. There are different requirements for determining the liquidity, risk tolerance, minimum rate of return on investment, and other factors for the funds of different natures. For example, there are great differences between the unemployment insurance fund and old-age insurance fund, and there are also great differences between the pooled fund and account fund in the old-age insurance fund. This requires investing social security funds in diversified and pluralistic ways to meet different requirements of the funds of different natures and actively explore investment management modes suitable for them to maximize returns.

Fourth, we should continue to optimize the investment environment for the insurance funds under the macro situation of building a harmonious society and highlighting the importance of improving people's livelihood. As we know, in the past decade, the basic old-age insurance replacement rate has constantly decreased from 77.2% in 1998 to 48.3% in 2007, and the gap between retirement benefits of workers of government organs and public institutions and enterprises is also expanding. To this end, the central government decided in 2007 to further raise the basic old-age pensions for enterprise retirees for another three consecutive years. Enterprise annuity as supplementary pension is an important part of the multi-level and multi-pillar social insurance system. Great achievements have been made in the market-oriented operation of enterprise annuity, but it is still necessary to continuously optimize the investment environment for enterprise annuity, vigorously develop the annuity market, and improve its yield to make due contribution to the benefit level and diversity of enterprise retirees.

Fifth, we should gradually establish a social security fund supervision system to realize the goal of establishing a social security system covering both urban and rural areas by 2020. The 17th CPC National Congress proposed to establish a social security system covering both urban and rural areas by 2020. Under the premise that other conditions remain unchanged, China's total GDP will reach 70 trillion Yuan or so in 2020, and with the continuous expansion of the coverage of the social security system, the balance of accumulated deposits of the social security fund will be more than 10 trillion Yuan, accounting for 15% of China's GDP in 2020. Due to such a huge balance of accumulated deposits of the social security fund, it is necessary to establish an effective social security fund supervision system. First, we should formulate and improve the relevant laws and regulations for social security fund supervision as soon as possible, tighten up the legal system, and carry out supervision according to law; second, we should constantly replenish the supervision team to adapt the mounting size of the funds; third, we should establish a supervision system mode suitable for the five basic insurance and multi-pillar pension fund operations; finally, we should establish a multi-sectoral collaboration and joint management of regulatory supervision system, especially for account funds and corporate pension funds with market-oriented investment operations, and draw lessons from the financial crisis taking place in the United States to nip such a crisis in the bud.

Sixth, we are facing a severe scarcity of supervisory resources. We should strengthen the building of the social security fund supervision team. The social security system as a macro system includes a number of subsystems, such as financing system, supervisory system, premium collection system, investment system, benefit distribution system, and supervisory system. In the past 10 years and more, the total accumulated amount of social security funds was not very large in size, there was no enormous pressure from ROI, and so we could still get on with the management level and supervisory resources. But the balance of accumulated deposits has increased by more than 20% each year since 1998 to reach 300 billion Yuan in 2001 and surged by more than 100 billion each year since 2001. Faced with such a rapid growth rate and such a scale, the former social security fund supervision resources prove definitely inferior and the original regulatory model is not viable.

From the perspective of regulatory resources, 1.5 trillion Yuan of social security funds (plus the enterprise annuity and the national social security fund) is a huge challenge for the central regulatory authority with only a dozen staff members, and the regulatory burden is seriously overloaded ("regulatory load" refers to the ratio of the number of officials of the regulatory authority and the number of insured or assets). By assets, each regulatory official in Europe manages 10 billion Euros on average, and foreign regulatory authorities are mostly independent. A comparable example is the National Commission for the Retirement Savings System (CONSAR) in Mexico. CONSAR has 170 staff members, each managing US$320 million. By the number of the insured, Chinese regulators each manage 10 million insured persons, which is hundreds of times higher than abroad. The State Administration for Pension and Retirement in Argentina, as a comparable example, has 183 staff members, each managing 51,000 among the 9.3 million insured persons in the country. The asset scale of social security funds will expand exponentially in the future, which requires increasing regulatory resources, enriching the regulatory teams at all levels, and improving the regulatory strength to adapt to the development of the social security system.

(Published in *China Population Science*, Issue 6, 2008)

Notes

1 The Ministry of Human Resources and Social Security, the National Bureau of Statistics: 2007 Human Resources and Social Security Development Statistics Bulletin, the website of the former Ministry of Labor and Social Security, http://www.molss.gov.cn/gb/zwxx/2008–06/05/content_240415.htm.
2 Ibid.

5 Deepening the reform and regulating the fund sources and behaviors of government investment

The *Decision of the CPC Central Committee on Some Major Issues Concerning Building a Socialist Harmonious Society* puts forward the principles to be followed:

> We must adhere to reform and opening up. We shall continue in the direction of reform to develop the socialist market economy. In order to meet the requirements for economic and social development, we shall promote economic, political, cultural and social restructuring and innovation. We shall open wider to the outside world, make the reform decisions more scientific and the reform measures more coordinate so as to establish more dynamic, more efficient and more open systems and mechanisms.

We should practically follow the guiding principles set out at the 6th Plenary Session of the 16th Central Committee of the CPC in economic work based on the characteristics of social and economic development at the current stage. Since the beginning of 2006, China's economy has operated steadily on the whole, but we are still faced with some problems such as an overly high growth rate and the scale of investment in fixed assets. From the stages of economic development in China, the current high investment rate has its objective inevitability, but based on the historical experience and international comparison, the investment rate in China has hit a record high in recent years and is significantly higher than those in developed countries and other developing countries. The high absolute growth rate of investment, the high investment-to-GDP ratio, and the undue role of investment in boosting economic growth are likely to result in overheating the economy in whole or in part.

Hungarian economist Janos Kornai analyzed the issue of recurring investment expansion in the socialist economies in *Economics of Shortage*. Kornai argues that investment is expansion-driven. He said, "In a socialist economy, no enterprise or nonprofit organization does not want to get investment, and there is insatiable demand for investment. Investment hunger is persistent. Once a completed investment temporarily satisfies the investment hunger, new hunger will soon produce and it will be more intense than ever". A drive towards expansion can cause investment hunger which will be sufficient to change a system to a shortage economy. After nearly three decades of reform, China's socialist market economy system has been basically established, and the problem of shortage has been basically solved. Especially for the general consumer market, due to the enormous involvement of the non-state-owned economy and fierce competition, the supply has exceeded the demand. However, Kornai pointed out that "investment hunger" persists, and the government-led investment impulse is still strong, which is largely related to the incomplete transformation of government functions, especially the investment funding sources and irregular investment behaviors of the local governments.

Relevant data show that in China's current investment structure, the state-owned and local projects still account for a large proportion. In the first half of 2006, state-owned investment accounted for 46.5% of the investment in fixed assets in urban areas and local investment 89.6%. Thus it can be seen that although the institutional background we are facing has changed profoundly, government investment is still an important mode. Undoubtedly, government investment plays a positive role in improving the infrastructure and boosting economic growth. However, it should be noted that, as the forming mechanism for government investment impulse is not eradicated (such as the pressure of performance appraisal on local governments and the role of the administrative cycle etc.), the investment funding sources and irregular investment behaviors of the local governments have resulted in a strong investment impulse of government, and the strong guiding role of government investment has also led to investment expansion in the whole society, which is the root cause for the high investment rate.

First, leveraged construction is quite a common practice for local governments. As the funding sources and scope of government investment are not currently strictly defined and there is no sound supervision mechanism in this aspect in China, some local governments blindly pursue GDP growth or vanity and image projects aiming at changing the images of the cities. They concocted various pretexts, bundled loans through various investment and financing companies, borrowed heavily from the banks, and invested heavily in infrastructure construction and in constructing training centers, plazas, green spaces, office buildings, and so on through a guarantee by the government or by the local people's congresses. These loans are large, long-term loans, and the current leadership does not care whether it has ability to repay in future. These loans have stimulated investment, but brought huge financial risks.

Second, the huge land transfer fees received by local governments are mainly used for investment in fixed assets. Research data show that the total revenues from land transfer in the whole country was 587.5 billion Yuan in 2005. In some areas, the net revenues from land transfers have accounted for over 60% of the extra-budgetary government revenues, and in some areas, the revenues from land transfers even have exceeded the fiscal revenues of the government. Land transfer fees have become the largest source of extra-budgetary disposable income of local governments. At present, land transfer fees are not subject to strict supervision and management because they are not fully included into the budget, so they have become the main source of funding for some local governments to blindly expand the urban construction scale and launch vanity and image projects.

Third, special funds are used illegally for construction. In recent years, major and serious criminal cases involving the illegal use of special funds have occurred from time to time. The occurrence of the "Shanghai Social Security Funds Corruption Case" has not only uncovered the corruption of illegal uses of various special funds to seek high returns and bartering power for money of some local governments and officials, but also reflected the regulatory loopholes.

Fourth, the government-led "undue investment attraction" makes it difficult to achieve the macro-control target of inhibiting the overly high growth of fixed asset investment. Undoubtedly, investment attraction plays an important role in local economic development. However, the local governments competed to promulgate the preferential policies to attract investment, which has become an unignorable problem in economic development. Some local governments regard investment promotion as the "top priority" in economic work, and some even take it as a political task to attract investment, assign it to various departments and officials at all levels and include it in the important indicators for performance appraisal. To attract investments, industrial land was transferred at low prices and even at "zero price" in some areas, which has not only led to vicious competition and redundant construction, but also paid a heavy price in terms of land, taxation, and resources etc.

Fifth, leveraged expansion of universities under soft constraints. Recent years have witnessed a surging wave of borrowing for colleges and universities behind the "admission expansion", the building of "university cities", and the implementation of the 211 Program. According to investigation, colleges and universities each have borrowed money ranging from 300–500 million Yuan to over 1 billion Yuan in the borrowing boom, and the total amount of money borrowed by colleges and universities in the country amounted to several hundred billion Yuan. In June 28, 2005, Li Jinhua pointed out at the 16th Plenary Session of the 10th National People's Congress that the results of audit investigation of the financial revenues and expenditures of the 18 universities affiliated to the ministries and commissions under the State Council in 2003 showed that many universities carried out large-scale basic construction, resulting in heavy debt burdens. By the end of 2003, the 18 universities totaled 7.275 billion Yuan, an increase of 45% over 2002, of which the debts incurred for basic construction accounted for 82%. In this borrowing boom, universities, banks, and local governments jointly sought interests. Just as what the experts said: "Local governments transferred land at a low price to support education and borrowed money from the banks to support the expansion of colleges and universities, which has not only solved the problem of inadequate education funding, but also boosted the GDP growth and the real estate market in the surrounding areas brought by the expansion of universities". The banks have also found a relatively "safe place" for the surplus deposits under the implicit government guarantee. Leveraged expansion of universities has become an important factor boosting local investment, but also led to a repeated occurrence of arbitrary charge collection in universities, and the banks are also facing huge bad debt risks.

Sixth, the transformation of profits into fixed asset investment by state-owned enterprises has also contributed to the high rate of investment. Since the fiscal tax reform in 1994, according to the relevant requirements, state-owned enterprises have not handed over their profits to the state. At that time, these requirements had their own rationality. But in recent years, state-owned enterprises are increasingly concentrated in oil and gas, electric power, telecommunications, railway transportation, tobacco, and other monopoly industries, and their monopoly profits are amazing. In the first nine months of 2006, the total profits of state-owned and state-holding enterprises amounted to 508.6 billion Yuan, among which oil and gas enterprises contributed 269.5 billion Yuan, accounting for 53%. The profits of state-owned enterprises, especially the monopoly profits of state-owned monopoly enterprises, mostly found their way into new investments, except for the part that was used as working capital and internal welfares. As the profits are completely disposed by enterprises independently, and investment orientation and investment decisions were made randomly, waste and loss resulted due to erratic decision-making.

In addition, the slightly expansionary fiscal policies have further stimulated the investment impulse of local governments. The proactive fiscal policies that had been implemented for six consecutive years since 1998 played a positive role in stabilizing China's economy, maintaining the economic growth rate, improving the infrastructure construction in the western regions, and adjusting the regional layout of productivity. However, the negative effects of the long-term implementation of the proactive fiscal policies cannot be ignored. In particular, with the expansion of the scale of government investment, the role of government in economic operation has gradually increased, while the economic regulation role of the market has gradually weakened. In recent years, the expansionary fiscal policies have been replaced by the prudent fiscal policies, but due to the rigidity of fiscal spending, we still need to continuously allocate huge funds for the subsequent construction of the previous treasury bond projects, so the fiscal policies retain some expansionary characteristics. The amount of long-term treasury bonds for construction issued was reduced from 80 billion Yuan in 2005 to 60 billion Yuan in 2006, and the allocations from the central government budget for general development increased by 10 billion Yuan. The allocations from the central government budget for capital construction reached 115.4 billion Yuan, remaining basically the same as in 2005. The fiscal policies with slightly expansionary characteristics have enhanced the investment impulse of local governments.

Historical experience shows that every drastic change in China's economic growth was closely related to the scale of investment. The government-led investment expansion played a prominent role in every investment fluctuation. We should correctly understand the characteristics of government investment during the transformation of the market economy system. Its guiding role is likely to lead to the rapid expansion of the overall scale of investment in the whole society. Therefore, we should follow the principles and requirements of the CPC Central Committee on building a socialist harmonious society, apply a scientific outlook on development, and make use of economic, legal, and administrative measures to continuously deepen the institutional reform, solve the problem of soft budgetary constraints institutionally, and eliminate the mechanism for forming the government investment impulse. We should strengthen the management of the use of various special funds, earnestly study and solve the issue of leveraged construction by universities and public institutions without considering their ability to repay the debts, and earnestly study and solve the issue of handing over the rational use of profits by state-owned and state-holding enterprises in the monopoly industries. We should regulate the investment funding sources and investment behaviors of the governments, state-owned enterprises, and public institutions from all aspects to ensure a reasonable growth of investment in fixed assets and promote stable and rapid economic development.

(Published in *the Journal of CASS*, November 2006)

6 The layout adjustment of the state-owned economy to be combined with economic restructuring

It is a drastic move to combine the layout adjustment of the state-owned economy with strategic economic restructuring. The layout adjustment of the state-owned economy and strategic economic restructuring are two important strategic tasks in China's economic reform and development. There is a close link between them, and they must be closely combined, planned on the whole, and implemented step by step so that they mutually coordinate and reinforce.

To meet the requirements of the socialist market economy and new situations, we should strategically adjust the layout of the state-owned economy to optimize resource allocation. Starting from scratch, the Chinese state-owned economy has experienced the development process from small to large and from weak to strong and made great achievements. It has made great contributions to laying and strengthening the foundation of China's socialist economy, promoting China's economic development, improving people's material and cultural life, and consolidating and strengthening national defense to ensure the smooth progress of China's reform and opening up. But for a long time, the state-owned economy has also been plagued with a number of problems such as an overstretched battle line, a huge number and wide distribution of enterprises, irrational organizational structure, low production capacity utilization rate, and low economic returns. These conditions cannot meet the need for the establishment of a socialist market economic system and do not adapt to the new situation of deepening the opening up. Therefore, we should, in the spirit of "doing certain things and refraining from doing other things", strategically adjust the layout of the state-owned economy through corporate restructuring, establishing joint ventures, invigorating small businesses, developing conglomerates, merger, bankruptcy, and other measures. We should focus on key areas to achieve optimal allocation of state-owned assets, improve the overall quality of the state-owned economy and increase the control over the state-owned economy.

With economic development, we have bidden farewell to the shortage economy, the problem of food and clothing has been basically solved, and the consumption demand and structure of urban and rural residents has changed dramatically. In recent years, the contradiction of irrational economic structure is increasingly serious. In terms of industrial structure, overcapacity is a serious problem in the processing industry, low-level repetition is a common phenomenon, the development of the high-tech industry lags behind other sectors, the transformation of traditional industries is still an arduous task, and the development of the tertiary industry also fails to meet the requirements of economic development. In terms of organizational structure, the industrial concentration is low, the level of specialization and cooperation between enterprises is on the low side and the size and structure of enterprises is unreasonable. In terms of ownership structure, we are still faced with an arduous task in adjusting the layout of the state-owned economy. We are faced with many new problems in the development of the collective economy and still have plenty of work to be done in the development of the self-employed and private businesses and other forms of ownership, especially in the slow development of the self-employed and private businesses in the central and western regions.

In terms of the regional economic structure, the phenomenon of structure convergence is increasingly serious, and the gap between the eastern and western regions is widening. In rural areas, we are also faced with an arduous task in agricultural and rural economic restructuring. The main tasks of strategic economic restructuring are as follows: to optimize the industrial structure and upgrade the agricultural, industrial, and service sectors; to reasonably adjust the productive forces and promote the coordinated development of regional economy; to actively and steadily promote urbanization and strive to achieve positive economic interaction between urban and rural areas; to strengthen infrastructure construction; to strive to improve the ecological environment; and to achieve sustainable development. Therefore, strategic economic restructuring is to optimize the allocation of social resources and improve the overall quality of the national economy in the new situation.

At a certain stage of economic development, there is a mutual adaptation relation between different forms of economic organization and industrial structure. The state-owned economy has played a significant role in accumulating social resources to conduct large-scale investment and developing technologically leading industries and industries of strategic importance to achieve the overall economic balance, laying a solid foundation for China's modernization. But in the meanwhile, the state-owned economy also has problems such as unreasonable industrial structure and regional layout. By combining the layout adjustment of the state-owned economy with the strategic economic restructuring, we can foster strengths and circumvent weaknesses and give full play to the advantages of the state-owned economy in capital-intensive and technology-intensive industries with significant scale effects and market stability and fully exert the roles of the non-state-owned economy in the labor-intensive industries with low capital and technical threshold, poor scale effects, and fierce competition. This requires combining the strategic adjustment of the layout of the state-owned economy with the strategic economic restructuring.

There are some common tasks in the layout adjustment of the state-owned economy and the strategic economic restructuring. Bankruptcy and closing are the only options for enterprises that cannot find any market for their products, entail long-term losses but are not expected to turn round, and suffer from the drying up of resources. Small coal mines, refineries, cement works and glass factories, and small thermal power plants that have been wasting resources, or are technologically backward, are manufacturing poor-quality products, and have caused severe pollution should also be forced to go bankrupt or close down. Only in this way can we solve the problem of low-level blind and overlapping construction. We should energetically advance the development of high and new technology sectors and the technical transformation of traditional industries to achieve an upgrading of products and industries. We should improve the organizational structure of enterprises through reorganization, coalition, and merger of enterprises to foster industrial conglomerates and groups. We must uphold and improve the basic economic system, with public ownership playing a dominant role and diverse forms of ownership developing side by side. We should speed up the infrastructure construction and layout readjustment of old industrial bases to fully exert their role in supporting economic development. The harmonious, regional urban and rural economic development should be achieved to narrow the economic development gap among the eastern, central, and western regions and between urban and rural areas. These common tasks also require combining the layout adjustment of the state-owned economy with the strategic economic restructuring to exert the role of the layout adjustment of the state-owned economy in driving economic restructuring and the role of economic restructuring in guiding, stimulating, and consolidating the layout adjustment of the state-owned economy.

We must give full play to the role of market mechanisms in the layout adjustment of the state-owned economy and the strategic economic restructuring. Undoubtedly, to accomplish these two strategic missions, the roles of governments at all levels must be fully exerted, including proposing and formulating the strategic goals, strategic priorities, procedures, and concrete policies and ensuring that these policies can be seriously implemented in practice. Especially, factories and mining enterprises that produce low-quality products, waste resources, cause serious pollution, or are not equipped with the conditions for safe production should be forced to close down; outdated equipment, technologies, and processes should be phased out; a portion of surplus production capacity should be cut; enterprises that entail long-term losses but are not expected to turn around or are insolvent should be forced to go bankrupt; and the government should play a decisive role. In addition to the economic and legal means, the government can also adopt the necessary administrative measures. However, under the socialist market economy, enterprises are the basic units of the national economy and main market entities, and the tasks of the layout adjustment of the state-owned economy and the strategic economic restructuring will ultimately be assigned to and accomplished by enterprises. Particularly the things in a range of autonomy of enterprises must be decided by enterprises independently.

The structure, mechanism, and quality of enterprise will directly affect the process and actual results of the two strategic adjustment missions. Presently, the vast majority of enterprises in China are large-scale backbone state-owned enterprises and state-holding enterprises. They have played an important role in economic development and technological progress in China and international competition participation and will also exert a dominant role in the strategic economic restructuring. Therefore, we must combine the two strategic adjustment missions with the establishment of a modern corporate system, the change of a corporate operation mechanism, the improvement of the quality of enterprises, and with the cultivation and improvement of the market system and form an independent mechanism for enterprises to optimize the allocation of resources and make a sensitive response to market demands and their changes so as to give full play to the guiding role of the market mechanism to enterprises and the basic role of the market in the allocation of resources.

Institutional innovation and technological innovation is the driving force and source of the layout adjustment of the state-owned economy and the strategic economic restructuring. Institutional innovation can break the shackles of the old system, make the relations of production more adaptable to the development of productivity, provide an institutional guarantee for the liberation and development of productivity and create a good mechanism for the layout adjustment of the state-owned economy and the strategic economic restructuring to smoothly push forward these two strategic adjustments and consolidate the achievements made. Therefore, the reform in planning, finance, banking, investment, science and technology, state-owned asset management, and other areas should be deepened to improve and strengthen macro-control. To deepen the reform of state-owned enterprises, enterprises should truly become corporate and market entities that enjoy full management authority, assume sole responsibility for its profits and losses, seek self-development and self-reliance, and truly change their operation mechanism. Medium- and large-size state-owned enterprises should, based on the direction of reform of establishing a modern corporate system, accelerate corporate restructuring, promote the shareholding system reform, and improve the corporate governance structure. A number of trans-regional, cross-sectoral, cross-ownership, and transnational conglomerates and groups with well-established main business, high management level and strong competitiveness should be fostered. A variety of ways should be taken to speed up the restructuring of SMEs and enliven SMEs.

Technological innovation is a source for maintaining the vitality of the national economy. Without the support from technological innovation and progress, it is difficult to get rid of the low-level, low-efficiency dilemma in the layout adjustment of the state-owned economy and the strategic economic restructuring to reach the purpose of adjustment. The layout of state-owned economy and the economic structure should be optimized and the overall quality of the national economy should be improved with technological innovation as the driving force. To actively promote the high-tech research of strategic significance, efforts should be focused on making breakthroughs in key areas such as information technology, biotechnology, new materials technology, and aerospace technology, and the independent innovation capability should be improved in some high-tech fields related to the lifeline of the national economy and safety. Major projects in high and new technology sectors should be implemented to improve the conversion rate of scientific and technological achievements. Technological renovation of traditional industries should be accelerated to promote technology and product upgrading in traditional industries.

Information technologies must be widely applied in various industries to accelerate the process of IT application vital to the national economy. Generic technologies, key technologies, and other technologies supporting structural adjustment and industrial upgrading must be energetically developed. Enterprises are the principal participants of technological innovation, and it is imperative to establish a system of technological innovation with enterprises as its center. Enterprises, especially large enterprises, should establish their research and development centers and increase input in research and development. Enterprises should develop products with their independently owned intellectual property rights and increase technology reserves. Industrial production, research, and development of technology should be combined, technological personnel in scientific research institutions and institutions of higher learning should be encouraged to join enterprises or enterprise groups, development and spreading of applied technologies should be intensified, and input into experimental application of new technologies should be increased so as to facilitate the translation of technological developments into real, productive forces. Effective measures should be taken to promote the development of science and technology enterprises.

(Published in *Qiushi*, Issue 4, 2001)

7 Studying and solving several major strategic issues in reform and development

After decades of hard work, especially sustained and rapid development since the reform and opening up, the shortage of goods we have long been plagued by has been basically solved. The Chinese society is shifting from subsistence to a comfortable life, the economic system from a planned economy to a socialist market economy, and the economic growth pattern from extensive mode to intensive mode, with tremendous progress having been made. But some new situations have also appeared and brought many new problems. We must study and solve some major issues of holistic and long-term significance to better promote the modernization drive in China.

1. Speeding up economic restructuring

With the rapid development of science and technology and a solution for the commodity shortage, China's economic structure is increasingly irrational, which has become one of the important factors restricting further economic development. Therefore, it is imperative for China to carry out economic restructuring and promote industrial upgrading and structural optimization. Comprehensive plans should be made and efforts should be intensified in this regard, otherwise we will get stuck in a passive situation in the fierce international competition in the future. Based on past experience, coupled with the revelation of the economic restructuring research in the world with the mega-merger as an important symbol, China's economic restructuring should focus on addressing the following issues in the next three to five years or longer:

The irrational industrial structure resulting from overlapped and blind construction in the past should be adjusted to realize the rational allocation of production capacity. Industries and product structures that are overly decentralized or fail to establish an economy of scale should be adjusted to address the problem that all enterprises, large or small, have an all-inclusive organizational structure; to develop specialized collaborative relationships; and to improve the economy of scale of enterprises and the degree of organization of the industry. Industries that are technologically backward, cannot find any market for their products, or have excess production capacity should be diminished to reduce waste of resources. Old industrial bases should be transformed and their economic structure should be adjusted with new technologies and new equipment. Preferential investment policies should be given to encourage investment in the western regions to reduce the economic development gap between the eastern and western regions and promote the rational distribution and coordinated development of regional economy. Up-to-date technologies and high technologies should be used to upgrade the traditional industries, and the development of high-tech sectors should be accelerated to improve the technical contents and added value of products. The development of the tertiary industry should be vigorously promoted. Particularly, effective policies and support measures should be adopted to accelerate the development of information, culture, education, tourism, community and intermediary services, and the relationship between technology-intensive and capital-intensive sectors and labor-intensive sectors to facilitate the continuous improvement of labor productivity and to alleviate the employment pressure.

In short, we should uphold the direction of the development of industries, products, technologies, enterprises, and employment structure etc. towards socialized mass production to meet the industrial and technological development requirements of the world. In the process of structural adjustment, we should give full play to the basic role of the market in resource allocation and avoid by all means returning to the old way and old model of the planned economy. In the past, overlapped construction was generated as a result of the planned economy, and if such an unscientific approach was adopted continuously for structural adjustment, the existing irrationality problem can hardly be resolved, but on the contrary, new problems may be created.

2. Improving the technological innovation capacity

In an increasingly fierce global market competition, to enhance the potential of China's economic development, improve the ability to withstand a variety of risks, and ensure long-term economic development, we must rely on scientific and technological progress and innovation and enhance the capacity of independent innovation to achieve a leap forward in technological development. This requires us to accomplish two tasks: to transform traditional industries by using modern technologies and to develop high-tech industries to claim the commanding heights in science and technology. These two tasks are the main direction of scientific and technological progress in the current and future period of time. To this end, we should actively promote the establishment of the national knowledge innovation system and select the right areas that can play a driving role in promoting economic and social development, safeguarding the national security, and improving the productivity and overall national strength so as to concentrate our forces to tackle the key scientific and technological problems and strive for breakthroughs in key areas and crucial links. Particularly, we should strengthen the innovation in the basic and key high-tech sectors, accelerate the development and application of high technologies in high-tech industries, especially emerging industries of strategic importance, and actively cultivate new economic growth points. In the meanwhile, we should accelerate the transformation of scientific and technological achievements into practical productive forces.

Enterprises are the principal participants in technological progress and technological innovation. Enterprises are the main bases both for research and development and for promoting the transformation of scientific and technological achievements into practical, productive forces. Large enterprises and conglomerates should establish their technological development centers and increase capital and personnel input to develop more new technologies and new products to meet the needs of development of enterprises.

We should accelerate the reform of research institutes so that they can be merged into and cooperate with enterprises in different forms or restructured into separate, new-type scientific and technological development enterprises with strong vitality and become the vital new forces in technological progress and innovation. In the meanwhile, social capitals should be guided to participate in scientific and technological development, and a risk investment mechanism for the development of high-tech sectors should be established to gradually form a diversified technology investment system.

Competition in the key high-tech sectors is competition for talents. We should attach great importance to the training of personnel, particularly the training of young technological professionals, and create better living and working conditions for them to grow and exert their abilities. We should establish the scientific and technological personnel incentive mechanism so that technology, management, and other production factors can participate in distribution, and provide ample rewards to scientific and technical professionals who have made outstanding contributions to give full play to their initiative and creativity. We should improve the policies to attract talents and encourage overseas students and talents to return home to work or serve the motherland in other forms. We should encourage scientific and technical professionals to establish technology enterprises, further cultivate and develop the good practice of respecting knowledgeable and competent people and advocating innovation, and create a favorable social environment for technological innovation and advancement.

3. Narrowing the income gap

We have formed a diversified distribution pattern with distribution according to work as the main form, "egalitarianism", "egalitarian practice of everybody eating from the same big pot", and other phenomena in distribution have been mostly overcome, but there are still some serious issues that need to be solved promptly. These serious issues include the following: (1) there is a tendency of over-inclination to individuals in income distribution in some place and social sectors, which has affected the country's fiscal revenue and resulted in unfair distribution; (2) although the uniform standards have been established for the wages of the workers of the party and government organs at all levels, there are some non-standard and even chaotic phenomena in the actual implementation and there are also enormous "gray" incomes; (3) the income of the employees of privately or individually-owned businesses and private and foreign enterprises and other high-income earners have not been adjusted effectively and there are big loopholes; and (4) the phenomena of misappropriating public properties and getting high illegal incomes by tax evasion and fraud, power-for-money deals, and other means are serious in some places, departments, and industries. In addition, the income gap between urban and rural areas and between the eastern and western regions should not be ignored.

If not timely addressed, the problems in income distribution will evolve into political and social problems. If all departments, local authorities, and entities set up their own "small exchequers" in income distribution, this will give birth to departmental protectionism and local protectionism, and the corruption phenomena such as "taking countermeasures against the decisions of the higher authorities" and ineffectiveness in implementation of the decisions will appear. Deng Xiaoping has always attached great importance to the issue of income distribution and proposed to encourage some people and some regions to get rich first. When some people and some regions get rich first, others will be brought along, and, through this process, common prosperity of the entire population will be gradually achieved. China is now in the primary stage of socialism and will remain so for a long time to come. We must uphold and improve the basic economic system, with public ownership playing a dominant role and diverse forms of ownership developing side by side, which requires upholding a diversified distribution system with distribution according to work as the main form.

On the one hand, we must adhere to the principle of giving priority to efficiency with due consideration to fairness and optimize the allocation of resources to promote economic development and maintain social stability. On the other hand, we must continue to improve the living standards of workers, peasants, intellectuals, and cadres with constant economic development to gradually achieve common prosperity. To implement a diversified distribution system with distribution according to work as the main form and combine it with distribution according to production factors will inevitably lead to differences in income among members of the society. There are always differences among things, and the society is developing in contradiction. To solve the issue of income distribution, we should abandon "egalitarianism" and the "egalitarian practice of everybody eating from the same big pot" in distribution and introduce the competition mechanism and actively promote development according to the requirements for development of the socialist market economy. In addition, we must take appropriate policy measures to protect lawful incomes, regulate excessively high incomes, ban illegal gains, and try to increase the incomes of low-income people and retirees to prevent excessive disparity in income distribution and fully arouse the enthusiasm of cadres and masses.

4. Promoting coordinated regional economic development

We must take effective policy measures and give play to the advantages and favorable conditions of all regions to promote the coordinated development of regional economy, which is the essential requirement for fully realizing the modernization and achieving common prosperity. After over two decades of reform and opening up, the economic strength in the coastal regions has been improved, and there are favorable conditions for economic development in these regions, so they should seize the opportunity to continuously accelerate the development and strive to realize modernization. This will help ensure and enhance China's economic strength and financial resources. After the national strength and financial resources have been enhanced, we can better support the development of the central and western regions. According to Deng Xiaoping's strategic thinking of "Two Overall Situations", the CPC Central Committee has made a major decision on promoting the development of the western regions.

The western regions cover a vast area and are rich in natural resources. There is a huge potential for development and a huge market potential. Implementing the strategy for the development of the western regions has a direct bearing and important practical and historical significance in expanding domestic demand and stimulating economic growth; on the national unity, social stability, and consolidating border defense; and on the coordinated development of the eastern and western regions to achieve common prosperity. We must combine the strategy for the development of the western regions with the three-step strategic goal, combine the support of the state to the western regions with the role of the market mechanism, combine the economic development of the western regions with the promotion of social progress, and combine the development with the opening up policy. In promoting the development of the western regions, we must focus on constructing transportation, telecommunications, energy, and other infrastructures and give special importance to the rational development and effective utilization of water resources; carry out comprehensive management and improve the eco-environment; adjust the industrial structure and promote the development of competitive industries to transform the resource advantages into economic advantages; give priority to development of science and technology and education; and strengthen personnel trainings to improve the quality of workers.

5. Attaching importance to ecological and environmental protection

With more rapid economic development, more importance should be attached to ecological and environmental protection. This is an important matter related to China's sustainable development and has a bearing on the benefits of future generations, so we must always take it seriously on a strategic level, correct the wrong practice of "economic development takes precedence over governance" and adhere to the policy of laying equal stress on economic development and environmental protection.

China has a vast territory, but limited arable lands, with arable land per capita far below the world average. We must make use of land resources economically and rationally, and more importantly, we must resolutely curb the phenomenon of indiscriminate use and destruction of arable land. To reduce soil erosion, curb the expanding land desertification and prevent flooding, we must gradually implement the policies for returning farmland to forests, returning the grain plots to husbandry, and returning reclaimed water from lakes back to its original state. We must attach great importance to rational exploitation and utilization of mineral resources, firmly close down small ore mining and processing enterprises that destroy resources, pollute the environment, and are without security measures. Although floods have always been a big worry for the Chinese nation, water shortages are increasingly becoming the constraints for agricultural, economic, and social development in China. In addition to attaching great importance to the protection and rational use of existing water resources, we must also step up to solve the problem of a severe shortage of water resources in some areas. The general requirement is to attach equal importance to utilization and conservancy, especially water conservation. We must proceed from a long-term perspective, give an overall consideration, make scientific comparisons and careful planning, and timely launch some major water conservancy projects.

Large cities are densely populated areas. Some large cities in China are facing the problem of severe pollution, so we must resolutely carry out comprehensive pollution control in these large cities and strive to achieve good results as soon as possible to improve the quality of life for residents in large cities and improve the economic development conditions.

6. Facing up to the challenges of economic globalization

Due to the rapid development of science and technology, the number of transnational companies is increasing and their influence is expanding. This has caused a change in investment mode and international division of labor; accelerated globalization in trade, investment, production, and finance; created closer international economic ties; and intensified international competition. Economic globalization is a double-edged sword, which has provided new conditions for the development of all countries and brought varying degrees of risks. Developed countries have significant advantages in the process of economic globalization, while the majority of developing countries, due to the low level of economic and technological development, are relatively disadvantaged as they have lower ability to make use of the opportunities and prevent risks. If their policies are improper, their economy will be at risk and under impact.

Therefore, faced with the economic globalization, we must actively participate and know how to protect ourselves and strive to transform unfavorable factors into favorable factors. We must grasp the new opportunities and face up to the challenges after joining the WTO and formulate the policies and measures to foster strengths and circumvent weaknesses. We must strongly develop a number of conglomerates with trans-regional, inter-trade, cross-ownership, and transnational operations and give full play to their important role in participating in international competition. In the development of a state-owned economy and a collective economy, we must encourage the development of a non-state-owned economy, make use of their flexible mechanisms, and give to play their active role in processing and foreign exchange-earning. We must give priority to improving the quality and competitiveness of enterprises; put in place effective practical measures for product development, technical processes, and management; and make effective use of the WTO rules to maximize protection of the development of emerging industries and infant industries in China.

7. Safeguarding our national financial and economic security

The Asian financial crisis warned us that we must pay special attention to safeguarding our national financial and economic security when further opening up the economy to the outside world. We must persist in reform and opening up, establishing a socialist market economy as our established policy, we must unswervingly push forward the great cause, and, in the meanwhile, we must seriously explore measures and methods to safeguard our national financial and economic security in the new situation of further opening up to prevent any eventuality. To this end, we must further promote the reform of commercial banks, improve the system, reduce bad debts, and block sources of losses; continue to rectify the financial order, further screen and reorganize the local financial institutions, and crack down on financial crimes; further improve the securities market and strengthen supervision; strengthen the training of modern financial management personnel and education on basic financial knowledge for leading cadres to raise the awareness of financial risks; and strengthen research on derivative financial products and financial instruments to take precautions beforehand. We must strengthen the research and management of debts, with particular emphasis on the research and management of external debts. The amount of external debts must match with our country's economic aggregate and fiscal revenue, and the types of external debts must have a reasonable structure. We must strengthen the management of foreign exchanges, improve the foreign exchange settlement system and the convertibility system under the current account and take a prudent attitude over the open capital market. In the adjustment of the strategic layout of the state-owned economy, the state-owned economy must keep the control position in the key enterprises in the sectors involving national security, natural monopoly sectors, sectors providing important public goods and services, pillar sectors, and high-tech sectors and give play to its leading role in the entire national economy. We must ensure that the intellectual property rights of some key, high technologies that have a bearing on the lifeline of the national economy are firmly held in the hands of the state.

(Published in *Guangming Daily* on May 2, 2000)

8   Reforming and improving the urban social insurance system in China

Social insurances cover many contents. In this paper, we mainly discuss how to improve the old-age, medical, and unemployment insurance systems to create a good environment for the reform of state-owned enterprises.

1. Conflicts between the traditional social insurance system and the establishment of a modern enterprise system

The traditional social insurance system in China is the product of the planned economy and also an important supplementary measure for the minimum wage system for workers in urban enterprises, especially state-owned enterprises, so as to vigorously promote the industrialization process in China. It has the characteristics of non-equity, non-efficiency, and non-socialization and does not comply with the requirements for establishing the socialist market economic system characterized by "emphasizing efficiency but not at the expense of equity". Its operating mechanism does not meet the objectives and direction of market-oriented reform of China's economic system. The entrepreneurial social insurance system, in particular, is contradictory to and conflicted with the reform objectives of establishing a modern enterprise system.

(1) Sharp contradictions and conflicts between the traditional social insurance system and the establishment of a competition mechanism for survival of the fittest

The main objective of the reform of state-owned enterprises is to improve the operational efficiency of enterprises and the national economy. Market competition, as the primary mechanism and means for optimizing the allocation of resources and improving the operational efficiency of the economy, will inevitably lead to violent differentiation among different enterprises. Enterprises meeting the market competition requirements will develop and grow, while those not meeting the market competition requirements will shrink, go bankrupt, and be forced to exit the market. Survival and death of enterprises is an inevitable result that the market mechanism acts on its own. Only in this way can we achieve a reasonable flow of resources and improve the operation efficiency of the economy. It is estimated that the state-owned enterprises that are insolvent or entail long-term losses but are not expected to turn around account for around one-third of the total state-owned enterprises, but the state-owned enterprises take on a series of responsibilities for their employees such as social insurance. In the absence of a socialized social insurance system, if these enterprises are forced to make large-scale redundancies or go bankrupt, their employees will lose the insurance and security provided by the enterprises, which will directly affect their lives and social stability. Lagging behind of the reform of the traditional social insurance system makes it difficult to establish a modern enterprise system, deepen the market-oriented reform, and makes it even harder for the enterprises to make redundancies or go bankrupt.

(2) The traditional social insurance system and the market have become the main bodies in allocation of labor resources, and there exist sharp contradictions and conflicts in the enterprise management mechanism promoting the rational flow of personnel

Due to the traditional employment system and the social insurance system, a sizable surplus of labor exist in state-owned enterprises, which is the so-called phenomenon that three employees share the job that can be accomplished by two employees. It is estimated that the state-owned enterprises in China have 20–30 million redundant employees. The marginal productivity of labor in a number of state-owned enterprises is even negative. According to a survey by the Economic Development Research Institute of East China Institute of Chemical Technology, around 78–98% of state-owned enterprises are plagued with the severe and lingering problem of labor surplus. In other words, almost all state-owned enterprises are facing the problem of labor surplus to varying extent.

Labor employment rigidity means having a solid allocation of labor resources. It blocks the two-way choice channel between individual workers and enterprises at the institutional level, and more seriously, it cannot undergo self-regulation in the adjustment of the industrial structure and the change in the supply and demand structure. According to the survey, the flow of the labor force into or out of state-owned enterprises each year before the reform accounted for only 3–4% of the total employees of enterprises. However, even in the lifetime employment system in Japan, 13% of the workers leave the enterprises where they work each year. The survey data show that the enterprises with a structural imbalance of labor force account for 63% of the enterprises that have been sampled. According to the survey by the Institute of Economic reform, enterprises have vacancies for skilled personnel. The redundancies are concentrated in auxiliary and unskilled workers. According to the structural redundancy calculations approximately accounting for 15–20% of the total number of employees on active duty, at least 15 million laborers nationwide need a two-way choice or restructuring.[1] The contradiction between vacancy and redundancy among enterprises is mainly caused by the lack of a corresponding adjustment mechanism after the primary distribution precipitation, and the contradiction between vacancy and redundancy inside enterprises is caused by the imbalance and lack of control of lifetime laborers in quality indicators. Without unemployment and mobility, there is no driving force to improve people's working enthusiasm and there is no further stimulus to enrich their own human capital. As a result, the dummy labor resources will form a huge social waste.

The traditional employment system and social insurance system have also resulted in the aristocratic phenomenon for workers in state-owned enterprises. On the one hand, there was serious unemployment in enterprises, but these workers behaved "aristocratically" due to employment insurance, and they picked easy jobs and shirked the hard ones, preferring the light workloads to the heavy ones and were unwilling to do the hardest and dirtiest jobs; on the other hand, the enterprises employed a large number of external temporary or contractual workers to fill those abandoned vacancies. In 1988, this kind of complementary workforce had accounted for about 3% of the total workforce and was growing at a rate of 9% forecast at that time.

The traditional social insurance system could hardly adapt to the development of a large number of non-state enterprises and was inimical to promoting the flow of laborers to non-state-owned enterprises. When the state-owned economy occupied a dominant position, as the wage system and grades were uniform in the whole country, the transfer of a handful of workers was also carried out in the national economy. This contradiction did not exist. But after 20 years of reform, great changes have taken place in the ownership structure in China. The proportion of the state-owned economy has greatly reduced. Taking the industry for example, during 1978–1988, the proportion of sales revenue decreased from 80.9% to 29.1%, total assets fell from 92.0% to 63.4%, and the employees fell from 60.7% to 24.5%.[2] This shows that more and more people were employed by non-state-owned enterprises, and non-state-owned enterprises have become the main places to absorb the workforce. The traditional social insurance system obviously could not cover these types of enterprises and their employees. It also caused a lot of obstacles to the mobility of personnel. In particular, there still exists identity discrimination for workers in this social insurance system, and it also violates the principle of fairness of the modern social insurance system. When people were worried about the impact of the unemployment of workers of state-owned enterprises on social stability, they failed to consider that the unemployment of the employees of other types of enterprises was also a serious problem. The market economy system without social insurance is clearly unstable.

(3) Sharp contradictions and conflicts between the sociality and mutual aid of the requirements of the traditional social insurance system and the modern social insurance system

As there are great differences among enterprises, especially between old and new enterprises, the insurance premium burdens are too light for some enterprises but too heavy for some others. This problem was not particularly serious in unified revenue and expenditure conditions, but it became very serious in the market-oriented reform. Many old enterprises had a large proportion of retirees, which caused serious burdens on the enterprises. Some enterprises owed the wages of their retirees and their medical expenses could not be reimbursed. This not only affected social stability, but also lead to the inability of enterprises to equally participate in market competition. This directly affected the restructuring of enterprises and hindered the reform of the enterprise system. Based on the basic principles of social insurance, the traditional social insurance system has lost the income redistribution function of social insurance. At the same time, it has lost the social adjustment and mutual-aid functions, which greatly reduced the ability of enterprises and workers to resist risks.

2. Progress and performance of the reform of social insurance system

(I) Progress and performance of innovation of social insurance system

The *Decision on Establishing a Unified Basic Pension Insurance System for Enterprise Employees* issued by the State Council in July 1997 and a number of important policies issued later affirmed the efforts made by different regions in exploration, summarized the experience of the pilot reforms and established the basic framework of the old-age insurance system.

1   Establishing the innovation principles and objectives of the old-age insurance system. That is, by the end of this century, a basic old age insurance plan shall be established, which will be adapted to the requirements of the socialist market economic system and be suitable for the various types of urban employees and individual employees. The sources of contributions will be from various channels, protection will be multi-tiered, the social pooling of funds will be combined with personal accounts and liability, obligations will be coordinated, and administration and provision of services will be socialized.[3] It includes the following contents:

(1) Wide coverage – the coverage will be expanded gradually from the workers of state-owned enterprises to workers of all types of urban enterprises and self-employed workers.

(2) Multi levels – mainly include basic old-age insurance, supplementary pension insurance for enterprises, and individual savings-funded endowment insurance. The basic old-age insurance is designed to guarantee the basic living needs of retirees, the supplementary pension insurance for enterprises mainly reflects the differences in distribution according to work, regional differences, and differences in the economic efficiency of enterprises; the individual savings-funded endowment insurance mainly aims to meet the security needs of workers at different levels and standards.

(3) Four unities – unified system, unified standards, unified management, and unified use of funds.

(4) Two combinations – combine social mutual aid and personal protection and combine equity and efficiency.

(5) Two correspondences – rights correspond to obligations, and the level of security and economic development corresponds to affordability.

(6) Two separations – separate administration from fund management and separate executive bodies from oversight bodies.

2   Establishing a mixed (partial accumulation system) funding mode. Presently, there are three main funding modes in the old-age insurance systems throughout the world: pay-as-you-go mode, full accumulation mode, and mixed mode. Before the unified mode was established in 1997, there were extensive debates in theory or in practice over what kind of funding mode would be selected by the basic old-age insurance system in China. In 1995, the central government promulgated simultaneously two reform schemes for the local governments to select and gave the local governments the rights to modify the implementation schemes as the compromise response to the debates. Therefore, before the unified funding mode was established, these three modes were actually in the test process.

The piloting of the three modes has accelerated the reform of the old-age insurance system and increased the probability of success for the system integration by the central government. However, different pilot programs, inconsistent contribution rates of personal accounts, uneven burdens on enterprises, low levels of social pooling, and other practical problems have also created many institutional barriers for establishing a unified, national, basic old-age insurance system. In July 1997, the State Council issued the *Decision on Establishing a Unified Basic Pension Insurance System for Enterprise Employees*, which clearly stipulates that the funding mode of "combining social pooling with personal accounts" should be implemented in China's basic old-age insurance system and requires other pilot modes to transform to the mode in a given time period.

3   Implementing seven unities for operation of the basic old-age insurance

(1) Unified contribution rate for personal accounts. Personal accounts should be established based on the contribution rate of 11% of the wages of employees, and all individual contributions should be included into the accounts, and the remaining balance should be transferred from the contributions of enterprises.

(2) Unified accounting interest rate. The accounting interest rate of personal accounts should be determined by the time deposit interest rate and wage growth rate.

(3) Unified contribution base. The total wages of employees should be their contribution base, and enterprises should pay contributions

based on the sum of the contribution bases of individual workers. For employees whose average monthly salary is above 300% of the local average in the previous year, the 300% above the local average should not be included in the contribution base; for those whose monthly salary is below 60% of the local average in the previous year, the base shall be 60% of the city average.

(4) Unified contribution rate. The contribution rate of enterprises should be no greater than 20% of their total payroll, and the contribution rate of individuals should be no less than 4% of their basic wages in 1997 and should increase until ultimately reaching 8%.

(5) Unified pension calculation and distribution method. Pension includes basic pension and personal account pension. The monthly payment of basic pension insurance accounts for 20% of the average monthly salary of the staff and workers in the previous year, and the monthly payment of personal accounts is the amount accumulated in the personal accounts divided by 120. If the cumulative premium payment period is less than 15 years at the time the individual participating in basic pension insurance reaches the statutory retirement age, he or she is not entitled to collect basic pension, and the amount in the personal account should be paid in a lump sum.

(6) Unified transitional method. Employees who started working before and retired after the implementation of the unified system are entitled to an additional pension for the transitional period. Usually, the additional pension for the transitional period is calculated based on average indexed monthly earnings (AIME) multiplied by a certain percentage of the contribution time of the employee (1.0–1.1%) to properly compensate for the working age and contribution time before establishing the personal account.

(7) Unified merger time. It would be generally accomplished in 1997 and no more than 1998 in some provinces.

4   Sectoral pooling was included in local pooling. Sectoral pooling and local pooling were two different forms of the old-age insurance system in the 1980s when the reform was piloted. Sectoral pooling was initially implemented in railway and other four sectors. In 1993, it was expanded to another six sectors including transportation upon approval by the State Council, thus forming the pooling pattern of 11 sectors. In the framework of the unified basic old-age insurance system implemented in 1997, sectoral pooling was separated from social pooling, the management cost expenditure was increased, and the sectoral-local competition for the level of insurance benefit caused new interest frictions and overwhelmed enterprises. In 1997, No. 26 Document issued by the State Council clearly specified the reform direction of including sectoral pooling in local pooling after basically realizing pooling at provincial level in the whole country. In August 1998, the central government officially initiated the handover

procedure. So far, the segmentation of the trap and block of the social insurance system that existed for a long time officially came to the end.

5   Provincial-level pooling was implemented for the basic old-age insurance system. Implementing provincial-level pooling was an important move to enhance the financial capacity and institutional security of the existing old-age insurance scheme. In 1991, a total of 13 provinces and municipalities in China implemented provincial-level pooling. But still more than half of the provinces did not implement provincial pooling, among which most regions still implemented pooling at the lower county or city level. At the same time, the regions that had implemented provincial-level pooling still had the problems such as irregularity and imperfectness, and even provincial-level pooling existed only in form. In 1998, the increasingly serious pension arrears throughout the country forced the State Council to decide to implement provincial-level pooling in the whole country by the end of the year. According to the arrangement of the central government, provincial-level pooling was implemented in two steps: the first step was to establish provincial-level regulating funds by the end of the year, and the ratio of regulating funds was determined by the provinces themselves based on the principle of ensuring that the pensions were paid on time and in full; the second step was to realize three unities in three years – unified enterprise contribution rate, unified management and use of funds, and unified intra-provincial social insurance management system.

(II) Progress and performance of reform of the medical insurance system

1   Establishing the objectives and principles of the reform of the basic medical insurance system. The basic goal is to establish a social medical insurance system in line with the requirements of the socialist market economic system based on the affordability of financial departments, enterprises, and individuals to meet the basic medical needs of workers. The basic principles are as follows: (1) the level of the basic medical insurance treatment must be consistent with the level of economic development; (2) the basic medical insurance follows the principle of universality to cover all urban employers and employees; (3) the premiums of basic medical insurance are shared by enterprises and employees, and the self-responsibility spirit is stressed through the personal account mechanism design; and (4) the basic medical insurance follows the principle of localization and socialization.

2   Establishing the funding mode combining social pooling with personal account

(1)   The basic medical insurance system adopts the funding mode combining social pooling with personal account, and the funds of basic medical insurance consist of pooling funds and personal account funds. The contribution rate of employers is about 6% of their total payroll, and the contribution rate of employees is generally 2% of their salary income.

The premiums of basic medical insurance paid by individual workers go entirely into their personal accounts. The premiums of basic medical insurance paid by employers are divided into two parts: about 70% is used to establish the social pool fund, and about 30% is diverted into personal accounts. Based on this calculation standard, the funds diverted into personal accounts amount to 3.8% (2% + 0.06 × 30%) of total wages, and the pooling fund will reach 4.2% (0.06 × 70%).

(2) Social pooling funds run parallel to personal accounts. The range of payment of social pooling funds and personal accounts are specified. Social pooling funds and personal accounts are managed separately.

(3) The entry threshold and cap line for social pool funds were established, and the constraint mechanism for the paid use of the pooling fund was designed. The decision provides that the minimum standard for paying the pooling fund is 10% of the average annual wage of employees in local areas, and the maximum payment limit is about four times that of the average annual wage of employees in the local areas. The medical expenses below the minimum standard should be paid by personal accounts or at the own expense of individuals. Those above the minimum standard and lower than the maximum limit should be paid by social pooling accounts, but individuals should also bear a certain proportion of the expenses.

(4) Establishing the framework for the government to regulate social pooling funds and personal account funds. The basic medical insurance funds are managed under special financial accounts and should be regarded as ear-marked. The social pooling funds should follow the principles of tax-and-spend, spend-and-tax and balance of income, and expenditure. The expenses of social insurance administration authorities should be included into the fiscal budgets of local areas, and the practice that the expenses of social insurance administration authorities are directly withdrawn from the funds was changed. The sound budget, financial accounting, and auditing systems should be established for the social insurance administration authorities. The medical insurance fund oversight organization in which the government, the insurer, the insured, the trade unions, experts, and representatives participate should be established to strengthen social supervision.

(5) A number of important measures should be taken to promote medical and pharmaceutical reform. To keep in line with the international practice, we should formulate the scope and standards of basic medical insurance within the institutional framework of basic medical insurance, including the Catalogue of Drugs for Basic National Medical Insurance and treatment items and standards for medical service facilities, to ensure the balance of payments of the basic medical insurance funds, and to determine the scope of medical services the funds can afford. Using designated medical institutions and drugstore management is practiced for the basic medical insurance. The

designated medical institutions and hospitals are determined by social health insurance regulatory agencies, and their rights, responsibilities, and obligations are specified through contracts. In the meanwhile, the competition mechanism is introduced from the medical service market and the drug supply market for basic medical insurance; the insured can choose a number of designated medical institutions for medical treatment or purchase drugs in a number of designated drug-stores with prescriptions. When medical institutions carry out an economic operation analysis and cost accounting, they should separate the management and accounting of medical services and drugs, and on this basis, they can reasonably raise the prices for medical treatment to reflect the value of their medical services and superb medical skills and completely correct the existing misconducts such as no separation between "medical services" and "drugs" and change the situation wherein a hospital subsidizes its medical services with overly expensive drug prescriptions,

(III) Establishment and performance of the unemployment insurance system

1   The unemployment restriction was broken conceptually so that the unemployment insurance system has become an extremely important social security system to support the institutional transformation. In the process of market-oriented reforms, China is facing unprecedented pressure in open unemployment and hidden unemployment. In response to the practical challenges of institutional transformation and social development, the unemployment insurance system is in the early stages of expansion, the implementation of the non-institutionalized re-employment projects, and the establishment of institutionalized unemployment insurance system in various provinces has effectively alleviated the urban poverty resulting from unemployment and laying-off workers. Presently, many provinces have generally established the regulatory agencies for unemployment insurance that separate the functions of government from those of institutions and initially formed the vertically and horizontally combined operation system integrating premium collection, unemployment registration, job training, job recommendation, self-help production, and payment of unemployment benefits.

2   The objective of wide coverage of unemployment insurance in the scope of the urban economy has been initially realized. In recent years, the coverage of unemployment insurance for urban workers has been expanded gradually from employees of state-owned enterprises to workers of enterprises with other forms of ownership, and the number of insured has increased from 95 million in 1995 to 110 million in 1996, an increase of 16%.

3   The contribution rate of unemployment insurance has been increased, and the amount of unemployment insurance fund is increasing. The

contribution rate of enterprises has been increased from 1% to 3% of their total payroll, and that of individual workers is 1% of their total wages. Since 1990, the revenue and expenditure of unemployment insurance is expanding, and Table 3.8.1 reflects this trend.

4   The unemployment insurance policies were implemented to promote re-employment of unemployed and laid-off workers. In the process of economic restructuring, China advocates positive unemployment insurance policies. Positive unemployment insurance policies mean that the existing unemployment insurance system should have two kinds of institutional ability, namely to guarantee the basic needs of the unemployed through the issuance of unemployment allowances and to positively promote the re-employment of the unemployed through taking a number of important public policy measures. The re-employment promotion ability of the existing unemployment insurance system is mainly reflected in the following three areas: first, the system has established the payment conditions conducive to re-employment. One of the qualifications for the unemployed who may receive unemployment insurance compensation is that the unemployed must have undergone unemployment registration and have requested new jobs, and the unemployment insurance compensation generally reduces by 10% for the unemployed who has been out of work for more than a year; the payment of unemployment insurance compensation will be ceased for the unemployed who has refused twice the jobs recommended by the relevant department or agency without justified reasons. Second, the state has established a complete re-employment promotion system integrating job-transfer training, job recommendation, employment guidance, and self-help production. Third, the system implements tax incentives for employers to encourage them to provide more jobs for the unemployed.

Taking the unemployment insurance system of Dalian in our survey as an example, to ensure the positive unemployment insurance policies, apart from paying unemployment benefits, a large proportion of the unemployment insurance funds are used for job recommendation, employment training and self-help

Table 2.8.1 Revenue and Expenditure of Unemployment Insurance in China during 1990–1997 (except 1992) (100 million)

Year	Total revenue	Total expenditure	Accumulated balance	Year	Total revenue	Total expenditure	Accumulated balance
1990	7.43	1.87	19.20	1995	35.3	18.9	61.6
1991	8.37	2.5	25.07	1996	45	27	79.6
1993	16.3	9.3	38.7	1997	46.8	36	90.4
1994	18	11.4	45.2				

Data Source: Ma Guonian and Liu Taiqin, *Unemployment and Unemployment Insurance*, published by Enterprise Management Press, 1997.

production. During 1986 to June 30, 1997, the unemployment insurance agency in Dalian collected a total of 372.15 million Yuan in unemployment insurance premiums and spent a total of 186.37 million Yuan, in which unemployment benefits amounted to 31.89 million Yuan, accounting for 17%; one-time regular relief funds amounted to 68.23 million Yuan, accounting for 36%; anti-poverty funds amounted to 7 million Yuan, accounting for 4%; medical expenses, funeral expenses, and maternity allowances amounted to 1.42 million Yuan, accounting for 0.8%. The above expenses for meeting the basic needs of the unemployed accounted for 57.8 % of total expenditure. The expenses for job-transfer training, job recommendation, and self-help production amounted to 30.05 million, 16.66 million, and 4.69 million Yuan respectively. The expenses for these three items to support reemployment of the unemployed totaled 51.4 million Yuan, accounting for 28% of total expenditure.[4]

3. Measures to improve the social insurance system

(I) Reasonably setting the contribution rates of enterprises and individuals in the existing social insurance system

In the process of establishing a modern, new social insurance system, how to set reasonable and appropriate contribution rates is mainly subject to the following restrictions: (1) the level and stage of economic development. Different stages of economic development decide different income levels of residents, and different income levels decide different contribution rates. The latter is the dependent variable of the former. (2) The target benefit levels of the new system. Higher target benefit levels inevitably decide higher contribution rates. Compared with the "high levels of benefits" of the traditional social insurance system, the existing system sets the "basic level" of the insurance benefits, which no doubt only needs modest contribution rates. (3) The affordability of enterprises. In the modern market economic society, enterprises are the main contributors of the social insurance system. The contribution rate beyond the affordability of enterprises will greatly harm the economic competitiveness of enterprises, so the practice of raising the levels of insurance benefits through "killing the goose that lays golden eggs" is obviously short-sighted.

If the above principles reflect the innovation process of Chinese social insurance system, then one of the main problems in the existing system is that some enterprises are unable to afford the increasingly heavy contribution rate. Based on the contribution rules of the existing system, the contribution rate of enterprises is 29% (20% for pension insurance, 6% for medical insurance, and 3% for unemployment insurance). However, due to the serious imbalance of pension burdens and redundant burdens in state-owned enterprises, especially medium-sized state-owned enterprises, the contribution rate of some enterprises is actually up to about 50%. The high contribution rate forces some enterprises to refuse to pay the premiums. The survey of the World Bank shows that the compliance rates of enterprises has reduced from 90% in the early 1990s to 70%

and 80% in 1994 and 1995 respectively. Moreover, so far this downward trend has shown no sign of rebound. The refusal of enterprises to pay the premiums poses a direct threat to the fund mobilization capacity of the existing system, thus increasing the risks of the system.

The refusal of enterprises to pay the premiums is mainly due to the unevenness in social insurance premium burdens among SOEs, especially the unevenness in pension burdens and medical burdens for the middle and old-age workers. In the premise that the central government does not bear the implicit social insurance debts, this situation can hardly be changed. Another problem related to this is the high administrative costs of the existing system. According to statistics, the local unemployment agencies withdrew 1.252 billion Yuan as management fees from the pension funds in 1994, an increase of 25.83% over the previous year, and the per capita expenditure of management fees was 33,800 Yuan, an increase of 12.67% over the previous year. In the same year, the expenditure of management fees of unemployment insurance agencies was 225 million Yuan, an increase of 38.89% over the previous year.

High management fees inevitably require high contribution rates. The problem is that within the existing government regulatory framework, it is difficult to maintain and increase the value of social insurance funds, but on the contrary, social insurance funds are suffering heavy losses. In 1994, the balance of accumulated deposits of social security funds was 37.699 billion Yuan, of which only 8.198 billion Yuan was used to purchase government bonds, accounting for 21.74% of the total balance, and a large part of the balance of funds were misappropriated for investment for other uses such as investment in capital construction and securities, with a considerable part being unrecoverable. The legitimate loss and illegal misappropriation of social security funds also makes it impossible to reduce the contribution rate of enterprises by maintaining and increasing the value of the funds.[5]

The above circumstances show that the existing system needs a longer process of reform; otherwise the systematic risks may make the social insurance system become the riskiest institutional arrangement.

(II) Expanding the coverage of old-age insurance

As far as the coverage is concerned, there is potential to expand. According to the relevant data, by the end of 1996, the coverage rate of the basic old-age insurance for urban workers was 78.4%, of which the coverage rate for state-owned enterprises (148.39 million employees) was 95.15%, the coverage rate for collective enterprises (29.57 million employees) was 51.47% and the coverage rate for enterprises with other ownership forms was 27.5%.[6] State-owned enterprises have the largest number of retirees, and their coverage rate is also the highest. Enterprises of other ownership forms (i.e. foreign-invested enterprises and private enterprises) were mostly established after 1980, so they have only a small number of retirees and their coverage rate is lowest. This shows that the basic old-age insurance has not been enforced as a legal system in all urban enterprises. According to statistics, the total number of workers who did not participate in the pooling by the end of 1996 was 24.14 million, and there were 1.16 million retired workers. Calculated based on the average wage of 6,145 Yuan and the average contribution rate of 23.58% in 1996, after the workers of these enterprises participate in the insurance, an additional pension fund of 35 billion Yuan will be collected. Each retired worker received 5,765 Yuan as pension benefits on average in 1996, and 6.7 billion Yuan was spent addition-ally for 1.16 million retired workers; a balance was struck between income and expenditure, the balance of newly-added funds was 28.3 billion Yuan, equiva-lent to 3.2% of the total payroll of 908 billion Yuan in 1996. That is to say, the withdrawal rate of basic pensions could be reduced by 3.2% in 1996. But this is the situation in which fund accumulation was not taken into consideration and pension income that year was used for expenses. Based on the pension expendi-ture in 1996, the proportion of the funds counted into the mutual-aid part ensures that the payment of pensions must account for 20%, but the unified system requires that the proportion of the funds counted into the mutual-aid part should be 17%, so there was still a 3% funding gap under provincial-level mutual aid. After the coverage was expanded, this part of the funding gap could be filled. The coverage was expanded in 1997 but the progress was very slow. In 1997, the coverage rate for employees of state-owned enterprises, collective enterprises, and foreign-invested enterprises and private enterprises was 96.6%, 53.8%, and 32% respectively.[7] When the contribution rate of unemployment insurance was increased, its coverage rate must also be expanded. The medical insurance system was also faced with the same problem after it was launched.

(III) Improving the collection rate

An important reason for the widening of the fund gap is unsatisfactory contri-bution. In 1996, the average collection rate of the premiums of old-age insur-ance was 92.5%, down 0.8% over 1995. It further decreased to 90.7% in 1997 and 82.7% in the first half of 1998.[8] By the ownership form, the collection rate of state-owned enterprises was 90.38% in 1996, down 3.22% over the previous year, indicating the poor performance of state-owned enterprises and their difficulty in affording for the insurance. The collection rate of collective enterprises was 90.11%, down 0.99% over the previous year, and that of enter-prises of other ownership forms was 96.04%, up 3.44% over the previous year, indicating that the affordability of enterprises of other ownership forms were better than state-owned enterprises. There was also great potential to increase the collection rate of unemployment insurance.

(IV) Improving the management of pooling accounts and
personal accounts

The two-line management system for revenue and expenditure of old-age insurance and medical insurance funds has been operated by establishing social pooling accounts and personal accounts. But there still exist many problems, especially for the management of pension funds. From the perspective of the relationship between social pooling accounts and personal accounts, there are three circumstances: first, social pooling accounts and personal accounts are mixed in use (see Fig. 2.8.1), and when the funds of social pooling accounts are insufficient, the funds accumulated in personal accounts will be used. Second, social pooling accounts and personal accounts are completely separated (see Fig. 2.8.2) and managed and operated by independent agencies respectively, and the two have no relationship except market behaviors (such as lending relationship). Third, the two are managed by an agency, but independent agencies are established for separate accounting (see Fig. 2.8.3).

Under the first circumstance, the establishment of personal accounts is only to make clear the amount accumulated in the personal account for each person, and the pension can be calculated and paid based on the accumulated amount. As the two parts of funds are mixed in use, in such cases, it is impossible to indicate the balance of social pooling accounts and the total amount accumulated in personal accounts, and when the funds in the current social pooling accounts

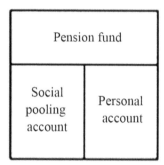

Fig. 2.8.1 Management Mode 1

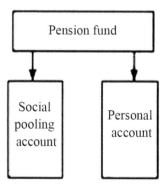

Fig. 2.8.2 Management Mode 2

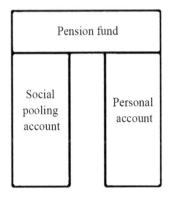

Fig. 2.8.3 Management Mode 3

are insufficient, the size of the gap of social pooling funds and the size of the "empty accounts" in personal accounts will inevitably be concealed, which is inimical to the government's pooling arrangements. In the second circumstance, social pooling accounts and personal accounts are completely separated and managed and operated by independent agencies, which is conducive to clearly specifying the sizes and responsibilities of social pooling accounts and personal accounts and conducive to the government's planning and arrangements of funds and solving the fund gap. But as relatively independent management and operation agencies should be established, it is necessary to establish a coordination mechanism for the two when pensions are paid. In addition, as old-age insurance is basic insurance, the risks for the independent operational of personal accounts must still ultimately be borne by the government. Under the third circumstance, it is required to achieve independent operation and management of personal account funds and mutual coordination between revenue and expenditure of pension funds, but poor management will lead to the first circumstance.

The management modes of social pooling account and personal accounts are shown in Figs. 2.8.1–2.8.3.

In handling the relationship between social pooling accounts and personal accounts, people have different points of view. Some people believe the existence of an empty account can be allowed and the payment crisis can be solved through the intergenerational transfer of an empty account. As personal account funds are operated through accumulation year by year and there is no need for lump-sum payments, there will be no payment difficulties before all the funds accumulated in personal accounts are spent (before 2008). The funds accumulated in personal accounts during this period can be used to fill the periodical gap of pension funds through borrowing or other means to achieve the intergenerational and intra-generational transfer of empty accounts. In such case, it is not necessary to separate social pooling accounts from personal accounts. Personal accounts are now in fact equivalent to risk reserves used to deal with the mutual-aid part and play the part of personal accounts of retirees. That is say, compared with pay-as-you-go, the establishment of personal accounts only provides an additional risk regulation and buffering mechanism. On the contrary, if social pooling accounts and personal accounts are completely separated, it is impossible to achieve this functionality. In such cases, the most serious problem with the existence of empty accounts is that this part of empty account funds cannot earn interest, or accounting interest must be subsidized by the government. However, compared with maintaining real personal accounts and the bearing of the mutual-aid gap by the financial department, the government only needs to bear interest subsidies, so the burden on government is clearly lighter.

We believe that the two should be separated completely so as to ultimately achieve independent management and operation. In order not to increase the pension contribution rate and to reduce the burden on enterprises, personal accounts are overdrawn in many places to address the over spending of social pooling funds, resulting in "empty account" of personal accounts. If such circumstances continue, it will be difficult to achieve the goals of the partially accumulated system, making it exist in form only. Therefore, measures should be taken as soon as possible to make personal accounts real accounts to achieve independent accounting and make explicit the fund gap. In the near future, pooling accounts should be separated from personal accounts to achieve independent accounting (see Fig. 2.8.3). After replenishing funds into personal accounts, we can consider establishing the independent personal account management agency (see Fig. 2.8.2) to arouse the attention of all social circles and seek ways to solve the problem as soon as possible.

(V) The government should pay the transitional costs of the institutional transformation represented by "empty accounts"

To realize the transformation from the traditional pay-as-you-go pension scheme, which has been running for 40 years, to a mixed mode, the most difficult problem we face is how to solve the implicit pension debt of the government representing the rights and interests of the middle- and old-aged workers. As a previous commitment of the central government, it constitutes the transitional costs of transformation between the two systems. Theoretically, there are two possible ways to pay for transition costs: intergenerational transfer payment and transfer payment of national public property.

1   The feasibility of the intergenerational transfer mode is analyzed as follows. The practice of diluting the transition costs through intergenerational income redistribution will face two major problems:

(1)   Whether this settlement mode is socially and morally fair. Undoubtedly, in the traditional pension scheme, the pension costs of middle- and old-aged workers have actually been solidified in existing state-owned

assets to form the national debts through "pre-deducting" and handing over to the state and through the investment behavior of the state. The transitional costs, as the national debts, ought to be borne by the state. The practice of paying the transitional costs through intergenerational income transfer payment is apparently to pass on the government debt to the younger generation. In this way, the "new comers" become the first interest losers in the new system, which is clearly unfair.

(2) Whether this settlement mode is financially viable. With the demographic transition in urban areas and the rise of the elderly dependency rate in the system, the maturity of the traditional pension scheme will force enterprises to contribute to the scheme at a constantly rising contribution rate. According to the survey by the World Bank, the average contribution rate in 13 provinces and 12 cities in 1994 was 23.5% and 25.9% respectively, far higher than the world's average level of about 20%. In addition, under the premise that the central government does not bear the responsibility to pay the transition costs, to ensure the paying capacity of the system "combining social pooling with personal accounts" in the process of population aging, even though the personal account funds are used to fill the fund gap in the scheme, the contribution rate of enterprises will also be kept at a high level of 30% after 2000. Such a high level of contribution is unbearable to the vast majority of state-owned enterprises.

With the contribution rate of enterprises hovering at high levels, the limited ability of enterprises to mobilize funds can hardly ensure the financial viability of the existing scheme. In other words, the gap between the pension fund supply and demand of the existing system is the root cause for the emergence of "empty accounts". Under the premise of retaining the shell of the mixed system, it may change the existing system into a veritable pay-as-you-go system, while the traditional pay-as-you-go system is unable to cope with the upcoming challenges of an aging population. Therefore, how to solve the "empty account" problem of personal accounts is an important issue related to the safety of the existing pension system.

2   To ensure the safety of the existing system, the only feasible way is that the government should give financial support to social security funds, and the alternative approaches include the following: provide financial allocations to fill the gap of social pooling accounts; issue special treasury bonds to fill the gap of social pooling accounts; set up special taxes, such as consumption tax, to fill the gap (this approach was adopted by Germany); and sell or lease part of state-owned assets, such as some SMEs and state-owned real estate etc. to repay the debts.

In the meanwhile, we must also be highly vigilant about the "empty account" problem of personal accounts in the reform of the basic medical insurance system launched in 1999. The personal accounts in the old-age insurance scheme are "accumulated accounts", and there is a relatively stable time cycle between income and expenditure. However, the personal accounts in the medical insurance scheme are "spending accounts", and the expenses of each insured person are uncertain just as the probability of prevalence is uncertain. In other words, the instant consumption characteristics of the basic medical insurance decides that the personal accounts in the system must be "real accounts" rather than "empty accounts"; otherwise, the excessive size of empty accounts will lead to the collapse of the existing system. Therefore, on occasion that the new medical insurance system will be launched, it is of strategic significance for the new system to keep personal accounts real accounts through raising the funds for part of the transitional costs.

(VI) Establishing an appropriate policy framework for enterprises to supplement old-age and medical insurances

In the existing old-age insurance system, the supplementary old-age insurance for enterprises belongs to a voluntary behavior of enterprises; it aims to provide higher insurance benefits for workers of an enterprise beyond "basic security" and also reflects or embodies different economic efficiencies among different enterprises. But in the implementation of supplementary old-age insurance, non-state-owned enterprises are generally reluctant to come up with a sum of money to set up supplementary insurance for their employees beyond the statutory basic old-age and medical insurance required by the state, because it would increase the burdens on enterprises, affect their competitiveness, and reduce the rate of return on investment. In real economic life, those that have a positive response to this kind of insurance are mostly the state-owned enterprises with good economic efficiency. However, in the premise that no unified policies and regulations have been issued by the state for these enterprises to withdraw the funds for supplementary old-age and medical insurance, it will bring about a lot of malpractices, such as the abuse of power by managers for their own personal benefits and heavy loss of state assets. Therefore, we suggest that the central government should establish a unified policy framework for implementing supplementary old-age and medical insurance for enterprises and set up strict restrictions that the fund can only be withdrawn from the collective welfare fund of an enterprise. In other words, if an enterprise has not established the collective welfare fund, it cannot withdraw the supplementary old-age and medical insurance fund. In addition, an enterprise should formulate a reasonable withdrawal plan and strict rules and regulations and carry out strict management.

(VII) Reasonably setting the overall level of social insurance

In 1998, the central government decided to implement provincial-level pooling for basic old-age insurance and required that this task should be accomplished in three years. In the meanwhile, some provinces and cities had also implemented provincial-level pooling earlier in the unemployment insurance system. The significance of provincial-level pooling is that, on the one hand, it can expand the contribution base of the existing system to enhance the financial ability and system security to cope with various risks, and, on the other hand, the social insurance burdens that are different in different regions and different enterprises can be solved through the majority rule. The universality and socialization principle of social insurance system requires that the system must be an open system. That is, it must cover all members of society. In this sense, provincial-level pooling is an intermediate stage of transition of the existing system to national pooling.

But the scope of medical insurance should be different. Establishing the socialized basic medical insurance system is one of the goals of the reform of the insurance system. Given the complexity of medical insurance and different economic development levels in different areas in China, the scope of social pooling should be moderate. In areas and prefecture-level cities with higher levels of urbanization and economic development, social pooling can be carried out at the prefecture level (including municipality, sub-provincial city, and provincial capital) to establish the basic medical insurance system based on prefecture-level pooling and supported by a provincial-level, risk-regulating fund. In areas with a lower level of economic development and urbanization, social pooling can start from the county level and gradually develop to the prefecture-level city when conditions are ripe. In the meantime, some large enterprises can be allowed to establish their relatively independent medical insurance companies. It should be noted that these insurance companies exercise some functions of the state and are independent, institutional legal persons. They must exist independently from the enterprises in accounting and management and accept the supervision and inspection of social insurance management agencies.

(VIII) Gradually loosening government controls over investment and operation of social security funds, especially pension funds

Presently, the central government requires that pension funds can only be invested in government bonds or be deposited in banks after enough cash reserves are saved for two months. However, the practice has proved that this kind of quasi-governmental regulation investments is unable to maintain and increase the value of the pension funds.

Pension funds are not allowed to invest in other areas. Presently, most banks in China are state-owned banks, and bank deposits and lending rates are decided by the government, the negative interest rates for the legitimate investment of pension funds means that the government will bear the ultimate responsibility for maintaining and increasing the value of the funds. If pension funds are allowed to invest in other areas, this means the investment institutions must be responsible for maintaining and increasing the value of the funds. Under the current situation of slack law enforcement and supervision and the volatility and immaturity of the capital market, it will be indeed a great risk to allow the pension funds to be invested in other areas.

But in the long term, on condition that the administration of old-age insurance is separated from investment and operation pension fund and a number of professional pension fund management companies are established, the diversified portfolio investment for part of the pension funds should be allowed. Based on China's actual conditions, we can establish a number of pension fund management companies and allow them to invest in stocks, corporate bonds, and other areas, which is conducive to the development and maturation of the capital market. Now the key issue is this: affected by local governments, the independent operation of fund management companies can hardly be guaranteed, and even if the fund management companies are operating independently, it is difficult to establish an effective incentive and monitoring mechanism for the fund operators.

With regard to whether it is possible to maintain and increase the value of pension funds through a diversified portfolio investment, we believe that this is possible if the political and economic situations remain stable and the market risks such as the Asian financial crisis do not occur. However, in the increasingly competitive international environment, it is difficult to avoid serious economic risks (though an exception could be made for the United States and the European Union in the future) and other countries or regional economic organizations that issue world currencies. Therefore, it is appropriate to take a more prudent attitude in fund operation and management.

(IX) Reforming the existing social insurance management system to truly separate administrative institutions from fund investment operators, executive agencies, and regulatory agencies

We recommend that, on the premise of maintaining a necessary government regulatory system, we can consider putting institutional investors under the management of the market. For example, Chile has cultivated a pension fund custodian market in addition to the existing system. That is, a number of pension fund management companies have been established to form market competition on the basis of the standardized information disclosure mechanism to reduce management prices and risks.

(X) Speeding up the legislative process of the social insurance system

In the early stage of innovation of the social insurance system, as the system construction is still in the pilot stage, we can have a number of schemes or solutions. However, after many years of pilot reforms, we should form a unified scheme, and the State Council should issue a document to standardize the scheme. After the document is issued, some adjustments and amendments can be made based on the actual conditions, and such adjustments and amendments should be confirmed by legislation. Social insurance legislation can be carried out based on the degree of difficulty of each item and actual progress of the system separately. We should first formulate the specific regulations and then establish the comprehensive social insurance law based on the regulations to establish an authoritative, legal framework for the operation of social insurance.

(This article is a chapter of *Research on reform and development of state-owned enterprises in China*, Economic Management Press, 2001, the title is newly added)

Notes

1 The comprehensive survey group of China Institute for Economic System Reform: *Reform: Challenges and Choice We Are Facing*, Beijing, China: China Economic Publishing House, 1986 edition.
2 *China Statistical Yearbook (1999)*, published by China Statistics Press, 1999.
3 The Decision on Establishing a Unified Basic Pension Insurance System for Enterprise Employees, *People's Daily*, August 27, 1997.
4 Zheng Haihang and He Chunlei, Social Insurance System: Review on the Dalian Model, *China Industrial Economy*, volume 1, 1998.
5 Yang Liangchu, Zheng Haihang, and He Chunlei, Some Thoughts on Strengthening Financial Management for Social Security, *Research on Financial and Economic Issues*, volume 1, 1997.
6 Mou Daquan, *Jointly Weaving a Safety Net*, Beijing, China: Economic Science Press, 1998, p. 87.
7 Released by the person in charge of Department of Legal Affairs of the Ministry of Labor and Social Security at the news briefing held on February 25, 1999, reported by *China Economic Times* on February 26.
8 Released by the person in charge of Department of Legal Affairs of the Ministry of Labor and Social Security at the news briefing held on February 25, 1999, reported by *China Economic Times* on February 26.

9 Accelerating the establishment of a new socialist market economy order

1. Necessity to establish a new socialist market economy order

The objective of China's economic reform is to establish a socialist market economy. The operation of a market economy not only requires an organization system that adapts to its operation mechanism, but also requires an economic order to ensure that the mechanism can fully function. If there is no such an economic order or such an economic order is not stringent, the actions of market participants, law enforcement agencies, and governments would not be in line with the norms of the market economy, thus hindering the normal operation and affecting the healthy development of the market economy. The rapid development of the market economy in China has broken the original order of the planned economy, and there is an urgent need to establish a new order of socialist market economy to ensure the normal operation, consolidation, and development of the market economy. In this regard, we have done some work, but are still far from meeting the requirements of the market economy. Lawlessness, failure to observe laws, misconduct of both parties in trade, law enforcement agencies and governments, and market disorder are very serious; commercial advertising is unworthy of the name; shoddy products can be found everywhere; intellectual property rights have been repeatedly infringed on; unlicensed vendors, tax evasion, and other phenomena still dominate the market despite repeated bans; collusion between officials and businessmen; mixing up the functions of the government and enterprises; power-for-money deals; and other phenomena could not be effectively curbed. This has not only brought a lot of social problems, but also tarnished the reputation of the market economy. Therefore, it is in urgent need of regulation to cure the market disorder.

2. Analyzing the causes for the current market economy disorder

The primary cause for the market disorder is that China is still in a period of transition from a planned economy to a market economy, and its economic operation mechanism is "multi-tracked". The planned economy system has been broken, but a sound market economy system has not yet been established. In such a special period, some economic activities are still carried out based on the mechanism of the planned economy, some economic activities are carried out based on the mechanism of the market economy, and some economic activities are carried out based on neither the mechanism of the planned economy nor the mechanism of the market economy. Some people make use of the loopholes of this "multi-track" system, which is likely to cause market disorder.

Another cause for the market disorder is that many people still lack a basic knowledge of a market economy because China has implemented the planned economy for a long time. For example, in production and operation, inadvertent IPR violations are common phenomena; when the joint-stock system was established, people did not know the difference between stocks and bonds, and some people regarded stocks as bonds and paid both principals and interests; in competition, some people did not know the boundary between fair competition and unfair competition and introduced some illegal means in competition. As for that sort of phenomena, except for a few people who commit an offense knowingly, the misconducts of most people were due to a lack of related knowledge.

The third cause for the market disorder is that there are changes in the thought of some people due to the impact of the market economy. The impact of the market economy on people is largely positive, which should be fully affirmed. While fully affirming its positive impact, we also should pay attention to the negative impact it brings. Under the planned economy, we stressed on products but disregarded goods, stressed on dedication but asked for no reward, stressed on national and collective interests but did not care about personal gains. Undoubtedly, these practices are wrong. But now some people have gone from one extreme to another. They introduced some things in the field of commodity exchange that should not be introduced, such as power, social status, social obligations, marriage, and even the human body, into the field of commodity exchange, and money worship began to flood. This ideological metamorphosis has a great influence on the market order.

The fourth cause for the market disorder is the imperfectness of the legal system. China's market economy has developed rapidly, but the laws and regulations on market management are far from meeting the requirements of the development situation. For example, to encourage and protect competition and prevent monopolies and unfair competition, there must be a law to protect fair competition; to prevent some entities and individuals from reaping huge profits, there must be an anti-profiteering law. So far, these laws and regulations have not been promulgated. With regard to the laws and regulations that have been promulgated, some are imperfect, and some have poor operability; there are conflicting policies from different departments, the responsibilities among law enforcement agencies and between law enforcement agencies and some administrative departments are not clearly divided, which leads to the serious phenomena of ducking responsibility, failing to observe laws, and slacking in enforcement.

The fifth cause for the market disorder is that there are a large number of small commodity producers. In China's urban and rural areas, small commodity producers account for a large proportion. Especially in the fields of living materials, macro regulation, economic development, and production and operation, small commodity producers still have a dominant position. These small commodity producers have low ideological and cultural quality, less money, and a strong speculative mentality. Many people do not understand and regard the market rules, and they dare to do anything just to make money. For example, the phenomena such as unlicensed business operations, production and sale of fake and inferior goods, nonconformity of goods and services to the standards prescribed by the State, fraud and deceit, racketeering, and tax evasion have mostly happened to them. In addition, these small commodity producers and operators have small business scales and are large in number and highly floating, which has brought a lot of difficulties to market management.

3. Establishing a new order of market economy is a systematic program

In China, accelerating to establish a new order of market economy has become an urgent issue of developing the socialist market economy. This is a very arduous and complicated task. In this regard, we should primarily focus on the following aspects:

First, we should deepen the reform and vigorously promote the development of the socialist market economy. With the deepening of reform, we are facing some deep-seated problems with the old system, which have increased the difficulty of reform. Without a tough fight, it is difficult to form a new system, and the normal order of the market economy can hardly be established. For example, to effectively solve the problems such as power rent-seeking, power-for-money deals, power-for-power deals, in addition to the appropriate laws and regulations, the most fundamental measure is to unswervingly continue to deepen the reform along the ideas of separating the functions of the government from those of the enterprises and separating the right of ownership from the rights of management to cut the ties between the government and enterprises, thoroughly transform the government functions, and enable enterprises to be become independent commodity producers. In short, the establishment of the normal order of the market economy will help to consolidate the achievement of the reforms and promote the development of the socialist market economy, and the establishment of a sound market economic order in turn depends on the deepening of economic reforms. The two tasks that are complementary to each other must be combined to achieve better results.

Second, we must carry out an education about the market economy for citizens. To carry out an education about the market economy for citizens is a very important measure for the development of the socialist market economy and the establishment of a new socialist market economy order. The priorities of this education should include at least the following three aspects: first, to carry out education of basic knowledge about the market economy for citizens, especially government officials, business owners, and managers; second, to carry out a wide range of legal education for citizens; and third, to carry out education in ideological quality and social morals for citizens.

Third, we should further establish and improve the laws and regulations for market management. To accelerate the establishment of a new order of the socialist market economy, we must further establish and improve market management laws and regulations, such as the market law (commercial law), anti-unfair competition law, and anti-monopoly law, to regulate the actions of traders, law enforcement agencies, and governments. In the meanwhile, to ensure that these basic laws and regulations are effectively implemented, there must also be special laws and regulations that match with them. It is an arduous and complicated task to establish and improve the laws and regulations for promoting the healthy development of the market economy. To accomplish this task smoothly, we can first issue some administrative regulations on a trial basis and formulate formal laws and regulations when the conditions are ripe, realizing that some existing laws and regulations can be amended and supplemented according to the requirements of the market economy, and some foreign laws and regulations can be used as reference.

Finally, we should strengthen the building of market administrative personnel and law enforcement officer teams. Based on the reform of government institutions, some cadres with high education levels and strong management competence can be attracted to business administration, law enforcement, economic arbitration, and judicial institutions.

(Published in *Guangming Daily* on June 3, 1993)

10 Discussion on the target mode of China's socialist market economy

The 14th CPC National Congress clearly stated that the goal of China's economic reform is to establish a socialist market economic system. This is a major breakthrough in economic theories in recent years, and has had a profound influence and a great significance in the economic development in China. However, we should also be keenly aware that there are some different modes of market economy in the world today, and which mode China will select for its socialist market economy or which mode China's socialist market economy is closer to will be an issue to be further discussed. This paper gives some superficial views in this regard.

1. Modes of market economy and their characteristics

Many scholars believe that the economic system is decided by the forms of ownership and the modes of decision making. More and more people believe that in the above two deciding factors, the latter is more decisive. For example, U.S. scholar Morris Bornstein believes that "the trend in study of economic system is: the importance of ownership as the key element in the role of the economic system is declining because resource allocation and income distribution patterns are more important". "Decision-making rather than ownership has become a central issue".[1] Another U.S. scholar Alan G. Gruch also holds "the decisive thing is not the ownership of production materials in law. The most important thing is the mode of economic operation and for whom it serves. In the two economic systems of capitalism and socialism, the question raised is the same".[2] Some economics textbooks in the U.S. also believe that "the economic behaviors of enterprises depend more on decision-making rather than ownership".[3] An example cited by these textbooks is that in the reign of Hitler, the German government implemented a highly centralized control over private companies, and there were great differences between the operation mode of these companies and that of private companies in other countries. On the contrary, now the state-owned enterprises in capitalist countries can be operated completely the same as private enterprises. Because of this, many scholars who are engaged in studies of comparison of economic systems divide the types of economic systems by the modes of decision making and classify the modes of market economy into the pure market economy (some people call it the free competition market economy), the state-intervened market economy, the state-planned market economy, and the former Yugoslav market economy (also known as market socialism).

The pure market economy is a kind of market economy in the early stage of capitalist development. In this economic system, production is on a small scale, there are almost no big monopolies, commodity prices are entirely formed by enterprises through competition, and the government rarely intervenes in economic activities. As this economic mode can no longer reflect the actual situation of the real economy, it is now just a purely hypothetical abstract mode in standard economics textbooks.

The state-intervened market economy is a mature market economy system. This economic system is practiced in many European and American countries, among which the United States and Canada are most typical. Its main features are as follows: first, some large and extra-large industrial enterprises have appeared in economic life. Some large industrial enterprises are also joint-stocked enterprises, which occupy a dominant position in sales in the industry. In addition to participating in the special industrial associations, these industrial enterprises have also joined the industrial federations. The industrial federations act as the spokespersons in dealing with the government, laborer organizations, and the public. In these industrial cores, a few large oligopoly enterprises and the highly concentrated commercial banking systems play a decisive role in the economic affairs of a country. Second, the organizations of labor market closely follow the form of industrial organization. Around the large industrial and economic centers, strong trade union organizations emerge as the times require. Their market power measures with the market power of large industrial enterprises. Especially in determining the levels of wage and employment, they play a very important role. Third, the prices of some products are no longer entirely decided by free competition in the market. Monopoly organizations, governments, and trade unions have a great influence on the formation of prices of some products. Fourth, the government has become an important part in economic life. Government employees take a greater proportion in employment, and the proportion of goods and services purchased by governments in GNP is on the rise. The government also has a number of public enterprises to provide the products and services for the society that private enterprises are unwilling to offer. Fifth, the government's economic management role has been enhanced. To regulate the economy, the government has formulated a number of laws, such as an anti-monopoly law, minimum income standards, and environmental protection law, to ensure fair competition and protect the interests of low-income people and the living environment of mankind. The government uses financial, banking, taxation, and other economic levers to intervene in the economy. Its objective is to combine microeconomic and macroeconomic policies to prevent the misallocation of economic resources, remove obstacles to achieve economic stability, protect large-scale production, and promote a more equal distribution of income.

The state-planned market economy is another type of mature market economy. This market economy system is practiced in France, Japan, Sweden, Norway, and the Netherlands. It has almost all the features of the state-intervened market economy, and the difference is that the state has less intervention in economy. The economy is regulated not only through economic legislation, economic leverage, and other means, but also through the national plans. Its basic features include the following: first, a national plan management agency is established to be responsible for collecting market information and preparing annual and long-term national plans. These plans are predictions of the GNP and its use for public and private consumption and investment in the planned period. The fiscal, monetary, price, and wage policies are matched with the plans to achieve the desired goals. Second, these plans are instructive, not directive, and they are realized through cooperation among various social classes and groups. Cooperation between the plan makers of the government and the managers of large industrial enterprises plays a key role in realizing these plans. Third, the market mechanism still plays a fundamental and decisive role in coordinating the daily decisions. Fourth, these plans have the information structure and power structure required by instructive plans.

Apart from the above three modes of market economy, Western scholars also called the former Yugoslav economic system a kind of market economy. It is built on the basis of corporate autonomy and social autonomy. Under this system, the joint labor grassroots organizations (enterprises) have greater autonomy in determining production, sale, distribution of profits, and other aspects; the state abandoned the practice of issuing mandatory plans to enterprises, and the joint labor organizations are responsible for formulating the plans based on the agreements in a top-down manner. These plans are not legally binding and can be adjusted by enterprises according to changes in the market; the pricing principle is also decided by enterprises based on the relationship of market supply and demand, and the market mechanisms play a major role in regulating the economy. Worker autonomy is implemented in enterprises, that is, the workers' committee elected by all employees is the highest organ of power in an enterprise, and managers perform work under its leadership.

2. Selection of socialist market economy mode

We have analyzed the four modes of market economy. Which mode will China select as its socialist market economy? Undoubtedly, we should not select the first mode because it is the mode of market economy suitable for the early stage of capitalist development, and it is now only practiced in a few special countries. For most countries, it has lost its value. Although the former Yugoslav economy system is known as a market economy, it was produced in the process of economic reform and has not yet taken shape, so it cannot be called a mature market economy. Practices have proved that this economic mode has many disadvantages, such as lack of strong macro-control by the government and lack of self-discipline and self-development mechanism in enterprises. Therefore, it is an inefficient mechanism, and we cannot take it as a target mode. The state-intervened market economy is a mature market economy, but as it is closer to the pure market economy than the state-planned market economy, it also has some major drawbacks. For example, in real economic life, there are still some areas where the "invisible hand" cannot work, and the economic levers can hardly play a regulating role in these areas. Even in those areas where the "invisible hand" can work, sometimes economic levers can hardly play an effective role. This is because, first, it is difficult for decision-makers to get timely and accurate information about the current economic situation, they can only make decisions based on the information reflecting the economic performance of the past, so biases are unavoidable. Second, statistical information may not be accurate. Third, decision making is often disturbed by political factors. Especially in countries like the United States, some major macro-control measures need to be approved by Congress. Some members of the opposition party in Congress tend not to cooperate with the government, so some major macro-control measures can hardly be introduced. Western scholars say this is the price to pay for democracy. Fourth, it also takes time to convince producers and consumers to act in the direction of macro-control. Practices have proved that the countries where this market economic system is practiced are unable to properly solve the problems that have existed since World War II, such as serious unemployment, inflation, and cyclical economic crisis. Because of this, in many Western countries, this market economy mode has lost its attraction as a national goal. In the recent decades, the governments of many Western countries have been seeking an economic system that is better and more viable than what is envisaged by the Keynesian Mainstream economists in the United Kingdom and the United States after the World War II. Therefore, some developed capitalist countries adopted another market economy system with more (rather than less) government intervention and economic guidance by the state. For example, the countries such as France, the Netherlands, Japan, Sweden, Belgium, Denmark, and Italy adopted a large number of plans to regulate the economy after the World War II. Although different Western countries have different national plans and experiences, they commonly adopt the development direction with greater national intervention and planning and have achieved success. Therefore, China's market economy mode, as far as the mode decision making is concerned, should be closer to the state-intervened market economy.

Another reason why China's market economy mode should be closer to the state-intervened market economy is that China's market economy will be built on the basis of the ownership structure with public ownership playing a dominant role and diverse forms of ownership developing side by side. Private enterprises are more compatible to the market economy, and, similarly, public enterprises, especially state-owned enterprises, are more compatible to national plans. In other words, compared with other enterprises, state-owned enterprises are more likely to accept the national plans. This has not only been proved by the economic practices in socialist countries, but also proved by the economic practices in capitalist countries practicing the planned market economy system. This is because in these countries, without exception, there are a considerable proportion of state-owned enterprises, which play an important role in implementing the national plans. Therefore, the state-planned market economy has an innate condition under the socialist conditions with public ownership playing a dominant role and diverse forms of ownership developing side by side. Undoubtedly, emphasizing the compatibility of state-owned enterprises to the national plans does not mean that state-owned enterprises are not compatible to the market economy. Indeed, under the highly centralized planned economy, state-owned enterprises have poor compatibility to the market economy, but according to the principle of "separation of ownership and control", the state-owned enterprises that have been restructured will have a strong compatibility to the national plans and the market economy. This has been proved by SOEs in capitalist countries.

China's unique social, cultural traditions are also the important factors urging us to adopt the state-planned market economy mode. As long as we have carried out some analysis, we will find that the social and cultural traditions of a country have a decisive influence on the formation of its economic system. Likewise, the types of market economic system selected by the capitalist countries are different due to their different social and cultural traditions. For example, as the social and cultural traditions of the United States are diverse and laissez-faire, the United States has selected the market economy system with relatively weak government intervention; on the contrary, for almost all the countries that have embarked on the road of a state-planned market economy, their social and cultural traditions have a strong nationalistic tendency or socialist thought. China has a history of two thousand years of centralized feudal society, so its social and cultural traditions have a strong nationalistic tendency. After the founding of New China, China has embarked on the road of socialism, and the socialist thought has been deeply rooted in the hearts of the people. In the meanwhile, China has accumulated rich experience in plan management in the 40 years of socialist economic construction. Undoubtedly, a highly centralized planned economy as an economic system should be abandoned. However, some experience and good practice acquired under this system are valuable assets and still very useful under the new market economy conditions and should not be fully denied by us.

3. Outline of China's socialist market economy mode

Although China's market economy mode is similar in many aspects to the state-planned market economy mode practiced in some Western countries, it is inevitably different from the market economy mode practiced in these countries due to the economic development level, social and cultural traditions, and the environment in China. Now, it is undoubtedly difficult to get a clear picture of China's socialist market economy mode, so we can only sketch out some of its outline.

(I) Enterprises have become independent commodity producers and formed their rational organizational structure. The difficulty for enterprises to become independent commodity producers lies in state-owned enterprises. After over 10 years of reform, although the autonomy of the state-owned enterprises in China has been expanded, they have not fundamentally gotten rid of the status of being an appendage of the executive agencies and are still unable to get the position of independent commodity producers. We must restructure the property rights relations of enterprises according to the principle of separation of ownership and control so that enterprises have the legal ownership rights to their properties through joint-stock and other means to make them real commodity producers that make their own management decisions and take full responsibility for their own profits and losses.

While restructuring the property rights relations of state-owned enterprises, we must reform and adjust the organizational structure of enterprises according to the principles of market economy and change the straight-line, grade-type organizational structure featuring vertical management to the network-type organizational structure with horizontal linkages. To this end, we should first form a reasonable ownership structure. The proportion of state-owned enterprises should not be too large, and they should be concentrated in railways, telecommunications, aerospace, basic materials, and a few military-industrial sectors. According to the experiences of foreign countries, the proportion of state-owned enterprises in various ownership structures should not exceed 30%, and otherwise, it is likely to form a monopoly and inhibit the role of the market mechanism. Second, a number of large enterprises and extra-large enterprises should be reorganized to form some conglomerates and trans-national corporations through equity-holding, professional collaboration, joint production and operation, and other means. The medium- and small-sized enterprises can be organically organized by these conglomerates and trans-national corporations. Third, the existing government agencies in charge of enterprises can be changed into the state's asset management organizations and industrial management organizations. The function of ownership of state-owned assets can be exercised by the state-owned assets management system. The system consists of the state-owned assets administration bureaus at all levels and their investment companies. The state-owned assets administration bureaus are the government agencies managing the assets of the state. They are mainly responsible for confirming and registering the properties of all the people; formulating and implementing various laws and regulations on possession, use, and allocation of state-owned properties; establishing and managing state-owned investment companies; and supervising the state-owned assets in cooperation with the relevant government authorities. State-owned assets supervision and administration bureaus only have a direct link with their subordinate investment companies and do not have a link with the production enterprises. In other words, the state-owned assets supervision and administration bureaus hand over the state-owned assets to their subordinate investment companies and these subordinate investment companies are responsible for holding and controlling the stocks of the production enterprises. In this way, the investment companies have become the intermediary organizations between the government administrative agencies and the production enterprises, thus properly solving the issue of separating the functions of the government from those of enterprises in the organizational system. In the meanwhile, we should establish the industrial associations, entrepreneurs associations, non-governmental organizations, and other economic unions and give full play to their role in industrial management and other aspects of macro-control. Finally, we must change the situation that all enterprises, large or small, have an all-inclusive organizational structure and promote specialized cooperation and alliances among enterprises to form the corporate organizational structure with large, medium and small companies working together to get high economic benefits.

(II) We must establish a sound and efficient market system; the basic characteristic of the market economy is that the market mechanism can fully exert its due role and become the basic means of resource allocation. To this end, the general requirements are as follows: the factors of production needed by enterprises should be gotten from the market rather than allocated by the government administrative agencies; all commodities must be exchanged through the market rather than allocated by the government administrative agencies; commodity prices must be formed through market competition and can reflect the relationship of supply and demand; monopoly operation must only be limited to a handful of natural monopoly industries, and there should be a fair competition between enterprises in other industries; and the economic decisions of enterprises are made in accordance with the market laws rather than are submitted to the government administrative agencies. To achieve the above general requirements, there must be a sound and efficient consumer market, a production factor market and an enterprise property market.

After over a decade of reform, China's consumer market has basically taken shape, and its basic characteristics are various forms of ownership and various modes of operation and various distribution channels; few circulation links; combination of centralized large-scale wholesale trade centers, shopping centers, and decentralized small-scale retail outlets; and a combination of an industrial product market and an agricultural product market. In the future, we must further establish and improve the market rules and break regional blockades.

The factor markets include many aspects, and it is important to establish sound production means, capital, and labor markets. In the production material market, we should thoroughly abolish the production allocation system, and like consumer goods, all means of production must enter the market. The means and channels of sale can be diverse, and products can either be marketed by materials enterprises or directly sold by producers. Materials companies marketing means of production must implement corporate management and should not enjoy any privilege. In the capital market, various specialized banks must, under the guidance of the Central Bank, implement corporate management. Banks have the rights to independently choose enterprises, and enterprises can independently choose banks. Bank deposit and lending rates can float freely within the range specified by the Central Bank. Specialized banks can break through the lateral facility channels among banks through bank bonds, regional bonds, commercial credit vouchers, and discounting among banks. Enterprises can also establish their internal banks or financial companies to raise funds by issuing bonds, stocks, and other means. In the labor market, we should further reform the existing employment system and personnel system, break the personnel department ownership system and corporate ownership system, and implement the labor contract system and appointment system. Employers have the right to recruit and dismiss employees in accordance with the relevant laws, regulations, and policies, and employees have the right to independently choose their careers. Except for the civil servants, the government will no longer have a unified system for wages and promotion, and this should be independently decided by enterprises. The level of wage should mainly depend on the demand and supply of labor, the level of economic efficiency of an enterprise, and the contribution of an employee to the enterprise. To safeguard the interests of workers, the social security system should be established to guarantee the basic livelihood of retirees and the unemployed. In the meanwhile, labor service centers should be established to help the unemployed to find jobs, carry out trainings, and provide employment guidance for them to enable them to meet the needs of re-employment.

The corporate property rights market is a necessary condition to achieve liquidity of stock properties of enterprises. It plays a decisive role in phasing out backward enterprises and production capacities to timely achieve the adjustment of the industrial structure and organizational structure. Therefore, a sound corporate merger and bankruptcy system should be established, including the liquidation and evaluation of assets, transfer of assets, and personnel arrangements.

(III) The government should maintain strong regulation for the economy

To meet the requirements of the market economy, in the macro-control of the economy, the government must adhere to the principle of separating the functions of the government from those of enterprises, the principle of macro regulation and micro deregulation, the principle of ensuring the leading role of medium- and long-term plans supplemented by annual plans, the principle of ensuring the leading role of indirect management supplemented by direct management, and the principle of ensuring the leading role of value-based management supplemented by physical management.

To ensure that macroeconomic management is more powerful and effective, the corresponding planning, finance, taxation, and financial systems compatible with the market economy must be established. A lean and efficient plan management agency whose main function is to prepare national plans and keep an overall balance should be established. But these plans must be comprehensive, broad-brushed, and resilient. They should mainly set the indicators in the planned period, such as economic growth, significant proportion relations, fiscal revenue, import and export, employment, and people's income levels. When making the plans, the planning agency should consult with conglomerates, industrial associations, economic federation, and other economic organizations to seek their views and get their support.

In terms of the fiscal and taxation system, a multi-level fiscal system with unified guidance from the central financial department and the local financial departments are relatively independent should be established. On the basis of clearly dividing the administrative power between the central and local governments, the tax-sharing fiscal administration system should be implemented. That is, we should clearly specify which taxes should be the income sources for the central government, which taxes should the income sources for the local governments, and which taxes should be the income sources for the central and local governments. The fiscal budget at all levels should implement double-entry bookkeeping and separate the current account from the capital account to avoid being confused and squeezed. If the governments at all levels are suffering the financial deficit, the financial deficit should be compensated by debts. The financial relationship between the state and enterprises should be completely separated. The government has no right to collect the profits from enterprises and is not obliged to bear the losses of enterprises. Meanwhile, the taxation system separating taxes from profits should be implemented. The tax system should focus on value-added tax, income tax, and resource tax and be supplemented by diversified taxes such as consumption tax. To ensure fair competition, the tax rates for all kinds of enterprises should be equal.

The functions of the central bank should be separated from those of the specialized banks, and the specialized banks should become the commercial banks for enterprises. The central bank should mainly exercise the macro-management function. To ensure that the central bank can independently exercise its functions, it can be separated from the government and led by the National People's Congress.

After the formation of the new macro system, to ensure the realization of the national macroeconomic targets, the country will regulate the economic activities through tax rates, interest rates, exchange rates, money supply, and other indirect means. In the meanwhile, the necessary direct means will be retained, including the following: to enact laws to regulate the economic activities of individuals, enterprises, and other groups; to approve the start-up, closing, and relocation of enterprises; and to determine the mode of operation of state-owned enterprises and delegate representatives to participate in the leadership organizations of enterprises. As the main consumer, the government plays a direct role in regulating the economy through the changes in purchases by the government, and we must also retain the necessary right to invest in order to carry out direct investment in infrastructure, cultural, and education construction, major environmental protection projects, and some regions and industries that need to be supported; also, some important materials in short supply needed by the state may be controlled through ordering or purchasing by the state although the state will no longer issue any mandatory national plan.

(Published in *China Industrial Economics*, Issue 3, 1993)

Notes

1 [US] Morris Bornstein, *Comparation of Economic Systems*, Beijing, China: China Financial and Economic Publishing House, 1989, pp. 13, 28.
2 [US] Alan G. Gruch, *Comparation of Economic Systems*, China Social Sciences Press, 1985 edition, p. 19.
3 [US] Richard G. Lipsy, *Economics*, the English version, Harper & Row Press, 1990 edition, p. 9.

11 Achievement and experience of the economic system reform in the major cities

China is a large country, so how to handle the relationship between industrial management and regional management is a hard nut to crack in economic reform. In the past, to strengthen the central government's centralized management, we had once put a large number of enterprises under the management of the central industrial departments and practiced the management system mainly based on "industrial management". To arouse the enthusiasm of the local governments, we have delegated a large number of enterprises to the provinces, prefectures, and cities and practiced the management system mainly based on "regional management". But the practices have proved that these two management systems are not successful. Since the 3rd Plenary Session of the 11th Central Committee of the CPC at which the reform and opening up policy was introduced, both scholars and practitioners have conducted extensive discussion and exploration. The 6th Five-Year Plan introduced in 1982 proposed the concrete task of "giving play to the role of the major cities in addressing the contradiction between 'industrial management' and 'regional management'". In the same year, the State Commission for Restructuring the Economic System started to pilot the comprehensive reform in the two medium-size cities of Shashi and Changzhou. In 1983, Chongqing as a typical large city was selected as the pilot city for the reform. In 1984, Wuhan, Shenyang, and other cities were also approved as the pilot cities. In October 1984, the CPC Central Committee affirmed in the *Decision on the Reform of the Economic System* the practice of addressing the contradiction between "industrial management" and "regional management" through giving to play the role of the major cities and improved this vision. The decision emphasized that on the one hand, the functions of the government should be separated from those of enterprises, and the industrial administration departments should streamline administration and delegate more power to lower levels, and industrial management should be turned into industrial management; on the other hand, after the functions of the government are separated from those of enterprises, we should give full play to the role of the cities and gradually form the open network-based economic zones of different sizes based on the cities, especially medium and large cities. Therefore, a reform scheme with Chinese characteristics to solve the contradiction between "industrial management" and "regional management" has gradually been formed. After the decision was published, the comprehensive reform in the cities had gathered pace. So far, the number of the pilot cities for the comprehensive reform nationwide has increased to 72. These cities have achieved remarkable results in the pilot reform and provided a wealth of experience in promoting the comprehensive reform of the economic system.

1   In the old economic system, the major cities were plagued with the most serious problem of segmentation and all kinds of contradictions. Whether we could make a breakthrough from the major cities would not only affect the pace of the economic reform but also decide the success of the reform. Based on the progress of the reform in the pilot cities in recent years, although it was very difficult, the originally rigid management mode was broken. A number of economically developed major cities such as Chongqing, Wuhan, Shenyang, Shijiazhuang, Nanjing, and Guangzhou have blazed their own paths through exploration and practice and made a series of breakthroughs. The main results of the comprehensive reform in the major cities include:

First, the multifunctional role of the cities has been restored and developed. In this regard, there were three changes in the understanding of the leaders of many cities: first, cities were no longer simply treated as production bases, and a variety of the functions of cities were recognized; second, a city must serve the entire economic zone it radiates rather than simply serve itself; and third, in the assessment and evaluation of the work of a city, we must attach equal importance to its gross output value of industry and agriculture and the size and strength of its radiating capacity. On the basis of raising the awareness, all the cities have made great progress. In 1979–1984, the number of employees in the tertiary industry in Guangzhou increased by 7.5% per year on average, and by the end of 1984, the output value of the tertiary industry accounted for 32% of its GDP. In the tertiary industries, businesses were developing rapidly, over 2,200 trade centers and over 400 production material trade centers had been established, and the retail outlets in the pilot cities had more than doubled. Some emerging tertiary industries, such as technology consulting, economic consulting, information services, and accounting and law firms had also developed, providing valuable services in production and technological innovation.

Second, the horizontal economic integration has been promoted. In recent years, with the development of the commodity economy, the horizontal integration among enterprises and cities and between urban and rural areas has gradually developed from small to large, from simple to complex, from near to far, from loose to tight, and from a low level to a high level, and have achieved remarkable results. For example, while vigorously promoting the integration of the local enterprises, Chongqing has positively promoted the integration with the southwestern areas and the areas along the Yangtze River. Nanjing has jointly established the economic coordination committee with 16 cities in the three provinces of Jiangsu, Anhui, and Jiangxi on the basis of equal consultation, voluntariness, and mutual benefit for extensive coordination in industries, transportation, travel, trade, finance, technology, materials, and other areas. Shenyang has established 25 enterprises groups involving 568 entities, 1,230 economic and technical alliances, and 289 industrial consortiums.

Third, the pattern of coordinated development of urban and rural areas began to take shape. After the system of counties driven by cities was implemented, the role of cities in leading and driving rural development was brought into full play, and the different advantages of urban and rural areas were combined to form the overall economic advantages. Taking Jiangsu Province as an example, after the system of counties driven by cities was implemented, the urban and rural economies were combined through uniformly organizing the specialized cooperation between urban and rural areas and the lateral integration in various forms, which has not only promoted the development of a large number of rural industrial enterprises, but also ensured the stable sources of agricultural raw materials and labor forces needed for urban industrial production. In 1985, 64 counties in Jiangsu province realized the industrial output value of 57.4 billion Yuan, among which the output value of rural industry accounted for 66%. The output value of the rural industry of 12 counties in Suzhou, Wuxi, and Changzhou where the rural industry was well-developed, including Wuxi, Jiangyin, Wujin, Shazhou, and Jintan, accounted for 71.6% of the total industrial output value of these counties. In 1985, the output value of the rural industry in Jiangsu Province reached 38.3 billion Yuan, close to the province's total industrial output in 1979. After Wuhan opened the door of the three cities (Wuchang, Hankou, and Hanyang), the surrounding suburbs and cities first benefited from the opening up. According to incomplete statistics, the total income earned by the three suburbs, four counties, and adjacent areas of Wuhan was up to 500 million Yuan from work and businesses each year. Chongqing adheres to giving play to the advantages of urban and rural areas and establishing the comprehensive technical cooperative relationship. In recent years, Chongqing has launched 1,022 urban-rural cooperative projects, and nearly 200 million Yuan was attracted to rural development, effectively boosting the development of township enterprises.

Fourth, the degree of economic opening was increasing. For example, Dalian has established the trade relations with more than 1,000 merchants in more than 40 countries and regions. The commodity exports have increased year over year. In 1986, the value of purchase of export commodities amounted to 1.48 billion Yuan and realized foreign exchanges of US$ 410 million, and the products were exported to 51 countries and regions. Technology and labor export has also been promoted. Since 1979 when Guangzhou implemented the opening up policy, it has established the trade relations with more than 5,000 merchants in more than 120 countries and regions and exported more than 1,000 kinds of commodities. The value of exports reached US$610 million in 1986, and this figure reached US$369 million in January to May this year, up 54.3% over the same period last year, and 100 export commodity bases have been established.

Fifth, urban construction has been promoted and the living standards of people have been improved. Many major cities in China are the old industrial bases. The idea of laying emphasis on production while disregarding the life and urban construction in the past has led to backward municipal utilities and infrastructures and "debts owed" to the livelihood of the people. In the eight years after the reform, urban construction and renovation has gathered pace in many cities, and the lives of the people have been significantly improved. In the past eight years, Nanjing has accelerated the renovation of the old districts and the construction of the new districts and built a large number of residential quarters, shopping malls, restaurants, hotels, and office buildings, and the living space per capita reached 7.38m^2 in 1985, ranking the front place in China. In the past eight years, Guangzhou invested a total of 1.197 billion Yuan in urban construction, 61% more than the total investment in the 29 years before the reform, the area of the residential buildings was over 1.25 times more than the total area of residential buildings in the 29 years before the reform, the per capita living area jumped from 3.8m^2 to 6.9m^2, the water supply capacity had more than doubled, and the road area added was also more than the total in the 29 years before the reform. In 1986, the per capita income of the employees in the whole city reached 1,778 Yuan, an increase of 1.5 times over 1978 and an average increase of 12.3% year over year, the per capita net income of farmers in suburban areas reached 752 Yuan, an increase of twice over that of 1978 and an average increase of 14.8% year over year.

Sixth, the productive forces were emancipated, the sustained urban economic development was promoted and the economic efficiency was improved. The economic indicators of the major cities in 1986 where the comprehensive reform was carried out increased substantially compared with those before the reform. For example, the GDP, national income, and gross output value of industry and agriculture in Chongqing increased by 74%, 72%, and 52% respectively in 1986 compared with those in 1982 before the pilot reform. In the four years after the reform, a total of 3.66 billion Yuan was paid to the state finance, an increase of 37% over the four years before the reform. After the pilot reform, the GNP, national income, and gross output value of the industry and agriculture of Wuhan increased by 12.7%, 11.2%, and 11.2% each year. Compared with 1978, the GDP, the gross output value of industry and agriculture, foreign exchange earned through export of products, and the fiscal income of Guangzhou increased by two times (an annual increase of 16%), 1.24

times (an annual increase of 10.6%), 3.5 times (average annual increase of 20.7%), and 1.21 times (an annual increase of 10.4%) respectively in 1986.

2   The comprehensive reform of the major cities in China is a great creation in the economic reform based on China's own national conditions. It is an important part of China's overall economic reform. Although the comprehensive reform has a short history, some experience has been accumulated thanks to the great support from the CPC Central Committee and the State Council and the courageous exploration of a large number of theorists and the workers of practical work departments.

(I) We must strike a balance between invigorating the cities and invigorating the enterprises. Invigorating the enterprises is the foundation of invigorating the cities, while invigorating the cities is the premise for invigorating the enterprises.

We must take enhancing the vitality of enterprises as the core of the reform. The comprehensive reform of cities is undoubtedly to invigorate the cities and give full play to the various functions of cities. However, enterprises are the direct reflector of the productivity, so only by invigorating the enterprises can we invigorate the cities. Therefore, the governments of the major cities can never seize all kinds of power granted by the central and provincial governments in their own hands on the excuse of invigorating the cities while continuing to regard enterprises as appendages to administrative organs and managing enterprises mainly through administrative means. They must make invigorating the enterprises the starting point and goal of the comprehensive reform of cities, take enhancing the vitality of the cities as the core of the reform, and promote the transformation of government functions, streamlining administration, and delegating more power to lower-level governments to actively create conditions for invigorating the enterprises. The practice of reform proves that the cities that can better strike a balance between invigorating the cities and invigorating the enterprises have achieved good results in the reform. Taking Chongqing as an example, Chongqing started in 1984 to rectify the administrative companies that intercepted the rights of enterprises and cut the intermediate links in management to ensure the autonomy of enterprises. Based on the idea of "strike reflection", Shijiazhuang always gives priority to invigorating the enterprises and strikes all departments through invigorating the enterprises and requires them to take appropriate reform measures, streamline administration, delegate more power to lower-level governments, and carry out reform internally and externally to enhance the vitality of enterprises.

(II) We must open the door of cities and adhere to opening up internally and externally.

As mentioned above, to bring into play the role of cities, we must form a number of open, networked economic zones of different sizes based on the cities, especially medium and large cities, so as to break the old system featuring sectoral and regional fragmentation and vigorously promote the development of commodity production. This requires that we must overcome the narrow-mindedness of the small producers and local parochialism, abolish the protection policies inimical to competition, change the past self-seclusion state, establish the concept of socialized production of the modern commodity economy, open the door and adhere to opening up internally and externally. That is to say, on the one hand, a city must allow and encourage the enterprises from other provinces and cities to sell their products and invest in order to establish enterprises in the areas under its own jurisdiction, establish various alliance relations, and attract all kinds of talents; on the other hand, a city must allow and encourage its local enterprises, products, talents, and funds to actively enter the markets of other provinces and cities and the international markets and develop and strengthen the lateral economic ties among enterprises, cities, and regions according to the objective requirements of the commodity economy. Otherwise, it is impossible to realize the goal of reform, and new sectoral and regional segmentations will be formed. At present, although this problem has not yet been thoroughly solved, some pilot cities have acquired valuable experience in the practice of reform. The experience mainly includes the following aspects: first, while opening up to the outside world, a city must strive to make a breakthrough through promoting the development of circulation and transportation. A city generally has various functions, including a production center, a transportation hub, a trade center, a financial center, an information center, or a scientific and cultural center. But from the perspective of the development history of a city and the relationship among its various functions, a city will first be a trade center, and with the development of trade, it will gradually become a transportation hub and a production base, while the functions of a city as a financial center, an information center and a scientific and cultural center in turn serve for production and trade. Therefore, when opening up to the outside world, a city must first develop businesses and promote the free flow of commodities, and to develop businesses, a city must also solve the transportation problems so as to ensure unimpeded circulation of commodities. Second, a city must fully open to the outside world. That is to say, a city must open not only to foreign countries, but also to other provinces, cities, and areas in China, and it must open not only the business circulation, but also other aspects such as industries, science and technology, information, and transportation; it must open not only individual enterprises, but also various industries; it must open not only to rural areas but also to small towns and large cities; it must open not only to the hinterland, but also to the border and coastal areas; it must open not only to economically underdeveloped areas, but also to the economically developed areas. By opening up, cities can learn from each other's strengths to offset their own weaknesses and compete with each other to encourage the forerunner and urge on those lagging behind. Third, a city must open up in all aspects. That is to say, it must open both the consumer market and the production material market; it must open the capital market, the technical information market, and the labor market to promote the rational flow of personnel. In short, the economic relations of commodities must be gradually developed into all areas and aspects of social reproduction. Fourth, a city must adhere to opening up in various forms. A general merchandise trading relationship, a fixed cooperative relationship, a joint production relationship, or a long-term or short-term collaborative relationship can be established. In short, any form conducive to the opening up can be used.

(III) We must closely combine the urban reform with the urban economic development and strike a balance between them.

First, we must properly handle the relationship between the reform and the economic development. The economic reform is a long and complicated process, the implementation of a number of major reform measures needs unified understanding and certain conditions, and even after the implementation of these measures, it will take a long time to get the results, while some serious problems should be solved as soon as possible in the current economic development. This objectively requires that a city must not only focus on studying and planning some major reform measures, but also embark on the "spark program" for the reform to obtain immediate effects.

Second, we must properly deal with the relationship between the goals of reform and the urban economic development strategy. The urban economic development strategy must be formulated according to the reform objective of establishing an open, network-based economic zone, and every city can blaze the way of reform with its own characteristics according to its economic development strategy. The economic development strategy of a city should be based on the city itself, but it should not be limited to the city itself. It should include the entire economic zone. This needs to be achieved through reform. We should establish the horizontal management system model characterized by the development of lateral economic ties to coordinate a city's development strategy and the economic development strategy of other areas in the economic zone and promote the reform based on the coordinated strategy.

(IV) Deepening the reform of major cities depends on the support of the macroeconomic reform.

In recent years, great progress and significant achievements have been made in the comprehensive reform of the major cities, but under the current situation, we are faced with increasing difficulties to deepen the reform. The reform of major cities has the nature of a comprehensive reform, but after all, it belongs to a local revolution which is subject to the national macro-reform process. For example, we have delegated the management of enterprises to the government at the city level. The ultimate goal of doing so is to separate the duties of the government from those of enterprises and reduce direct government intervention in production and operation activities so that enterprises will become producers and operators that make their own management decisions and take full responsibility for their own profits and losses under the control and guidance of the national plans. However, under the current system, many enterprises must still carry out production according to the mandatory plans, the basic materials needed by enterprises are also allocated in a unified way, and a number of other enterprise powers are still in the hands of the competent authorities. In such a case, the behaviors of enterprises are mainly guided by the administrative departments, not by the market. This shows that to deepen the reform of major cities, we must carry out a major reform of the macro system. Presently, there is an urgent need to reform the planning system and the supplies system to reduce the mandatory plans, and the key materials that are in short supply can be put under control through ordering by the state. The experience of some major cities in establishing the production material market should be gradually promoted, and the financial market must be opened positively. In the meanwhile, we must adhere to the principle of lifting price controls on some commodities while readjusting price controls on others and actively promoting the price reform. Only in this way can we constantly deepen the reform of major cities to achieve the desired goals.

(Published in *Economic Management*, Issue 12, 1987)

12 Institutions of the economic management need transition and modification

With the highly centralized management system, an economic administration organ tends to put enterprises under its complete control by administrative means. As an enterprise is production-oriented, and its main task is production, the economic administration organ sees commanding or directing manufacturer's production process as its main job. Practice over years has proved that quite a few drawbacks are present in this way of economic administration organs managing enterprises.

As reform is deepening, an enterprise as a cell of national economy begins to witness changes of its nature and status from merely a manufacturing entity to a relatively independent commodity production and management, and from merely a manufacturing type to a production and management type. Accordingly, it is required that reform be carried out in the superstructure and that economic administration organs be transformed from a simple command-giving type to a guidance- and service-oriented type.

Such transformation will lead to the following changes:

First, there should be a change in the main administration functions. Under the highly centralized management system, an enterprise, merely a manufacturing entity, is deemed adjunct to an economic administration organ of the government that directly commands production of the enterprise. When the nature of the enterprise turns into a production and management type, the main functions of an economic administration organ will in general shift to coordination, balance, service, and supervision, notwithstanding its different division of labor and specific responsibilities.

Second, there should be a change in administration priorities. It may include the following: 1) originally, the economic administration organ could hardly concentrate on macro-economy management since priority was given to governing micro economy. This is one of the reasons for unchecked construction, redundant construction, and proportional imbalance. The successful transformation of the economic administration organ into a guidance- and service-oriented nature will minimize government's intervention in production and management activities of the enterprise to ensure the latter's independent management under the State plan. Economic administration organs should place great emphasis on macro-economic control, such as controlling significant proportional relations; investments and key construction projects; striking a balance between finance, credit, foreign exchange, and critical supplies; and making reasonable arrangements for industrial development and productivity throughout the country, to ensure the coordination and balance of the national economy development as a whole. 2) Previously, the economic administration organ focused on realizing near-term objectives and fulfilling monthly, quarterly, and yearly plans, and paid little attention to setting and achieving medium- and long-term objectives. After shifting to a guidance- and service-oriented nature, the economic administration organ will focus its attention on realizing medium- and long-term objectives, studying long-term economic development strategies, setting medium- and long-term development goals, and establishing significant technical-economic policy to achieve these goals. 3) In the past, the economic administration organ focused on the scheduled production output of an enterprise, i.e. the more products it produces, the higher the growth rate of output value, and the better the economic effects. As a result, production was severely divorced from marketing; varieties and designs of products became fewer and fewer; and quality degraded while prices soared. After shifting to a guidance- and service-oriented nature, the economic administration organ will focus on improving economic benefits not only by balancing and coordinating macro economy development and strengthening our various economic relations to avoid major decision-making misplays, but also by adopting various measures to facilitate enterprises in developing new products, in increasing varieties and designs, in improving product quality, in reducing consumption, in paying close attention to market changes, in meeting market needs, in minimizing costs, and in increasing profits.

Finally, the administration approach should also change. Previously, it was by giving mandatory plans and other administrative orders that the economic administration organ governed enterprises. After shifting to a guidance- and service-oriented nature, the economic administration organ adopts such methods as economic leverage, economic legislation, and supervision to govern production and operation activities of an enterprise, notwithstanding necessary administrative interventions, in order to encourage the advanced enterprises, but spur those that are backward; encourage the development of products in short supply, but impose restrictions on products in excessive supply; encourage the development of new products, but eliminate outmoded ones; and encourage the application of advanced technologies, but get rid of obsolete, outdated ones.

To practically achieve the function transformation of economic administration organs requires streamlining administration and delegating power to the lower levels so that they can free themselves from governing such economic affairs as the daily production-supply-marketing and the human, financial, and material resources of an enterprise.

Streamlining administration is preconditioned by delegating power to the lower levels. Since the founding of New China, we have simplified government organs more than once, but we have not yet achieved anticipated goals; instead, the more they were downsized, the more complex and overstaffed they became. The root cause for this phenomenon is that streamlining administration did not synchronize in time with delegating power to the lower levels. In fact, the former should be preceded by the latter.

There are a number of powers that an economic administration organ can delegate to the lower levels, but the following two are of ultimate importance:

1   Administrative jurisdictions over enterprises pertaining to all industrial departments under the Central Government and those under the Provincial/District Governments should be transferred to administrative organs of large- and medium-sized cities. Practice over years has proved that direct intervention by industrial departments under the Central Government and those under the Provincial/District Governments may make government shift its focus towards concrete issues and affairs of an enterprise, over-looking and even impairing industrial management, and that enterprises who are directly subordinate to the organ are more accessible to preferences covering production plan, material supply, technical transformation, and investment than those who are not, which may prejudice the overall arrangement of production according to objective demand, quality of performance, and economic efficiency of the enterprise, and may also compromise the development of specialized collaboration and economic consortium based in a city. For this reason, most of the industrial departments under the Central Government and those under the Provincial/District Governments should not exercise direct jurisdiction over enterprises, with exception to those provinces or districts which are economically and industrially backward and embrace fewer large- and medium-sized cities. These administrative jurisdictions over industrial enterprises should be delegated to organs in large- and medium-sized cities.

2   The rights to lay down yearly plan should be transferred to enterprises. At present, the yearly plan and quarterly plan of an enterprise are under the jurisdiction of economic authority; the enterprise is merely entitled to work out its production operation schedule. Whereas it is a tough job to work out and get released a yearly plan due to frequent alterations, there often occurs an embarrassing phenomenon that "a yearly plan is usually formulated in a whole year". In this case, it seems impossible to streamline administration and invigorate enterprises when jurisdictions delegated by the State are not implemented. On this ground, the State's plan management of industrial production must switch from "a yearly plan supported by five-year plan" to "a five-year plan supported by a yearly plan". Thus, the State will only issue a five-year plan (with a list of annual targets) to enterprises and use the fulfillment of tasks specified in the five-year plan as criteria of assessment; while at the same time publishing economic information and developing some economic incentive and development-controlling measures to guide production and management activities of enterprises. In this way, the State will largely control finance, revenue,

credit, foreign exchange, critical materials, amount of investment, and key construction projects in addition to five-year plans; and the rights to product and manage will be transferred to enterprises. According to the State five-year plan, market demands, and actual conditions, the enterprise can develop a yearly plan on its own and report it to competent authority for record or approval. The competent authority will merely coordinate imbalanced issues between enterprises. Not only will this method enable the economic administration organ to concentrate on the study of strategic and comprehensive problems and enhance industrial management, but also enable enterprises to have more autonomous rights in making plans. It also creates necessary conditions for enterprises to become relatively independent commodity producers and operators.

Besides delegating powers to lower levels or transferring part of their powers to enterprises, the economic administration organs can hand over some transactional, power-irrelevant activities to civil trade associations/guilds for democratic management, e.g. carrying out fishing expeditions in an industrial situation; putting forward a proposal of industrial development planning; recommending or drafting technical equipment policy, laying down conventional guild regulations; providing enterprises with technical-economic information, consultation, and personnel training; summarizing and popularizing advanced technology and managerial experience; organizing competition and peer rating between enterprises, etc.

After the power of economic administration organs is delegated to lower levels, adjustments shall be made in regulatory agencies and their functions to perfect industrial administration system. By administrative functions, the government's economic administration agencies can be divided into three systems: functional management, industrial management, and competent authority of enterprises.

There are many governmental function management agencies. By main functions, they can also be divided into three subsystems:

1   Adjustment-balance subsystem: includes such sectors as planning, price control, taxation, banks, labor wages, and finance. For each sector in this subsystem, its job functions need to be further defined and job methods need to be improved, but there must be a more authoritative comprehensive department to coordinate all economic leverages. The planning commission may be an appropriate candidate because it makes plans, takes charge of the successful execution of plans, and has regulating measures to assure such execution.

Now that the planning commission is entrusted with comprehensive management of all economic leverages, it should be authorized to act as a veritable "commission" that involves price control, taxation, banks, labor wages, and finance sectors, and will make plans and coordinate various economic leverages under the leadership of finance and economy group.

2   Coordination-service subsystem: includes such sectors as economic committee, railway, communication and transportation, electric power, goods and materials, business, and foreign trade. In this subsystem, the economic committee plays roles varying from coordinating managerial activities covering communication and transportation and energy suppliers so that they provide essential material conditions for production and management activity of an enterprise, to summarizing, analyzing, and regularly publishing economic information provided by all sectors as references for enterprises to make their yearly plan and other economic decisions.
3   Supervision subsystem: includes such sectors as auditing, industrial and commercial administration, statistics, and finance banks. Audit sector should become a comprehensive supervisory sector. This subsystem needs to be consolidated in order to transform economic administration organs; particularly, the audit sector in charge of overall supervision needs to be improved and enhanced. In addition, the government supervision needs to be combined with judicial supervision so that it can play the role of an economic court.

The industrial management sector of the government means industry ministries under the Central Government, industry departments under the provincial, municipal, or autonomous region governments, and industry bureaus in large- and medium-sized cities. After the industry ministries under the Central Government and industry departments under the provincial, municipal, or autonomous regional governments no longer take charge of enterprises, these government organs will be downsized or merged, and will exercise the functions of industrial management.

After the administrative power of supervising enterprises is transferred to large- and medium-sized cities, the competent authority thereof must take the change and the industrial bureaus thereof must exercise the functions of competent administration for enterprises. However, the managing contents must be streamlined sufficiently by doing the following: 1) execute plan management for enterprises by issuing a uniform, scientific, and comprehensively balanced five-year plan to coordinate and balance the yearly plan of the enterprise. The five-year plan (including production, marketing, goods and materials, energy resources, labor wages, capital construction, technical transformation, etc.) may be proposed by relevant department but must be released to enterprises after being reviewed and approved jointly by the planning sector and competent authority for enterprises. All directives and instructions given by relevant sectors must not be released to enterprises until selected and sorted by a competent authority. 2) Guarantee that the competent authority makes available the material conditions for enterprises to execute the mandatory plan of the State and bears economic losses incurred to enterprises due to decision-making mis-play. As long as the competent authority it has the right to release plans and give directives, it is obliged to help enterprises address all problems concerning the execution of plans and directives and will be economically and legally liable for the correctness of these plans and directives. 3) Appoint or dismiss director/manager of an enterprise. The director (manager) of an enterprise owned by the whole people will be appointed, dismissed, or examined by the competent authority; this is one of important symbols to differentiate it from one under collective ownership. Due to a double identity of the director of the enterprise owned by the whole people (he or she manages the enterprise on behalf of both the State and the staff), the competent authority must respect a system of democratic centralism when appointing or dismissing the director (manager). If the director (manager) is elected or nominated by staff representatives, the election or nomination will be subject to the examination and approval by the competent authority; if he or she is designated by the competent authority, the designation will be recognized on the Workers' Congress after he or she serves for some time. The aforesaid procedures also apply to the dismissal of the director (manager). 4) Execute economic and administrative supervision of enterprises so that they can totally accomplish mandatory plans laid down by the State, resolutely implement all policies and guidelines of the Party, and strictly comply with all economic laws and regulations of the State; in addition, enterprises will be rewarded or punished contingent on their performance.

When the industrial administration organs have made the adjustment in their functions in the ways as mentioned above, the systems, including balance adjustment, coordination service, and supervision, will be consolidated, and the functions of industrial management and competent authority will be modified. All this will pave the way for transforming the economic administration organs from a production-commanding type into a guidance- and service-oriented type.

(Published in *Economic Management*, Issue 10, 1984)

13 Discussion of strengthening industrial management

For a long time, we have only paid attention to the management of enterprises by competent departments but neglected industrial management, resulting in poor industrial management. This has resulted in fragmentation, multi-leadership, mutual restraint, overlapped production and construction, and other problems. While the reforms, such as streamlining administration, delegating more power to lower levels, and giving to play the economic organization role of cities, are carried out, strengthening industrial management has become an urgent issue in the management of various industries. The following is some of our superficial opinions.

1. Defining the concept of industry and industrial management and distinguishing industrial management and management by competent departments

The management of industries of the state is divided into the management of enterprises by competent departments, management by integrated departments, and industrial management according to the division of functions of all government administration departments. We are quite clear about management by competent departments and management by integrated departments. As industrial management and management by competent departments were combined into one in the past, people only pay attention to management by competent departments but know little about the concept of industrial management and its tasks.

To make the definition of industrial management clear, we must first clearly define what makes an industry. We hold that an industry means an industrial category forming according to the nature and characteristics of products (services) manufactured by enterprises and their different roles in the national economy. An industry has the following three characteristics: the first characteristic is variability. An industry is developed with the expansion of industrial production, scientific and technological progress, and social division of labor. In addition, with the development of productive forces and deepening of division of labor, new industries will continue to emerge. On the one hand, the division of labor is "to transform into a special branch of industry not only the making of each separate product, but even of each separate part of a product – and not only the making of a product, but even the separate operations of preparing the product for consumption".[1] On the other hand, due to scientific and technical progress, new technologies, new materials, new processes, and new products will appear, and thus some new branches of industry will emerge. The second characteristic is hierarchy. The classification of the branches of industries is somewhat like a biological classification which divides biological organisms into phylum, class, order, family, genus, species, and so on. Branches of industry can also be divided into several levels based on products. For example, according to the current taxonomy, the branches of industry in China can at least be divided into four levels: primary classification (broad classification), secondary classification (medium classification), tertiary classification (rough classification), and quaternary classification (fine classification) (as shown in Fig. 2.13.1). The third characteristic is combination. There are different methods for industrial classification. In other words, different industrial systems can be formed according to different classification methods. For example, in the Western countries, it is classified by industries, but it is classified based on two major categories in China. But no matter what classification method is used, a scientific industrial system should be formed.

Industrial management means to coordinate and monitor the related economic activities in the entire industry through the government's industrial administration department and non-governmental organizations and provide a variety of services for the entire sector to promote the healthy development of enterprises in the industry under the guidance of the national plans. Therefore, the industrial management and management of enterprises by competent departments serve two different kinds of functions. Their main differences are reflected in the following aspects:

(I)   Industrial management should reflect not only the general functions of economic management of the state but also the democratic management function of the enterprises in the same industry. Its main tasks should include following: formulate the industrial development plans; formulate sectoral technical and economic policies and industrial production and construction standards; collect, analyze, process, and transmit technical and economic intelligence and information; give suggestions on using economic levers to regulate the production and organize various technical and economic activities for enterprises in the industry; check the production technologies in an industry; supervise the enterprises in the industry to implement the national plans, principles, and policies; and summarize and exchange the advanced experience of the enterprises in an industry in production technology and management. Management by the government competent department mainly reflects the corporate management functions of the owners of production materials of all people. Its main tasks should include the following: issue on behalf of the state the plans that have been comprehensively balanced (including plans for production, sale,

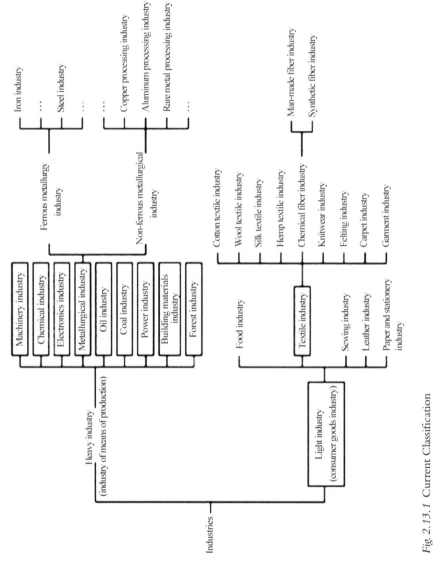

Fig. 2.13.1 Current Classification

materials, energy, labor and wages, capital construction, and technological modification, etc.) and various instructions and directives to enterprises; appoint, dismiss, and manage directors and managers of enterprises; create necessary external conditions for enterprises to accomplish the plans; and supervise the business activities of enterprises.

(II) Industrial management is to exercise the management function not only for the enterprises in an industry, but also for some activities of the competent department of these enterprises; while the competent department should only exercise the management function for the enterprises under its management.

(III) An enterprise may be under the management of several industrial administration departments. For example, if the products of an enterprise belong to three different industries, it will be under the management of three industrial administration departments, and each industrial administration department exercises hierarchical management. But there should be only one competent department for an enterprise.

(IV) Industrial management has two organizational forms: governmental and non-governmental, while the government department is the only competent department for enterprises.

2. Establishing two different kinds of industrial management systems

(I) Improving the industrial administration departments of the governments at all levels

1   Adjusting the affiliation of industrial enterprises and separating the industrial administration department from the competent departments of enterprises.

First, all the central industrial ministries and the industrial bureaus of all provinces and autonomous regions are in principle no longer in charge of enterprises, and a small number of enterprises that should be directly managed by the central government can be put under the charge of the State Economic Commission. But there should only be a small number of such enterprises, which can only be limited to the following: first, the enterprises that need centralized management due to the industrial characteristics, such as large-scale oil, petrochemical, and power enterprises; second, the large-scale key enterprises with high product yield, high planned distribution proportion, wide collaboration and matching areas, and significant impact on the national economy, such as conglomerates in the ship and auto industries; third, the heavy machinery and large whole-set equipment manufacturers, which should carry out production according to the mandatory production plans and distribution plans issued by the state, such as manufacturers of large-scale power generation equipment, large-scale machine tools, and other products.

Second, the management of most of the enterprises directly under the central ministries and the enterprises directly under the provincial governments should be delegated to the major cities. But the major cities should also change the situation that the industrial administration department and the competent department are combined into one. In large cities, the management bureaus for enterprises of public ownership should be established as the competent departments in charge of enterprises. In medium-sized cities, the economic commission may directly act as the competent department in charge of enterprises.

Third, the governments at the county level should be in charge of small, state-owned industrial enterprises. They mainly process local raw materials into products to serve for local economic development and improve people's living standards. To arouse the enthusiasm of the counties and to promote the development of local industries, these enterprises can still be affiliated with the counties, but the industrial bureaus at the county level should be canceled, and the economic commission at the county level should be in charge of enterprises.

Fourth, the affiliations of the trans-city and trans-regional conglomerates should be determined according to the extent of relations between their main production and economic activities and the regions where they are located. In general, a conglomerate should be under the jurisdiction of the city where its leading factory or company is located. A conglomerate should be in charge of its affiliated factories.

Fifth, a dispatched agency under a province is not the government at a certain level, so it should not be directly in charge of enterprises. In the area that has been transformed into a city directly under the jurisdiction of the provincial government, the enterprises formerly affiliated to the area should be under the charge of the municipality. In an area that has not been transformed into a city directly under the jurisdiction of the provincial government, some enterprises can be put directly under the charge of the county where they are located.

After the above adjustment, the original industrial administration departments of the central and provincial governments and the governments of the autonomous regions and municipalities will only exercise the function of industrial administration department of the government.

2   The government's industrial administration departments should be adjusted according to the principle of centralized management. As shown in Fig. 2.13.1, the establishment of the existing industrial administration departments is unreasonable due to the following factors:

  First, at the primary level of classification, no ministry has been established for the heavy industry, but the ministry of light industry has been established, which is asymmetric at this level.

  Second, light industry can be divided at least into three branches of industries at the secondary level, namely food, textile, and daily necessities, but only the Ministry of Textiles is established at this level. In such practice, the textile industry is actually considered parallel to the light industry, as if light industry does not include the textile industry. This is obviously unscientific.

Third, seven ministries have been established in the heavy industry (excluding the military sector), but only two ministries have been established in light industry. This is obviously related to the practice that undue emphasis was put on the development of heavy industry, while the development of light industry was neglected. In recent years, we have corrected the practice and idea that undue emphasis was put on the development of heavy industry, while the development of light industry was neglected. The structure of light and heavy industries were adjusted so that the proportion of light industry is more reasonable, but such tendency has not been corrected at the institutional level.

To solve the above problems, the existing industrial administration departments must be adjusted. In the adjustment of government's industrial administration departments, the following principles should be taken into consideration:

First, we must ensure the scientific base of the system. The setting of administration departments of the government in all industries must be at the same level as industrial classification so as to form a scientific industrial management system.

Second, we must take into consideration the size of an industry and the varieties and complexity of products in the industry. In general, the larger an industry, the more varieties and complexity of products and the heavier the management tasks will be. An independent administration department should be set up for a large industry. On the contrary, similar industries should be combined, and a department should be set up for the management of several industries.

Third, we should lay stress on the key industries. That is, it is better to set up the management authorities for the emerging industries and industries whose development needs to be particularly encouraged.

Fourth, we must adhere to the principle of "streamlining, uniformity, efficiency, conservation and anti-bureaucracy".[2] If an organ can accomplish the management tasks, we should not set up another unnecessary organ; if an organ at the primary level can accomplish the management tasks, we should not set up organs at different levels. According to the above principles, the existing industrial administration departments can be adjusted as follows:

(a) According to the current industrial classification in China, it is suitable to set up the government's industrial administration departments at the secondary level. This is because in industrial classification at the primary level, there are only two industries, i.e. the heavy and light industries, and if the government's industrial administration departments are set up at this level, the scope of management is too large, which is inimical to industrial management; while if the government's industrial administration departments are set up at the tertiary level, there are too many industries, so it is impossible for the government to set up so many industrial administration departments. Therefore, the government's industrial administration departments should only be set up at the secondary level in industrial classification, so the Ministry of Light Industry that is set up at the primary level of industrial classification should be revoked.

(b) In the light industry as a broad sector, the Ministry of Textiles should be retained, and the Ministry of Foods and the Ministry of Consumer Goods should be newly established. The establishment of the two new ministries is not only to meet the requirements of sectoral classification, and more importantly, it is to adapt to the development of the new situation. With economic development and an improvement of people's living standards, the food and consumer goods industries are witnessing rapid development, and their position in the national economy is becoming increasingly important. In 1982, the output value of the food industry accounted for 18.59% of the country's gross output value of industry, rising from the fourth place to the third place, next only to the machinery and textiles industries. Moreover, in these two industries, there are many small branches, the products are complicated, and they are closely related to people's lives. As a result, the industrial management of these industries is an arduous task, but the establishment of two industrial administration departments is conducive to the healthy development of the industries.

(c) The seven ministries under the heavy industry as a broad sector are all established in the secondary level of industrial classification, which is in line with the requirement for industrial classification, but the Ministry of Petroleum Industry, the Ministry of Coal Industry, and the Ministry of Power Industry can be merged into the Ministry of Energy Industry. This is because, although the products in these three ministries are important, they are relatively unitary, and after the separation of the functions of the government from those of enterprises, their industrial management task is not arduous, so their combination will not weaken the industrial management.

(d) Based on the requirements for industrial classification, the centralized management of industries should be implemented. Industrial overlap will appear no matter which method of industrial classification is used. For example, according to the existing industrial classification, bicycles, sewing machines, watches, and so on fall into the machinery industry or the consumer goods industry; electronic watches fall into the consumer goods industry in light industry or the electronics industry in heavy industry. Therefore, after the adjustment of industrial administration departments, we must also adjust the management scope of industrial administration departments according to the requirements for industrial classification and implement centralized management. For example, the garment industry should be classified into the Ministry of Textiles Industry, and bicycles, sewing machines, refrigerators, and other household appliances can be classified into the consumer goods industry.

The adjusted industrial administration departments are shown in Fig. 2.13.2. The industrial government administration departments of all provinces, municipalities, and autonomous regions as well as the major cities should also be adjusted based on the above principles. At the county level, due to the small industrial sector, the lowest level of industrial management should not be given this level of competence, so you cannot set up an industry management department.

3   We should properly define the functions of the industrial administration departments of the government at all levels and implement hierarchical management. The central industrial administration departments and local industrial administration departments should implement hierarchical management. Although the industrial administration departments at all levels have no direct leadership relationship, the industrial administration departments at a higher level have the power and responsibility to provide instructions to the industrial administration departments at a lower level. The industrial administration departments at a lower level should receive the instructions from the industrial administration departments at a higher level and should also ensure that the guidelines, policies, regulations, and directives formulated by the industrial administration departments at a higher level are concretely implemented. The scope of functions of the industrial administration departments should be clearly defined. The central industrial administration department should be mainly responsible for formulating major technical and economic policies, the national industrial development plans, the layout of key industrial enterprises, the standardization, serialization, and generalization of products and parts, and the quality standards for important products and other tasks; the local industrial administration departments should be mainly responsible for formulating local industrial development plans, the layout of ordinary industrial enterprises in the area, and the local product standards and other tasks. In addition, the central industrial administration departments can carry out the overall management while exercising various functions, while the local industrial administration departments must carry out more concrete management.

(II) Establishing and improving various industrial associations[3]

(III) Rectifying and reforming the industrial companies

Industrial companies are a special form of organization in the industrial economic management system in China. Most of these companies are administrative in nature, play the role of industrial competent departments of the government, and appear as corporate identities. In the past, they played a certain role in industrial management, but with the deepening of economic reform, they are afflicted with increasingly serious maladies. First, these industrial companies intensified the problem of non-separation of government administration and enterprise management. The government administration departments

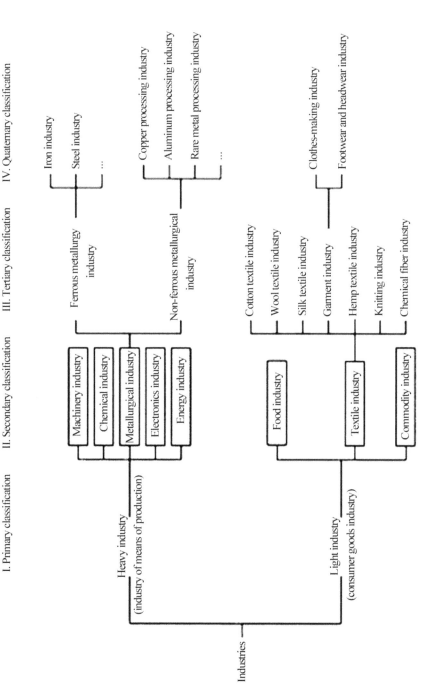

Fig. 2.13.2 Adjusted Classification

and enterprises are two kinds of organizations that have different natures and functions: the government administration departments are administrators, while companies are subordinates. As these two kinds of organizations with different natures are merged together, they must exercise the government's management function and corporate management function, which will inevitably exacerbate the problem of non-separation of government administration and enterprise management and affect the economic benefits of enterprises. This runs counter to the reform direction of separating the functions of the government from those of the enterprises. Second, this has increased the levels of management and affected the enthusiasm of factories and enterprises. These industrial companies are sandwiched between the government's industrial administration departments and factories and enterprises; the majority of them have become subordinate administrative agencies of the government, but they do not have the power of the government authorities and cannot effectively solve the problems of enterprises. Especially in the past two years, many industrial companies that were eager to achieve the transformation into enterprises continued to expand their scope of management and took over the power from their subsidiaries, but they were unable to solve the production and management problems of factories and enterprises. This has exacerbated the conflicts between these companies and the factories, the factories called them "second mother in law" or "tap company", while the government's industrial administration departments regard them as the leaders of factories and enterprises, so these companies are sandwiched in the middle and become the focus of conflict between the higher and lower levels. Third, industrial companies are "grotesque" organizations that exercise a number of functions, and they want to take charge of everything, but are unable to do so, so they performed badly in managing anything and many things under their charge were left uncared for. This has affected work efficiency. Therefore, to establish two different kinds of industrial management systems, it is necessary to rectify and reform the industrial companies.

Industrial companies have the following three ways out:

First, they must develop into enterprises, which is currently the expectation of many industrial companies. But from the perspective of the development prospect, except for a few industrial companies, it is difficult for the majority of industrial companies to realize this goal. At first, the products of the factories in many industrial companies vary widely, and many factories have no intrinsic link in production technology. For example, the products of a daily-use chemical company in a city covers dozens of "daily-use chemical products" that are almost unrelated in production, including toothpastes, soaps, and cosmetics. It is undoubtedly very difficult for such an industrial company to serve as a unified production and operation entity. Second, the majority of industrial companies are too large in scale and have too many factories, and the production of the factories are mostly enclosed or semi-enclosed and mutually independent, so it is very difficult to carry out unified accounting and enforce self-responsibility for their own profit and loss. If the industrial companies are too large in scale, we will have the situation where everybody "eats from the same big pot", which is not conducive to mobilizing the enthusiasm of factories and workers. Third, the enterprises in the same industry are organized within a company, which is neither conducive to competition nor convenient for management. In particular, some national, industrial companies cover the major companies in the same industry and form a monopoly. Fourth, if an enterprise is too large in scale, it is incompatible with the management in the current stage in China and is inimical to improving the economic efficiency.

Second, industrial companies should develop into industrial associations. This is the most practical and effective way out for most industrial companies. At present, China's industrial management really needs these organizations, and these organizations have not been established in many places. Based on the future development trend, with the continuous deepening of the institutional reform and expansion of enterprise autonomy, the industrial companies will gradually disintegrate, and some will develop into industrial associations. This is because some enterprises inside the industrial companies are likely to break the boundaries of the industry and establish a number of cross-industrial alliances, such as industry-industry alliances, industry-business alliances, industry-trade alliances, and industry-research alliances. These alliances may be loose at the beginning, and their affiliations do not change, but once they become the "community of destiny", they will separate from the industrial companies and become close corporations or general factories that are directly under the management of the relevant government departments. Some enterprises that have close links in production and operation in the industrial companies will gradually unite and establish some corporate joint organizations in the companies, and after these alliances have grown up, they will also divorce from the industrial companies and exist independently. Some factories and enterprises in the industrial companies will gradually develop into large-scale joint ventures or independent factories during production and operation by relying on their own strength, and they will also break away from the leadership of the industrial companies. In this way, the industrial companies' existence will not be significant and thus can only evolve into private industrial associations.

Third, industrial companies that were unable to be developed into enterprises or evolved into industrial associations should be dissolved as soon as possible.

(IV) The relationship between strengthening industrial management and giving play to the role of major cities in organizing the economy should be correctly handled

We must effectively combine strengthening industrial management and giving play to the role of major cities in organizing the economy. This is the key to the success of restructuring the industrial organization system, so we must address the following problems:

(1) Major cities should be the hubs combining the vertical and horizontal relations.

Vertical relations mean the management of enterprises by the state, which includes the management of enterprises by the competent departments and the comprehensive departments and industrial management. They embody the function of economic management by the state, which mainly reflects the economic ties between the central and local governments and between the state and enterprises. Horizontal relations mean the economic ties among enterprises and among cities, which reflect the requirements of the commodity economy and the relationship between commodity exchanges.

Vertically, the central ministries and the industrial bureaus of all provinces and autonomous regions no longer take charge of enterprises, and enterprises will be under the charge of the cities. Accordingly, the plans, energy, and materials required to accomplish these plans and the funds for the technological transformation of these companies should also no longer be issued or allocated by the former departments to which they are affiliated, but should be issued or allocated directly by the planning departments at all levels and arranged by the cities uniformly. In particular, industrial management must also find its way to the cities and the enterprises gathering in the cities through a variety of technical and economic policies, plans and production, and technical standards. Horizontally, as industrial enterprises are mainly concentrated in the cities, the cities are the centers of trade, transportation centers, and finance, and intelligence information, science and technology, and culture, so the various economic ties among enterprises, among cities, and between urban and rural areas must be established and developed by relying on the cities.

(2)   Improving the industrial planning coordinated with the urban planning.

We must strengthen industrial management and give play to play the role of industries. First of all, we must do a good job in enterprise planning, break regional segmentation and sectoral separation, and closely combine the industrial planning and regional planning centering on the cities. The State Council should set up an authoritative group for industrial planning, bring together the persons in charge in the relevant departments and regions to jointly study and formulate the plans of the key industries, especially the plans of the large industries, so that the plans formulated are holistic, strategic, policy-based, scientific, and authoritative. After the industrial plans are approved by the state, the production, construction, adjustment, restructuring, technological innovation, and other major economic activities of the relevant departments and regions should be carried out based on the requirements of the plans. In execution, if any significant change occurs, it is necessary to go beyond the requirements of the plans and carry out arrangements or modify the plans, and the original planning group or industrial administration department should bring together the stakeholders to jointly study the situation and make decisions and in order to not respond blindly.

When formulating the industrial plans, we should not only take into consideration the immediate output value, output growth, and arrangement of construction projects, but also include the development and the layout of production capacity for a longer period of time; the technological development and product upgrading; the specialized cooperation and regional division of labor; the development of key products and products in short supply; the organizational structure adjustment; and the technical transformation and so on. In addition, we must study and formulate various policies and standards to ensure the implementation of the plans, such as the policies for technologies, equipment, technical standards, construction standards, reasonable scales, and production batches, etc. With these plans, policies, and standards, the industrial administration departments will give support to the production and construction activities in line with the plans, policies, and standards, and on the contrary, they will restrict those that are not in line with the plans, policies, and standards. In this way, we can control the production capacity and reduce conflicts in production arrangements.

(Published in *China Industrial Economics*, Issue 2, 1985)

Notes

1 *The Collected Works of Lenin*, Vol. 1, Beijing, China: People's Publishing House, 1984, p. 161.
2 *Selected Works of Mao Tse-tung*, Vol. 3, Beijing, China: People's Publishing House, 1991, p. 850.
3 For the related content, please refer to the *Journal of China Industrial Economics*, issue 1, 1984.

14 A brief discussion on the local protection policies

In the economic development in the past, there was a guiding principle that a large area or even a province should establish its own independent economic system. Under the guidance of this thought, some local governments had adopted for many years a kind of "protection" policy in the development of the local economy: they did not allow the purchase of products that could be produced locally from other regions; they tried to create conditions to produce the products that could not be produced locally, and made efforts to improve the self-sufficiency level and gradually reduce dependence on other areas. At that time, these policies were regarded as important measures to protect the local industry and promote local economic development. Now, it is believed that on the contrary, these administrative measures that violate the economic laws have actually hindered the development of the socialist commodity economy and intentionally or unintentionally dismembered the unified socialist market, making some inexpensive products unable to enjoy a good sale. In some local markets, where the commodities had low quality and high prices and were available in only a few varieties, the public was dissatisfied. Such "protection" policies, in essence, were to protect the backwardness and should be abolished in the adjustment and reform of the national economy.

1. The "protection" policies have protected the backward natural economy and are inimical to the division of labor in social production and to fully exerting the advantages of various areas

China has a vast territory and a large population, and the natural conditions, resource conditions, and the level of economic development vary widely. Taking agriculture as an example, due to the different natural conditions, it is suitable for growing rice in South China, while it is suitable for growing upland crops in North China. In some provinces, it is suitable for growing cotton, while in some other provinces, it is suitable for growing sugar cane or for the development of animal husbandry. From the perspective of resource conditions, some provinces have rich oil and coal reserves and are suitable for the development of oil, coal, and chemical industries, and some provinces have rich iron ores and non-ferrous metals and are suitable for the development of the "gold industry". Shanghai, Tianjin, Guangzhou, Jiangsu, Zhejiang, and other coastal provinces and cities have a relatively strong industrial foundation, well-developed transport conditions and strong technical forces, which is conducive to the development of light industry and high-tech and new products. Therefore, the development of the local economy should suit the local characteristics and conditions, which is a very important issue in theory and practice.

Marxist political economics pointed out that with the socialization of production, the small-scale production and operation mode must be changed, and the productive forces should be allocated scientifically according to the local characteristics so as to establish the industrial structures that can exert their advantages. That is to say, it is impossible for any place to produce everything and achieve self-sufficiency in everything. This requires breaking the boundary of administrative division and forming a unified, socialist domestic market to allow unimpeded access and sale of products from different areas under the guidance of the national plans. Chins is a unified socialist country that has destroyed the feudal separatism, and the whole national economy is an interrelated and indivisible unity. This is undoubtedly very conducive to the unified planning and rational layout of the national economy. We give equal importance to the division of labor and cooperation, seek advantages and avoid disadvantages, and organize social production. However, the "protection" policies were contrary to the objective requirements and artificially created the barriers. Under such policies, the governments in some areas blindly resisted the entry of products from other areas, laid one-sided emphasis on improving local self-sufficiency level regardless of the objective and subjective conditions, and even regarded this as the goal of economic planning. They forced themselves to develop the products and industries that were not suitable for the local conditions, but they were unable to vigorously develop the products and industries suitable for the local conditions, resulting in the unavailability of raw materials of some industrial products, technical problems, high costs, low profits, and heavy losses in some areas and low crop yields, high costs, and low farmer income in some other areas. This practice could also cause a chain reaction, affecting the economic structure in various areas and even the whole country, leading to the situation that every province, prefecture, or county, large or small, operates independently and has an all-inclusive organizational structure. The country's economic system was completely cut into many small pieces, hindering the overall balance and rational distribution, obstructing economic cooperation and economic exchanges between regions, and turning the national economy into a backwater economy. This has actually protected the backward, small-scale production and operation modes and the self-sufficient natural economy.

2. The "protection" policies have protected the backward production conditions and management modes and are inimical to the use of new equipment, new technology, and scientific management modes

Presently, the economic benefits of products differ greatly in different provinces or regions. Taking fuel consumption as an example, a ton of standard coal can produce 606 five-pound warm bottles in Jiangsu and Zhejiang, but only produce 74 such bottles in Guizhou, and 56 such bottles in Inner Mongolia; the coke consumed by per ton of iron pan is 190–220kg in Shandong and Liaoning, but it is up 1,000kg in some areas. In general, the production conditions for the products with poor economic effects are relatively poor, the technical and management level is relatively low, the equipment is outdated, and the techniques are backward. However, why are they able to survive? Except for some products that are in short supply, most of them are associated with the "protection" policies. They resist the products from other areas and implement the "monopoly" prices internally. These price policies are contrary to the law of value and negate the basic principles of an equal exchange of an equal amount of labor. In this way, the prices of some similar products with the same value vary greatly because of their different origins.

As a result, the enterprises with backward technological and management level can earn high profits although their products are of low quality and at high prices. This makes the managers of some backward enterprises complacent and helps develop an inert, dependent, and conservative attitude, so they will not take the initiative to improve the production conditions and management level of enterprises. A few years ago, in order to fill the gap in the production of cotton/polyester fabrics, a province invested heavily to establish a polyester staple fiber factory. However, due to the outdated equipment, backward technologies, and low level of management, the prices of the products were one third higher than those of similar products in other places. The textile factories that used this kind of raw materials were unable to maintain normal production, and the commercial sector suffered the loss of hundreds of thousands of Yuan due to marketing these raw materials. Therefore, the textile factory and the commercial sector asked to introduce raw materials from other areas, but the competent department did not agree with a view to protect the local industry. Under the protection of these policies, the fiber factory feels justified and contented. It has not reduced the prices of its products, but on the contrary, it sold all products at the same prices regardless of their quality. Under such circumstances, how can we urge enterprises to upgrade their old equipment, use advanced techniques, and improve their technical and management level?

3. The "protection" policies have protected the backward and outdated products and are inimical to the upgrading of products and the development of new products

The purpose of socialist production is to maximally meet the material and cultural needs of the economic growth of the entire society. The needs of this kind of economic growth are reflected not only in the number of products, but also in the quality, specifications, and varieties of products, and require the industrial sector to produce more and more new products to equip the other sectors of the national economy and meet the extensive needs of people's living standards. But in the past three decades, China's industrial sector performed poorly in this aspect. Putting aside the means of production, there are many problems with the industrial products necessary in people's daily life, regardless of quantity, quality, and varieties. The products that remained unchanged for many years can be found everywhere, low-quality products are flooding the market, and new products, new colors, and new varieties are rare, some remaining in the stage of "samples, exhibits and gifts" for a long time. There are many causes for these phenomena, but they are highly related to the implementation of the "protection" policies. Due to the "protection" policies, some enterprises lack the external drive for competition, and the barriers for isolation have been created in the backward areas. Good products are unable to enter to these areas, but self-produced products, bad or good, can be sold out, just as the saying goes "the daughter of the emperor needs not worry that she cannot soon be married". Now that they need not worry about the sale of the old product, why should they try to develop new products and upgrade old products? Some advanced regions have the conditions and ability to develop new products, but due to limitations of the market and lack of competitors, new products will not bring them more economic benefits. Therefore, they need not spend more money and manpower in the development of new products. In addition, these "protection" policies have also blocked the exchange of new products among different regions, cut off the regional economic ties, made the regional trade relations abnormal, limited the eyesight of people in a narrow range, and made them arrogant. At the new product exhibitions held in recent years, the participants from many provinces and cities said that the exhibitions have opened the horizons and showed them the strengths of others and their weaknesses, and some products that they felt were "not bad" locally were really bad when compared with others' at the exhibitions. Therefore, the product exchange among regions helps improve product quality and the development of new products, so it is extremely useful.

The appearance of these "protection" policies has their historical and practical reasons. China's socialist economy is not built on the advanced capitalist commodity economy, but developed on the basis of an extremely backward semi-colonial and semi-feudal, small-scale peasant economy, which resulted in congenital deficiencies of commodity economy. In the three decades since liberation, due to our misunderstanding of socialist economic forms in theory, lack of understanding on the development of commodity economy, some shortcomings in the management system, and some specific economic policies, we have made some mistakes in work, resulting in acquired deficiencies in the development of the socialist commodity economy. Now, under the correct guidance of the Party's ideological line, the adjustment and reform of the national economy is being carried out in an active and steady manner. In this process, the "protection" policies are bound to be abandoned. In order to adapt to the new situation of the modernization drive, it is currently necessary to further explore commodity competition and how to deal with the issue of "backwardness".

Marx believed that commodities are born levelers, and free competition is an objective law of the development of the commodity economy. Commodity competition, on the one hand, has accelerated the polarization of society, and on the other hand, promoted the development of social productivity. The feudal society where the natural economy dominated has to be replaced by the capitalist society (where the commodity economy is highly developed), while the capitalist commodity economy characterized by the private ownership of means of production and socialized production will be replaced by the socialist commodity economy built on public ownership of the means of production. This is the fact that has been proved and will continue to be proved by the history. Over the years, due to our prejudice against the commodity economy, we have mistakenly classified "commodity", "competition", and other economic categories into capitalist categories and set restrictions for them, greatly suppressing the extrinsic force for the development of commodity economy. Now, we are increasingly and keenly aware that the commodity economy exists in a socialist society and we must strongly develop the commodity economy. Therefore, the competition law will continue to play its due role. The policy of implementing planned regulation and market regulation based on the public ownership of the means of production makes it impossible for the competition law to "endlessly" play its roles, but still exists as a natural attribute of competition law – natural selection and survival of the fittest – in the commodity itself. Since it is a commodity, it should unconditionally show itself in front of customers so as to determine the people's choice. In addition, if enterprises as commodity producers do not have some competitive edge in the socialist market due to poor business operation and are unable gain some profits, corporate producers and operators deserve some economic penalties. We advocate that commodity producers in different regions and different sectors must compete for survival and development, to foster strengths and circumvent weaknesses, and make use of and rely on the external power of competition to promote commodity production. Therefore, we must abolish the "protection" policies, open the doors, change the unitary-channel and exclusive operation into multi-channel and inclusive operation, and turn the monopoly market into a unified market.

Some people, especially some people in economically backward areas, are worried that the good commodities from other areas will flood and occupy the local market after "opening the door" and overwhelm the local industry. If we do not change the style of "official workers" and "official businessmen", then this danger will continue to exist. However, as long as we are aware of the basic laws of commodity economy and good at organizing commodity production and the circulation of commodities, then the worry is unnecessary.

First of all, the economically backward areas have their own advantages. "You fight your way and I fight my way". As long as the economically backward areas concentrate their manpower, materials, and financial resources according to the local characteristics to produce some products that can exert their advantages, make use of the unique natural resources and native products, and develop the products that are in short supply domestically, they will be able to promote the development of the local advantages. For example, the wool textiles and leather products in the hinterland areas and the wooden products in North China have strong competitive edges after improving the quality and varieties. In addition, competition has created the conditions for alliance. The backward areas can take the advantage of their own raw materials and establish joint ventures with the advanced areas, implement product and profit sharing, or implement "compensation trade" under the principle of equality and mutual benefit, or exchange the technologies, equipment, and products from the economically developed areas with raw materials.

Second, China is a large country with a population of 1.3 billion, but its economy is relatively backward, and there is a vast domestic market. After the good products from other areas are introduced to the local area, the local, "native" products can participate in the competition, and the direction of the products can be changed to develop mass products and occupy the rural market. This requires us to be good at doing business and improve the market forecasts to adapt to market changes.

Finally, the state will implement the policies to encourage competition and help the backward areas. The imbalanced economic development in various areas is an objective reality. The state does not protect backwardness, but should support the development of some emerging industries in the backward areas in a planned and focused way based on comprehensive planning so as to fundamentally change the economic structure. In addition, we should make use of economic levers, and provide preferential policies in investment, taxation, and profit distribution to promote the economic development in the backward areas.

On the road ahead, there are a lot of difficulties and resistances, but the objective law of the development of the socialist commodity economy will not be changed by people's subjective will. Outdated and backward things will ultimately be obsolete despite of "protection". "River cannot be stopped by mountains; It will flow to the east". Under the guidance of the national plans, we should abolish the "protection" policies, break the market barriers, develop the local economy according to local conditions and division of labor, foster strengths and circumvent weaknesses, and advocate and protect competition according to the development law of the socialist commodity economy to promote scientific alliances and the development of the entire socialist economy.

(Published in the *Journal of Graduate School of Chinese Academy of Social Sciences*, Issue 1, 1981)

Index

For Product Safety Concerns and Information please contact our EU
representative GPSR@taylorandfrancis.com
Taylor & Francis Verlag GmbH, Kaufingerstraße 24, 80331 München, Germany